SAMS
Teach Yourself
Today

e-Parenting

SAMS
Teach Yourself
Today

e-Parenting

Using the Internet and computers to be a better parent

Evelyn Petersen
Karin Petersen

SAMS

201 West 103rd Street, Indianapolis, Indiana 46290

Sams Teach Yourself
e-Parenting Today

Copyright © 2000 by Sams Publishing

International Standard Book Number: 0-672-31818-0

Library of Congress Catalog Card Number: 99-067046

Printed in the United States of America

First Printing: January 2000

03   02   01   00   4   3   2   1

Trademarks

Warning and Disclaimer

Acquisitions Editor
Jeff Schultz

Development Editor
Alice Martina Smith

Managing Editor
Charlotte Clapp

Project Editor
Carol Bowers

Copy Editor
June Waldman

Indexer
Sheila Schroeder

Proofreader
Tony Reitz

Interior Designer
Gary Adair

Cover Designer
Jay Corpus

Layout Technician
Stacey Richwine-DeRome
Ayanna Lacey
Heather Hiatt-Miller

Table of Contents

Dedication

Dedicated to the e-Parents and e-Children of the new millennium.

Foreword

The multi-generational authors deliver an insightful, obviously exhaustive work that introduces the concept of e-Parenting with clarity and sensitivity.

For those of us facing the responsibility of raising children in the new millennium, this book is a treasure trove of helpful guidance. A wonderful combination of information and advice that is concise and practical while also on the cutting edge of our information age.

Using technology to enhance the parenting experience—which would probably give our grandparents a coronary—is as practical today as castor oil must have been at the turn of the previous century. There is a misconception that e-Parenting means less hands-on involvement and interaction between parents and children. The authors shatter this myth by emphasizing that this brave new e-World is one to be shared, embraced, and celebrated together.

The wealth of information and resources included here makes this book an invaluable tool. The care and enthusiasm of the authors make it a pleasure to experience. It's scary to think of the hours the authors must have spent crawling around the Web for worthwhile sites to include and review. Lucky for us they did! It is their thorough work that makes this book one you'll want to keep handy the next time you log on.

David Katzner

President

The National Parenting Center

Acknowledgments

A heartfelt thank-you to our significant others for their patience and support during the writing of this book. And a sincere thank-you to Jeff Schultz, Alice Martina Smith, and others at Macmillan USA who believed in the concept and vision of this book and helped us bring it to reality.

INTRODUCTION

Sams Teach Yourself e-Parenting Today is the first parenting book written to assist today's parents with the particular challenges of raising children in an increasingly high-tech e-World.

We'd like to tell you about why we wanted to write about e-Parenting. We are a mother and daughter team, ages 63 and 33. I grew up in the 1950s, and even though I have used the PC for 16 years as a parenting columnist, early childhood educator, and author of six books, I still feel like a novice in terms of the workings of my PC, the Web, and the Internet.

Our daughter, Karin, grew up right along with the PC and the Internet. She uses these tools as an integral part of her daily life, yet she is close enough to my world to be my bridge and my teacher. When Macmillan USA approached me with a proposal to write about e-Parenting, I knew I could not do it without Karin's e-World perspective, any more than she could write a parenting book without my perspective of 40 years experience in child development, family life, and education.

It seemed to us that writing this book together would not only be an adventure and a challenge, but would also give readers a truly unique perspective of e-Parenting...a blending of a mother's and a daughter's views on practical parenting in the e-World.

We have tried to use an approach that encompasses and blends the perspectives and challenges of today's parents with solid parenting practices that have stood the test of time.

Many of today's parents are already computer and Internet savvy, but just as many will not be as computer literate as their children are. For this reason, our style also incorporates a tutorial or "learn as we go" approach. A lot of what we wrote in this book was discovered along the way, which emphasizes how easy it is to *just do it*—dive in and learn. That's how an e-Parent begins the journey.

We want to emphasize that this book is *not* a "computer book" and that our intent is *not* to teach you how to use the PC. Our intent is to share commonsense, practical parenting information with you and to show you various ways to use the PC and Net to help make your parenting even more effective and enjoyable.

We want to help parents who are not yet fully comfortable with the e-World to feel more confident in using the PC and Net with their children in enjoyable and meaningful ways. But at the same time, we want to make parents aware of both the advantages and the potential dangers of the Internet.

Our intent is to assist parents in using the PC and Net as *one of* their parenting tools; we present ways to use virtual-world technology to help teach children to do critical thinking and to make wise, informed choices in their best long-term interest.

In this book, you will learn the following:

- e-Parents work smarter, not necessarily harder.

- e-Parenting, like any good parenting, is a skill. Some parents learn this skill naturally and quickly, whereas others need more tips and practice.

- More and more resources, services, and businesses are moving to cyberspace; e-Parents need to know their way around cyberspace to get what they need or want for their families.

- More options for enjoyment, learning, and fulfilling activities abound on the Net than you might have ever imagined.

- The PC and Net can help you show an interest in your children in new ways, enjoy them in new ways, and teach them skills you want them to learn in new ways.

In closing, we must give the disclaimer that although we have described step-by-step searches and identified many Web sites, these sites and the process of Net searches are always changing. What comes up in a search one week may not come up the next because Web content is continuously changed and updated. URLs (Web site addresses) change constantly. So use our guidance and suggestions as examples, use them in good faith, and use them as a jumping-off place for your *own* creative exploring. Enjoy!

PART I

Getting Started

CHAPTER 1

Being an e-Parent

In this chapter we're going to talk about the basics of good e-Parenting…just what *is* it?…and about the ways the basics of good parenting stay the same in any time and in any culture. However, the e-World does bring some new challenges to e-Parents and their children.

Parents want kids to learn to make choices in their best long-term interest. Can the Net help parents and kids use technology to make more informed choices? Or will kids be confused by the wealth of information and make poor choices? How will the e-World affect the basics of good parenting?

You know you can have fun with your kids using the PC and the Net. But how can the Net be helpful in teaching kids what you believe and what you think they should know? Read on….

Parents are often unsure of themselves and their parenting skills. They love those babies and are filled with joy over each small step of development, but somewhere, way in the back of every parent's mind, he or she wonders what will happen later, when the babies become children and the children become teens.

It doesn't matter whether you're a young, new parent or have become an "instant" parent in a step or blended family; you still have a few anxieties. You wonder whether you have what it takes to be a parent over the long haul. You wonder whether you can find the time to be a good parent or whether you really know enough about kids and parenting to do the job.

Be reassured that this kind of wondering is the first step to good parenting…and it is a giant step! It means that you know the importance of parenting and that the job will take time and commitment. It means that you know parenting will be fulfilling, but you also know that it won't always be easy. Wondering about the

What You'll Learn in This Chapter:

▶ How good parenting transcends cultures and technology

▶ What's different about e-Parenting

▶ How to be a better e-Parent

future of your kids means that you *want* to do good parenting, so you're already halfway there!

Good parents the world over, at any time in history, have always had the same kinds of fears about their parenting you have now. Parents who care—not just about their kids, but about the "job" of parenting—tend to learn very fast and do very well. One reason for their success is that they are open and willing to learn about good parenting, just like you are.

Other parents may say, "It was easier to do good parenting in the old days. Technology keeps changing our lives and increasing the pace; the information overload eats up our time. Life's more stressful, so it's harder to do good parenting." Our answer is this: Parents who want excuses have been using *that* one in some form or other ever since the dawn of time. Parents who want results just figure out ways to get them.

We say that your success as a parent, as with most things, depends on the way you look at and respond to the challenge. If you have children, they are here *now*. The electronic world, the e-World, is here now too, and we are a part of it. The future won't wait for you to think it over and adjust. You have to parent your children *now*—and tomorrow, and the next day, and the day after that. We cannot change or hold back the future, so let's jump in and use it to our advantage. Let's make the most of our growing e-World opportunities to do the best e-Parenting we can do!

You don't have to decide to be an e-Parent—you already are one. You are a parent of a child or children, and you live in the e-World. You realize that the e-World constantly affects your life and your children's lives and that its impact will undoubtedly increase. So you are also an *aware* e-Parent.

Because you are reading this book, we know that you are a parent who is always looking for ways to be an even better parent. You know that what you do as a parent *does* make a difference in the way your kids turn out. You realize that parenting is not getting any easier, so you are looking for information and resources to help you cope with the challenges. This book will give you lots of help.

But first, we need to say a few words about what good parenting is and about the ways e-Parenting is both similar to and different from the traditional concept of good parenting. We need to see how e-Parenting can make our parenting easier and more effective. We need to become even more aware of the spectrum of possibilities for using e-Parenting and e-World resources to do the kind of parenting that will help our kids succeed in the new millennium.

Are Good Parenting and Good e-Parenting the Same?

Good e-Parenting is built on the kind of love and caring that involves action and purpose. Good e-Parenting is not passive; it requires involvement. It means giving children guidance, experiences, and opportunities that will help them grow into successful adults. Good e-Parenting is not as hard as you may think. Just practice three simple basics that all good parents have been doing for a very long time:

- Maintain a loving, genuine interest in your children

- Have a desire to share what you believe with them

- Cultivate a willingness to teach them what they need to know

As you see, these three behaviors are easy to understand and easy to do, especially when children are young. The only hard part is that you have to do these things consistently and *keep on doing them* every day—not just when your children are young, but as they grow into the school and teen years. e-Parenting and e-World resources will help make this process easier.

The Good e-Parent:
The world may have changed, but the basics of good parenting are much as they have always been. Good e-Parenting is the same as good parenting.

Only Young Once
Over the past 50 years, researchers have learned that parents are the child's first and most important teachers. Parents have the greatest impact on their children in the early years; after about age 8, peer influence plays an increasingly greater role. In terms of an entire lifetime, the window of opportunity for parental influence is small. That's why it's vital to use good e-Parenting techniques to make the most of the opportunities in the early years.

e-Parenting Basics Are Timeless and Universal

The basics just listed are the same things parents do and have done all over the world. They're the same things parents did in the 1950s and the same things that parents did in the days of early humans. When we think about early peoples, we usually have mental images of clans or families sitting around a fire, engaged in rituals or in telling stories and legends. These stories and legends taught children "what their parents believed in" and helped teach guidance and self-discipline.

Early parents taught their children hands-on survival skills from a young age, teaching them "what children needed to know." Early parents had vested interests in producing offspring who would survive and continue the clan. And everyone in the community, including those with special roles, showed an interest in the children. Throughout history, parents continued doing the basics of good parenting in ways that matched their own needs and in ways that meshed with the societal structure of that time.

In the 1950s, almost all the information children got came from their parents and families. It is not surprising that there was little debate while children lived at home. Because children had so little information from other sources, they could not compare other views and opinions to those of their parents. Most children shared their parents' opinions and beliefs without questioning them until they were adults.

Centers of Family Life:

Historically, children and what they were learning and doing were of daily interest to the family, second only to the activities of the major breadwinner.

Children of the 1950s learned what their parents believed in and what their parents believed the children should know at the family dinner table, during get-togethers with family and friends, while helping with daily household routines, and while participating in family leisure activities that were based on face-to-face conversation and interaction.

The opportunities to do good e-Parenting have never been greater than they are today! We have e-World resources for doing parenting basics that were previously undreamed of and unimaginable.

And, trust us on this one: We also have more time to do good e-Parenting than we think we have.

Of course, it's true that the things e-Parents believe in may be more complex than ever before. The list of things we think our children should know may be much longer and more challenging than it was in the past. We may have to place a higher priority on showing an interest in our children and use multitasking techniques to make the time we spend with children count in several ways. In addition, e-Parents need a certain kind of mind set.

e-Parenting Is a Frame of Mind

Some of you who are reading this chapter may be looking for some enjoyable options for leisure activities or for "neat" ideas to use with your children. As authors, we want to make the point that this book—and the process of e-Parenting—is much more than that.

e-Parenting is a frame of mind, an approach to today's parenting that says, "I am willing and able to be involved in guiding my children, not only in the real world, but as they learn to use technology." Why? Because you want your kids to use technology in ways you approve of and in ways that promote your children's skills and best interest.

Yes, the basics of good parenting and e-Parenting are easy, but parenting e-Children may be difficult if you give them no guidance in positive ways to use e-World skills. e-Kids will have few problems with the technology itself, but the use of technology without good e-Parenting can cause problems that may make parenting harder.

To make parenting easier and better for today's families, we believe that starting to do e-Parenting *today* is a must. If we don't, we are putting our children's futures at risk. We need to use new methods and new platforms for doing e-Parenting that will help kids grow into successful adults.

What's New and Different About e-Parenting?

The two biggest changes we have to deal with as e-Parents in an e-World are increases in information and choices. We have to be able to deal effectively with information and choices ourselves and do the kind of e-Parenting that helps our children know how to do it, too.

e-Parenting and Information

The e-World has brought us a gift: the gift of masses of information, much of which will be helpful to our e-Parenting. But some e-Parents are looking this gift horse in the mouth. "The information is great, but...."

The quantity of information available tends to overwhelm us as it flies about in our heads and disturbs our sleep. It assaults us constantly with unrelenting speed; it invades and interrupts our thinking and our doing. We hate to ignore any of it because we might miss something. We might need that information if it's good, and we still have to do something with it if it's bad.

Touch It Once:

Managers used to call this approach to dealing with information and data the "touch-it-once" method: Toss it, file it, or answer it immediately.

In other words, we cannot make the information go away; we have to deal with it. As e-Parents, we have to learn to assess information quickly, act on it, discard it, or file it for later use.

Dealing with the information overload is often hard for us. Will it be harder in the future? When our children are young adults, will they be dealing with even more information than we are? Perhaps the amount of information won't be a problem for them; they will be used to it. But will kids recognize *good* information?

We know we need to teach our children how to sift, sort, discard, and save information. But much more important is teaching them to evaluate and save the *kinds* of information that will be useful to them.

As they grow, they will know how to push all the right buttons to operate various devices. But they need to know more than how to operate *tools*; they need to be able to use technology and information in ways that will teach them new *skills* and improve the quality of their lives.

As our children grow into adulthood, learning to recognize good information and have systems for organizing it will be even more crucial.

We e-Parents are lucky. The tools for teaching children how to deal with information comfortably and competently are built into our daily lives with the PC and the Internet. These technologies can give us a whole new platform for coping with information and doing good e-Parenting.

We can turn information overload into an asset. We can use the Internet to our advantage by teaching children how to recognize and evaluate good information—a survival skill for the new millennium that our kids need to learn.

You may be wondering just how and where you can begin to teach children the skill of sorting and dealing with information. Here is an example:

Begin teaching the skill of sorting information in a concrete, hands-on way. Invite your children to go through the daily real-world snail mail with you and learn how to recognize and discard "junk" mail. Help them recognize correspondence and bills. Show them where you keep those items until you answer the letters or pay the bills.

Reduce, Reuse, Recycle:
If you are an advocate of ecology and the environment, involve your children in the process of properly storing clean paper and junk mail for recycling.

If you have a file drawer and folders for these two types of mail (a bills folder and a correspondence folder, for example), you can show your young children how information can be sorted, organized, and accessed on a PC. On a PC, information can be filed and stored in easily accessed electronic folders.

You are teaching the first step of a life skill your kids will use every day of their lives. Sorting real-world mail teaches your kids to use concrete thinking skills. When they actually use the computer to file information in the correct e-folders, they will be using both concrete and abstract thinking skills.

As soon as children are using the PC regularly, help them read, delete, or save email messages into folders. (Most email systems have a folder option.) Do it together. Make a folder for each family member for email and other information they want to save.

Trust Begins with the Small Stuff

Some e-Parents can ask an older child to help out by sorting the email, deleting the "junk," and putting other messages into individual family member folders. A child who believes that you trust him or her to do this chore will feel pretty special. Try it. You can always check your personal filing cabinet or your trash/recycle bin to see whether your child inadvertently deleted something you need.

In Chapter 4, "Using the PC and the Net to Nurture Self-Esteem," we talk about making personal folders for family members as part of a self-esteem-building technique. Right now, we are just heightening your e-Parent awareness of a new platform for parenting.

e-Parenting and Choices

The other big change in our world that creates a need for good e-Parenting is an increase in the complexity of decision making. As you know, more information inevitably leads to more choices. The e-World gives us more choices than humans have ever encountered before or even thought possible.

So many options can be a good thing or a bad thing, depending on whether we see choices as an opportunity or a burden. Again, we can use this challenge to help us teach children how to make good choices.

Good parents have always known that teaching kids to make wise choices in their own long-term best interest is a top priority. After all, we aren't going to be around every time the child has to make a decision.

Teaching kids to make good choices is a *really* long-term parenting task. You start out gradually by giving young children daily opportunities to make choices they can handle.

- Choose between these two cereals

- Choose one of three outfits to wear

- Choose which friend to invite for a visit

As children get older, we encourage them to make more difficult choices and also to accept responsibility and consequences for the choices they make.

- Choose to have a pet and accept the consequences of taking care of it or not

- Choose to use up your entire allowance on candy and then have none left for anything else

- Choose to try out for a team sport and risk rejection

- Choose to try or not try a cigarette

- Choose to go or not go to an unchaperoned party

In the fast-moving and sometimes dangerous e-World we live in, it is not just "a Good Thing" to have children learn to make wise choices. Today it is *crucial for* children to learn how to make choices in their own best interests.

In the 1950s, a bad choice would probably not have been dangerous to a child's health and well-being; in the new millennium, making the right choice may sometimes be a life or death matter.

As an e-Parent, you can use the PC and the Internet, as well as real-world experiences, to teach children the skill of making choices. In Part II, "Raising Better Kids Using the Internet and Computers," we give you some more examples. Here are just a few:

- Early on, teaching your child to make good choices may take the form of helping the child choose the time of day to use the PC with you, pick one type of appropriate game out of three games, select the type of software to use that day, or choose which software to buy when three options are available.

- Later, choice making will include which Web sites to visit (or not visit), what kinds of software are most useful, where to find help with a homework assignment, what kinds of information searches to do, and more.

These virtual-world choices parallel the child's choices in the real world—and the virtual world of the Net and PC can also help the child make more informed choices. What sport shall I pursue? What hobby should I choose? What kinds of friends do I want? Who are my heroes? What gift should I make or buy? Should I do volunteer work in my free time? Children can make more informed choices on these issues by using the Internet to do some research. And after they've found information on the Net, they have to evaluate it by asking questions such as these: How can I get a second or third opinion on this? How can I check these facts to see whether they are true? When was this information updated? Who wrote this article, and what qualifications do they have?

Ask Questions Now:

e-Parents can help kids evaluate the information they gather by teaching them to ask questions about what they are reading and helping them get information from more than one source.

At an early age, children will be using computers in school. When they're home, they'll soon outdistance their parents in clicking and using the technologies of the PC and Internet.

This situation explains why e-Parenting *now* is so important. Schools can teach children techniques, but they cannot spend time teaching them to make wise choices in their best interests. Schools may not teach kids how to recognize and evaluate good information. When you have an abundance of information and choices, choices are much more difficult to make.

Only e-Parents can use both the real world and the platform of the virtual world to teach children how to recognize and use good information and how to make wise, healthy choices in their best long-term interest. Start e-Parenting today.

How Can I Do a Better Job of e-Parenting?

First, stop worrying. You are a good parent and a good person. You will always be ready and able to learn and to grow, and you are flexible enough to adjust to the inevitable changes that e-Parenting will bring you. What you need to do now is relax, pat yourself on the back, and take a new look at those timeless parenting basics at the beginning of this chapter.

Here they are again, written from an e-Parenting perspective. When you finish reading them, you will know that *you can do e-Parenting*. And you will be anxious to read Chapter 2, "Why a PC Can Be More Useful to Families Than a TV."

Show a Genuine Interest

You will be on your toes and constantly aware of all the tiny but important daily opportunities you have to show an interest in your children. Good e-Parenting means taking advantage of every opportunity to show an interest in your kids, using both real and online parent-child experiences to do it.

Showing a genuine interest also means that you always remember that any and all time you spend with your children really counts. Every minute you spend, every conversation you have, every joke you share, every smile you exchange, every touch on the shoulder, and every word of praise you say, is a way to show interest and is an investment in their future—and yours.

Provide Guidance

You will provide your *personal* guidance as well as guidance that uses available online resources.

Guidance means sharing the things you believe in and sharing things you think children should know. Guidance means modeling and demonstrating as well as talking and telling.

> Guidance means using the PC and Net together. It means using your e-Parenting skills to get your kids to ask themselves questions about the information they find and to help them learn to evaluate and choose good sites to visit.

Here are other important ways to provide your guidance.

Share What You Believe

The PC and Net can help you share what you believe is important in life with your children. Here are some examples.

- If you think creativity is important, you can go online and use keywords such as *creativity*, *kids*, *crafts*, and *paint* to bring up Web sites that may have what you're looking for. Try different keywords as you narrow your search. You may even try typing the words *early childhood* or *parenting* in a search box to find sites where creative activities for young children may also be listed. You and your child may be able to do this activity together.

- You can go online to teach your child about health and fitness, good grooming, or protecting the gray whale. Your child can learn about clean water, rain forests, other cultures, helping homeless people, or adopting homeless pets. The possibilities are endless, and the discovery and learning process is *fun*.

More Than One Way to Search:

The Net has many search engines. They all operate differently and bring up results differently, depending on your keywords and the topic you are searching. Use at least two engines in every search. See Chapter 3, "Using the PC and Net to Nurture Creative Problem Solving," for hints about using search engines.

Share Things You Think Your Children Should Know

Part II of this book will give you some more specific examples of real- and virtual-world strategies to teach your children important life skills and attributes. Meanwhile, here are some general examples:

- You can use the Net to help teach your child why daily exercise is a wise choice. Exercise improves fitness and appearance, both of which impact self-esteem. Self-esteem is something all parents value and want their children to have. Parents can nurture self-esteem in specific ways, so in a sense, they can "teach" it, just as they can teach the skill of problem solving.

- You can use the Net to help your child find other children who have a similar interest, such as scouts (the skill of working with people).

- You can use the Net to help your child cope with a fear of bats by learning some of the good things bats do (the attribute of self-esteem).

- You can use the Net to find out why the leaves change color (the skill of problem solving).

- You can use software on the PC to find out what different animals sound like or where they live (the skills of problem solving and doing research).

Have Fun Together

e-Parents and children should enjoy each other.

Your child needs a strong and secure relationship with you and a sense of connectedness to the family group. The child also has to be able to enjoy you and play with you.

You probably know that if fun and laughter are missing from a relationship, and if you don't enjoy the time you spend with someone, the relationship won't grow or last. It's the same with a parent-child relationship. Fun is important.

Keep Your e-Parenting Balance

You want to do the kind of e-Parenting that will prevent most problems in the teen years and ultimately turn out children who will be your friends when they grow up. This goal means keeping your e-Parent roles in balance. Be a calm, firm e-Parent when guidance is necessary, but also be a fun and playful e-Parent whenever possible.

Be a Parent First and a Friend Second

Sometimes single parents become so dependent on their children as friends that they forget they are parents.

Be careful not to put a child into the role of confidante or best friend. Don't tell a child things he or she really can't understand just because you want someone to talk to.

Just when the child thinks this "adult" role is great, you may want or need the child to be back in the little kid role again. Flipping roles this way is very confusing to children. Don't give them roles or information that are not age appropriate. Have heart-to-heart talks but stick to subjects your kids can handle.

You can easily find other adults to talk with on the Net; in particular, you can reach other single parents at parenting sites and through search engines, bulletin boards, and newsgroups.

Take Advantage of the PC and the Net

Take every opportunity you can in the early years to set the pattern for using the PC as a family-togetherness tool. Keep the PC in the family room, den, kitchen, or hobby room—anywhere you and the kids gather. This way, someone will always be nearby when anyone is on the Net, and the PC will be easy to use as a medium for doing things *together*.

Find Out More About Things You Both Already Like

Do searches and find sites about your child's heroes, interests, hobbies, sports, favorite Disney characters, or favorite stories. You can share your own special interests with your child, too, by using the Net and Web sites that show your child real photos or that use video and sound to take you there.

Get Virtually Up Close and Personal with Free Willy

You and your kids can visit Keiko, the orca that was the star of the *Free Willy* movies. The Oregon Coast Aquarium site has a good section devoted to Keiko and his story. Go to *www.aquarium.org* and click the *Keiko News Central* link. You can see what it would be like to ride on Keiko's back, hear and view news reports, hear the sounds he makes, view video clips of him in his new home in Iceland, and sign Keiko's farewell book. There's even a Keiko Kids Club geared for younger school-age kids.

Other examples of using the Net to investigate areas of interest are to visit virtual museums, exploratoriums, and art galleries with your kids; visit a live concert venue; or watch live Web cams at zoos. The operative words here are *fun* and *together*.

If you and your kids explore the Web together, you're likely to come across really cool sites like this one at www. aquarium.org, *where you can experience what it would be like to ride on the back of an orca whale.*

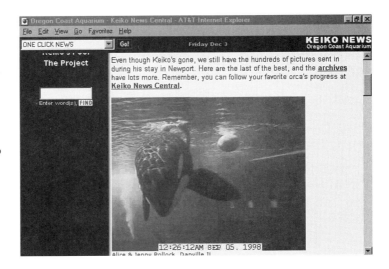

Discover Totally New Interests

When you and your child have time to spend together, "surf the Net." Your journey may take you to other lands or cultures. You can find new recipes to prepare together; you can discover books to buy and to read, science experiments to try, or creative activities to do.

Summing Up

We hope that this chapter has piqued your interest in e-Parenting and has made you stop and think about why it is so very important to be an e-Parent today.

This chapter introduced the three parenting basics you will see applied in many ways throughout this book. You also learned about the ways that access to unlimited information in the e-World has affected parenting.

We also talked about the big challenge of e-Parenting: helping kids learn to make informed choices in their best long-term interest. To achieve this big goal, we don't take quantum leaps—we just have to do lots of small, everyday things to make it happen. For instance, we have to be there for kids and guide them as they learn to evaluate information and make choices.

We have to give our children supervised practice in making bigger and bigger choices—and wiser choices—in the real world and in the virtual world. We have to be there for them when they make mistakes, too. One way to motivate good choices is by making sure that kids accept the consequences of bad ones.

We hope you see why we suggest that one way to help kids deal with information and to make informed choices is to have the PC and Net in your family room or den. This strategy also makes the computer more easily available for family fun.

Speaking of fun, that is one of the three e-Parenting basics: Show a genuine interest, provide guidance by telling kids what you believe in and what you think they need to know, and have fun together.

CHAPTER 2

Why a PC Can Be More Useful to Families Than a TV

As a part of getting started—and as a further enhancement to the e-Parenting state of mind—this chapter talks about two technological wonders: television and the personal computer. We're going to look at four areas of our lives in which television and personal computers have affected parenting over the past two decades—and continue to affect it. We're going to compare the ways computers and television affect family togetherness, entertainment, consumerism, and self-image.

Keep in mind that technology of any kind comes with its own opportunities, advantages, and disadvantages. Technological equipment, appliances, and operations are not bad or good in and of themselves. However, the ways that people use technologies can have positive or negative effects.

As authors, we believe that e-World technology offers a wide range of opportunities for good e-Parenting. e-Parents need to know that the electronic devices we take for granted and use every day in our homes actually *do* affect parenting, family life, and the ways children learn our values.

Family Togetherness

Each of us probably has a somewhat different picture of family togetherness. To us, it is simply time that family members get together to enjoy something…maybe they play games, bake cookies, have a picnic, work on a project, watch a sports event or watch a movie together. If the people involved are enjoying each other, and if whatever they're doing is relaxing or fun, it is family togetherness.

What You'll Learn in This Chapter:

- ▶ Whether or not the TV and the PC can enhance the way the family interacts
- ▶ Whether or not you can make the TV or PC experience an educational one
- ▶ Whether or not online and TV advertising can strengthen a child's sense of values
- ▶ Whether or not the TV and PC affect your child's self-image

Television and Togetherness

Interestingly enough, when television first became widely available, it was used every day to bring families together. Every afternoon or evening (daytime TV programs were sparse back then), all the family members would gather around the tube and watch a program, comment, laugh, and discuss the relevance of a show to their own lives. Television snacks became popular, adding zest to the family activity and enhancing the enjoyment of everyone present.

Friends and neighbors who as yet had no television sets gathered in homes that did have sets. The children benefited from the feeling of belonging to this extended family and neighborhood group, and they conversed, laughed, and snacked along with the adults.

TV Habits Then and Now:

Compare the 1950s picture of family and neighbors gathered around a TV set to today's neighborhoods, where most folks don't know their neighbors' names. Communal TV watching used to help children feel happily connected to a family and to a neighborhood.

As families became more and more affluent, they continued to place television sets high on their lists of things to buy. They bought second and third sets for different parts of the home.

At the same time, the television industry recognized and began using its tremendous marketing power to change wants into needs in the minds of consumers. In addition, the industry began using the consumers' fast-growing incomes to create more and more diverse programming. As consumers spent more money on the products advertised on TV, more sponsors jumped on the bandwagon of TV marketing. Soon, networks had more money to spend, so they created more and more diverse programming that targeted specific ages and consumer groups.

Result? Television is no longer an electronic catalyst for family togetherness; it is increasingly a technological wonder that causes isolation of family members, each with his or her own favorite programs and separate places to watch them. How many sets live in *your* house?

Exceptions occur when families verbally or tacitly agree to watch a special event, continuing show, or video together. During the 168 hours in a week, only a few hours are spent with television as a focus for *family* togetherness.

For years, television has often been used as an "electronic baby sitter," occupying young children while their parents or other family members spend time elsewhere. What is disturbing about this trend is not only the lack of family togetherness but also the lack of value assigned to what's being watched. If parents are not present, no one can comment, debate, or contradict the values the television is "tube feeding" the child. And children believe that everything they see on TV is true.

TV Violence Affects Kids:

Researchers are still arguing about the effects of television on children's behavior, but plain old common sense tells us that children should not be spectators of sex and violence.

TV as Teacher

Have you ever thought about your TV set as a teacher? It can be a really good or a bad teacher, and it can also be a teaching tool in an e-Parent's hands.

To children under age 5, everything the TV says is perceived as true. Research tells us that children cannot consistently separate fact from fantasy until about age 5. Fictional television shows, commercials, trailers, wild talk shows, and the soaps may be entertainment to adults, but to children these broadcasts are a way of learning what adults do, what adults think is good, and what adults think is funny.

Using TV as a constant baby sitter or as background noise is not good e-Parenting: The TV can become an uninvited guest in your living room, teaching children values that may not be yours.

You don't realize that it is talking all day, telling kids what is bad or good, what they need, what is cool or sexy, what kinds of people are successful, how to treat women, that doing mean things to people is funny, that outrageous behavior is normal....

If a real person were in your home telling your kids these things, you would be saying, "Hey, wait a minute! That's not true." You would be making sure that your kids knew what *you* believe. You should be telling your kids which things on TV are real and normal and which are exaggerations or half truths.

TV is not "just entertainment." It is a powerful tool that can teach values and influence thinking. So why not take that tool and use it the e-Parenting way?

e-Parents can use TV as a tool to help their e-World kids. Watching TV with your kids and discussing what you see—even if it's only a 30-minute show a day—can actually help them think about, question, and talk to you about what they're viewing. We'll say that again: *Kids will think about, question, and talk to you about what they are viewing.*

When kids do think about what they're watching, they are actually using the same *critical-thinking tools* you want them to use when they access the Internet.

So, e-Parents, please spend that 20 to 30 minutes a day talking to kids about what they are seeing and hearing on TV. Help them use some of the following strategies to encourage their critical thinking. Your kids need to practice using critical thinking and evaluation skills in everyday life and in their online experiences.

- Have the kids log everything they watch for three days and then tell you just one important thing they learned from each show, no matter what kind of show it was.

- Notice illusions that influence you. For example, the laugh track is an illusion to convince you that something is funny. Turn off the volume during a sitcom and see whether the things being done are actually funny or not.

- Keep track of the winners and losers on several shows. What kinds of people are portrayed as winners and losers?

- Talk about a different way for a particular story to end.

- Count and list the ads and sponsors of one hour of prime-time public television and compare them to the ads and sponsors in one hour of prime-time network television.

- Compare the kinds of ads that appear on sport shows and to the ads that appear on sitcoms. Which shows advertise beer? Which shows advertise cars? soft drinks? cosmetics? Talk about why.

- Talk about the rudest or silliest behavior you saw on TV during the week. Who were the show's sponsors? Do you know how to contact them? (*Hint:* Through their products.)

The PC and Togetherness

e-Parents who have the mind set to recognize opportunities for e-Parenting, and who want to use these e-World technologies to promote family togetherness, can certainly see the implications of *not* pursuing these approaches.

As personal computers become less expensive and more common and as the "programming" options of software and the Net become more prolific, the technological wonder of PCs could go the way of television—that is, PCs could increase isolation among family members.

e-Parents who value family togetherness will want to know how to prevent this situation. They will want to know how to use computers and the Net to bring parents and children together. Other chapters in this book provide many ideas for making this happen. For now, let's just get our awareness and imagination going with a few examples.

- **Enjoy parent–child PC activities.** Many e-Parent–child activities can be done with the personal computer, starting with how to turn it on and off properly and how to "go to" a personal folder or a place on the Net. Many simple software programs can (and should) be used with the parent and child as partners. Many children's programs have lots of built-in positive reinforcement (such as familiar images, fantasy fun, bright colors, and easy ways to click or navigate) and are easy for adults to enjoy with their children.

  As children get older and become junior partners in choosing software and using the Internet, parents can and should remain actively involved.

  The computer activity examples we share with you in later chapters will assist you in doing all three e-Parenting basics at the same time. Time management is important to busy e-Parents!

- **Play family games.** You can also bring family members together with family games—not only in the real world but also on the computer with software and the Internet.

- **Stay in touch.** e-Parents and children can bring the extended family and friends together on an ongoing basis with simple PC and Internet strategies such as email, family Web sites, and newsletters.

e-Parenting Multitasking:

If you're savvy, you can use the PC to do all three e-Parenting basics: Show an interest in your kids, provide guidance as you teach children what you want them to know, and have fun together!

Entertainment or Programming

We usually think of TV viewing as entertainment, even when we choose something educational to watch. The different choices, or the options for what we can watch, can be described as *programming*. With our personal computers and the Internet, the options (or choices of programming) are comprised of all the software we have and all the sites we can access. With television, we have less control and fewer choices about the programming that is offered to us.

e-Parenting Choices and TV

e-Parents know that their roles in controlling television programming are very limited. Networks, communications, and cable companies—and their commercial sponsors—decide what programs and entertainment options are available to us on the tube.

Although e-Parents and children have access to some programming options that include education and the arts, travel, the environment, and some great children's programs (think public television and *Nova*), television programming as a whole has become more superficial, more violent, and more sexually explicit over the last decade or so. Parental controls of what children are able to watch are also limited.

From what parents are writing to us or telling us, the technological parental controls for TV are not very effective. It may also be that parents just don't want to bother monitoring their children. Even if they *do* want to monitor, they usually can't be there all the time. The latest polls say that kids watch more than *five hours* of TV a day.

Perhaps more important, when children and parents watch television, they are usually *spectators*. Rarely are they in an active participatory role—except in the case of interactive television programming, which at this time has very limited accessibility.

e-Parenting Choices and the PC

On the other hand, e-Parent choices of programming with the PC are unlimited. There are many kinds of software for every purpose and age group—and the list keeps growing. In addition, the

Net provides unlimited options for things to do, see, and learn about. One search often leads to another—and the possibilities are endless.

You can find lists of good software in libraries, in book stores, and on the Internet. You can do searches to find the particular kinds of software programming you want.

The National Parenting Center (www.tnpc.com) is a wonderful place to start your search for quality software.

Approved Software

Many parents want more than lists of software; they want to know whether the software in which they are interested in purchasing has been approved or tested by other parents. The National Parenting Center (*tnpc.com*), which went online in 1991, is the oldest parenting site on the Internet. Since 1995, TNPC has been testing products for parents and children through its Seal of Approval program. Independent testers and parents evaluate software products based on level of appeal, desirability, design, interactive stimulation, price, and other essential elements. The center issues three Seal of Approval reports annually (spring, fall, and holiday).

All Seal of Approval reports are listed online in a searchable database where you can find winning products reviewed by child's age, price, description, and so on. Parents can learn about books, toys, crafts, baby products, Seal of Approval Web sites, computer software, and new technologies. Go to *www.tnpc.com* and click *Seal of Approval Reports* for an annotated list of recommended software.

TNPC has many other pages of excellent information and archives of hundreds of parenting topics. In this huge database of browsable articles, you can search by any number of fields (such as topic, age, title, author, and keyword).

From the TNPC home page, click the Seal of Approval link and then select the report you want to view (in this example, we selected Fall 1999). Click the category button for the products you are interested in.

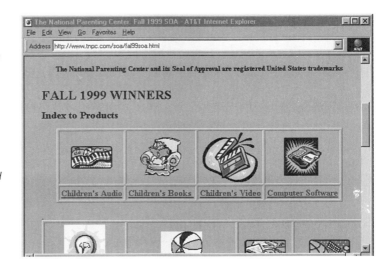

More Sites of Good Software:

Another source of reviews of sites where good software can often be found is www.netmom.com. Also check out www.NetFamilyNews .org.

In addition, when they are using the PC, the parent and child are in active roles. They are *not* spectators. No matter what they are doing, they are "in charge" participants in an activity they choose to do.

Doing things together doubles the fun and gives e-Parents many opportunities to converse with children about what they are learning or doing. In turn, these conversations help children learn what their parents believe is important.

Advertising and Shopping

Both television and the personal computer have ways of encouraging us to go shopping and ways to advertise their products. But if we are the kinds of shoppers who do comparison shopping, or the kinds of shoppers who want to know a lot about the product before we buy, which technological wonder gives us the most useful information, the PC or the TV? Which one gives us the most options?

TV Commercials and e-Parent Options

We would certainly agree that television is a land of commercial interruptions. A half-hour show, on the average, is now only about 19 minutes long; the rest of the time is commercials—about 6 or 7 of them during every "break."

Some commercials are deliberately vague so that you keep watching to try to figure them out. Others try to draw you in with color, sound, and pizzazz; still others are only a few seconds long so that you can see them before you click off with the remote.

All these commercials give purposeful, powerful messages that try to make you believe their products are things you *need*, not just things you may want.

To television's credit, more commercials than ever before focus on the family, portray diverse families, and show positive images of parent and child interactions. Today many celebrities are also making excellent public service announcements that give children and parents good information and often mention supportive resources that can be found on the Internet. In addition, more and more companies of all kinds are launching Web sites and placing their URLs at the end of their TV commercials.

But what real and useful information about the *products* do the commercials provide? Very little. Limited information about the products promotes impulse buying and uninformed choices. This behavior is something e-Parents will not want to encourage in their children.

Sometimes parents have the option of finding out more about a product by going to the Web site listed on the television screen. e-Parents and children may use this site to try to find out more. In general, however, you will get little useful information from TV commercials or from the technological wonder of television itself.

The PC and e-Parent Shopping Options

On the PC, however, advertising is quite a different story. Most "ads" on the Internet or at Web sites are small, quiet, and unobtrusive. They are often in the form of banners or small pop-up windows and can easily be ignored. Sometimes, however, the commercials can be intrusive, but most ads are in the form of banners you can try to ignore or pop-ups you can actually close. With TV however, you have no choice; you have to wait until the commercial ends.

About Web Sites:

When we evaluated Web sites to include in this book, it was important to us that ads, banners, cutesy graphics, and so on did not interfere with the mission of the site or its content.

On the other hand, if e-Parents want information about a product they might want to purchase, their PC options for gathering useful information are nearly unlimited. And e-Parents have tremendous opportunities to teach children how to make informed choices about purchases by using the PC and Net to do just that.

e-Parents can do searches to look at many examples of a particular product and can compare similar products from many companies. e-Parents can read articles describing tests of products, such as are done in the *Consumer Report* magazine; often they can read the comments of actual consumers of the product! e-Parents can learn about warranties, about related products, and even about environmental or health issues that may be related to the product. Talk about an informed choice!

And there is extra icing on this cake. While e-Parents are showing their children how to gather useful information before making buying decisions, they are also demonstrating that they *value* informed choices and believe that they are important.

The Value of Informed Choice

When young and school-age children grow into teenagers, e-Parents will be very glad that they taught their teens the value of informed choices and set a family pattern of making informed choices. When children learn to make informed choices early, and the process becomes a natural part of their everyday lives, they will be more likely to make well-informed choices as teens.

In addition, the conversation or discussion that goes on between parents and children as they use the PC and Net together gives parents a chance to talk about wants and needs—and the *difference* between them. Understanding this difference is an important life skill for e-Children, and teaching this skill is an important aspect of good e-Parenting! This type of conversation would rarely take place while watching TV.

e-Parents, you *do* know the difference between wants and needs, and you also know how to explain that difference to kids. Just *do* it. (At our house, parents pay for the "needs," and kids save up money for "wants." Delayed gratification is what real life is about, most of the time. And kids need to learn that.)

e-Parents may want to note that kids often have trouble knowing the difference between wants and needs. The problem gets worse when parents give their children what they want when they want it, a practice that does not improve family communication or prepare children for life in the real world.

Self-Image

How children feel about themselves—their self-esteem—is another issue important to e-Parenting. Self-esteem makes a life-long difference in children's attitudes and the ways they cope. It affects success in school, relationships, jobs, health and fitness, leisure activities, and life in general.

Self-Esteem and the TV

Children learn very little about themselves from most sitcom shows, although some are very entertaining. Children may learn many interesting things from the children's and educational television programs that are available, and an interest sparked there may lead to both real-world and virtual-world activities that promote self-esteem. For example, watching a young gymnast on TV may lead a child to learn more about gymnastics, pursue it as a sport, and enjoy success.

But how do children project themselves and their ideas about themselves into most of the programs they watch? How do the regular things they watch (cartoons, sitcoms, commercials, and other shows) affect their self-image?

Concerned e-Parents take the time to watch and discuss television shows with their children and monitor what they are watching. But even e-Parents are not there all the time.

Children also get very clear messages about themselves from TV commercials. Most of these messages tell kids that something is wrong with them or lacking in them and that they need to buy particular products to be okay or strong or pretty or handsome or smart or good.

Children may not be able to express the fact that they feel somehow not okay but are affected enough to often ask their parents to buy particular products, saying that they (the children) "need" them (the products). Think about that.

Self-Esteem and the PC

The PC, along with e-Parenting, provides many ways to help children (and parents) feel good about themselves. Just the fact that the parent and child are active participants in PC activities with control over what they are doing, instead of being spectators, is a big plus.

Chapter 4, "Using the PC and Net to Nurture Self-Esteem," provides more specific examples of ways to use the Net to enhance self-esteem. But here are a few general ways for e-Parents to use the PC and Net to build self-esteem in their children.

- Using various software and Internet programs that lead to enjoyable activities where the child feels successful—an "I can do this!" feeling.

- Creating the child's own Web site, containing ideas, likes, dislikes, pets, best friends, hobbies, and photographs.

- Creating the child's own page on a family Web site.

- Making personal folders in which the child can store email, favorite sites, and original creations.

Summing Up

In this chapter, we have seen how the use of two technological wonders that are a part of daily home life can affect our children and our e-Parenting. We can *use* the TV and the PC to help our children learn life skills and important values.

The ways we use these and other technologies help us share our values, attitudes, and beliefs about life with our children. Being aware of these issues and opportunities helps e-Parents make informed choices about the best ways to use the "good stuff" of the e-World in their e-Parenting.

In the four chapters of Part II, "Raising Better Kids Using the Internet and Computers," e-Parents will learn lots of ways to teach their children the skills they think their children should know. The life skills or attributes most parents want their children to have are creative problem solving, self-esteem and self-confidence, getting along with people, self-discipline, and the ability to take responsibility.

Read on to find out more about e-Parenting techniques that can provide this kind of guidance.

PART II

Raising Better Kids Using the Internet and Computers

CHAPTER 3

Using the PC and Net to Nurture Creative Problem Solving

This chapter contains many ideas for ways to nurture creative thinking and problem solving. We'll give you some ways to start practicing these skills with your kids through real experiences with nature and science, with art media, with real and play money, and with foods and kitchen experiences.

At the same time, we will be emphasizing ways you can help kids practice critical-thinking skills when you encourage them to compare, evaluate, and make choices. This chapter focuses on ways to enhance or expand on creative-thinking skills by using the PC and the Internet with your children.

What Is Creative Problem Solving, and Why Is It Important to e-Parents?

Creative problem solving is a special kind of thinking which we call *process thinking*. It's the kind of thinking kids do when they put different bits of information together and process it to figure out something. It is the kind of thinking children are doing when you can see the wheels turning in their heads. You're a parent; you know what we mean.

Creative problem solvers are also divergent thinkers. They are always open to possibilities. They see many sides to a question, many "right" answers, and many ways to solve a problem. The world our e-Children will inherit will need leaders who are divergent thinkers, doers, and creative problem solvers.

What You'll Learn in This Chapter:

▶ Why teaching your child creative problem-solving skills should be an important goal

▶ How to use real-world and virtual-world activities to teach creative problem-solving skills

▶ How to use open-ended media to teach creative problem-solving skills

▶ What the "experts" say about the PC and the Net as educational tools e-Parents know how important creative problem solving is to their children's success as adults and want to give e-Children experiences that help them practice this kind of thinking.

The kinds of experiences that promote problem solving or "figuring it out" are discovering, creating, inventing, constructing, comparing, classifying, and experimenting.

Notice that these are hands-on experiences. Children get even more out of these experiences when e-Parents are involved, and when they ask open-ended questions and make comments that encourage and expand the child's thinking process.

Open-Ended Questions

Open-ended questions have more than one answer, and the person asking the question should not know the answers he or she will get. The answers may not be what you expect! Open questions precipitate (or you could say "are catalysts for") imagination and process thinking.

"What is this color?" is a closed question. "How does yellow make you feel?" and "What do you think will happen if we...?" and "What are some things we can do with this color?" and "What does red make you think about?" are all open questions. As you see, open questions encourage real thinking, not rote answers. e-Parents can and should stimulate creative problem solving by asking children open questions often. Most three-year-olds respond to them well; fours and up love them.

Whenever the child must imagine something, such as moving an object in his or her mind to a different place before answering the question, the open question is more advanced and sophisticated. More process thinking is required.

Consider this example: "You told me lots of things you can do with this table. But what if you had this table at *your* house? What would you do with it there?" You can see that the use of imagination makes the thought process more complex. This type of question is like a riddle, and four- and five-year-olds love open questions as much as they love riddles. Children ages four and five love riddle-type questions. Riddles are also good ways to stimulating process thinking.

Just playing Mozart for babies or young children will not produce thinkers and problem solvers. In fact, some scholars are now questioning the validity of the "Mozart effect." New studies are in the works (the original study was done with college students).

Hearing classical music from a very early age is great and has been found to calm "hyper" babies, but learning for young children is still based on *doing*, not on listening or watching.

Research has proven that even babies do cognitive or process thinking as they assimilate knowledge about their world through the senses, and they also learn from experimenting and trial and error. Young children are born eager to learn and are learning *all the time*, no matter where they are.

And they are not passive learners; they are not "sponges." No, they are active learners, more like Pac Man, gobbling as fast as they can. It's up to e-Parents to make sure that their children are learning the right things.

One more thing…. As you may have guessed, creativity and cognitive thinking are related. Both kinds of thinking and doing require open attitudes and divergent thinking processes, which is why creative experiences are so good for kids. These experiences stimulate and reinforce process thinking.

So what does all this mean to e-Parents? We hope you will agree that creative problem solving is a good skill for your kids to know and that you will want some tips on how to nurture this skill.

Adults Benefit, Too:

Even adults remember only about 50 percent of what's presented when they hear or read about it, but they retain 90 percent when they *do* something.

How to Nurture Creative Problem Solving by Blending Real-World and Virtual-World Activities

Creative problem solving surfaces in daily life in many ways. It may mean looking at something from a different perspective, or using a material in a new way, or constructing something completely original to "fix" something else. People of all ages are full of creative problem solving potential, and kids are no exception.

e-Parents can help their children sharpen their creative problem solving skills in the real world and in the virtual world. Sometimes an interest is sparked on the Net that the child can carry into the real world with an engaging activity. Just as often, a real-world project can be enhanced with an online activity.

Children practice their creative problem solving skills when they use open-ended media, when they make natural science discoveries, when they do science experiments, when they pretend, and even when they help in the kitchen. In many of these real, hands-on experiences, the Internet can play a part.

Simple Science

Science is mostly about observing something very intently and telling what you see. With kids, that means looking and handling and touching and smelling. Science is also about asking "What might happen if…?" and then trying it (experimenting) to find out what *does* happen.

You can see that the basics of science are simple. Science is focusing one's interest on something, observing it, telling about it, experimenting to see what might happen, and telling what did happen. This is the bare bones of the scientific method, and children are natural scientists! Science makes kids process information and figure things out.

Because science activities practice creative problem solving, here are some ideas for nurturing that kind of thinking in your child.

Weather

The wheels turn in children's heads whenever they are doing any type of experiment or science activity. One everyday science activity is observing the weather. Daily weather affects all of us, and it's something that everyone, everywhere, observes and talks about.

e-Parents and their young children look out the window or check out the weather each day, just to know what kinds of clothes to wear or whether to take a raincoat. At child care centers, teachers often start the day by discussing the calendar and weather.

e-Parents can expand on a young child's interest in the weather by making a daily "weather check" part of the child's morning routine. The child can place a symbol or sticker (or draw a symbol) in the corner of that day's space on the calendar to indicate rain, snow, fog, sun, wind, or clouds.

At the end of the month, the calendar record (which is a type of graph) will give the e-Parent opportunities to discuss concepts like *how many*, *more*, and *less*, and also to ask the child why he or she thinks they had so many rainy days, and so on. (When children compare and evaluate, they are using critical thinking!)

If there are older kids in the family, the older siblings might take the information gathered by the younger kids and make graphs or discuss seasonal weather trends.

e-Parents can help children expand this science activity by making a simple rain gauge, using a wind sock and compass to find wind direction, and checking the daily temperature on an outdoor thermometer. The child can record this information on the calendar, too.

Children age 5 and older love recording information they gather, and they may even want to do experiments like these, which also practice figuring things out:

- Bring in some snow and record how long it takes to melt. What if you put it in the refrigerator? or the freezer?

- Make gelatin and put half in the refrigerator and half outside. Record which one jells first. If you repeat this experiment on a colder or warmer day, does the answer stay the same?

- Make a few things out of clay and put one item in the shade, one in the sun outside, one on the window sill, and one in a cool, dark place inside. Compare the differences in the time it took them to dry and how they look. Talk about why.

- Paint a section of the side of the house, driveway, or sidewalk with a big wallpaper type brush and bucket of water. See how long it takes the water to evaporate on days with different kinds of weather.

e-Parents will quickly see that observing the weather can lead both young and school-age children to other science experiments and discoveries about the elements of water and air.

▼ **Try It Yourself**

e-Parents can also take simple science experiments to new levels by using a PC and the Internet. Here are some ways to nurture creative problem solving in the e-World.

1. Fire up your PC and, with your junior scientist beside you, go to the Internet. Type the URL www.weather.com to load the world weather page.

2. When the weather site opens, your child can see the weather anywhere in the world. Click the thumbnail map of the United States or pick a country from the pop-up list box to get current information about the weather in your selected location.

3. After viewing weather data, your child may want more information. Click the *Learn More* button on the left side of the screen to open the More About the Weather page.

4. Click the Storm Encyclopedia link. You'll see many severe-weather topics. Under tornadoes is a pull-down list of many topics. If you choose *tornado safety*, for example, you can learn how to practice staying safe in a tornado. Then you can actually practice the tips with your child.

   Select other topics to learn about wind, clouds, hurricanes, and so on—or you can go back to tornadoes and choose *tornado formation* or *storm chasers*.

Another interesting weather-related site is the Science Learning Network (www.sln.org). At this site, children can learn more about air, wind, and light. They can do the following:

- Learn how to do a hands-on project using fruit to create light

- Make a pinhole viewer to see images carried by light and find out why the images are upside down and backwards

- Make an anemometer to measure wind speed, using ordinary objects found around the house

On the Science Learning Network site, you and the kids can see slide shows, guess what is under the microscope, learn about the physics of water and the science of cycling, and learn about energy concepts as presented by some of The Atoms Family characters.

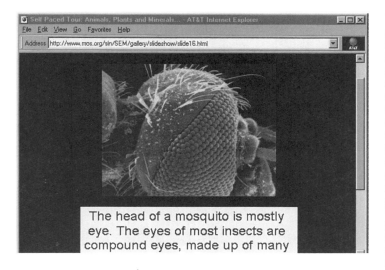

The head of a mosquito is mostly eye. The eyes of most insects are compound eyes, made up of many

This interesting game on the Science Learning Network (www.sln.org) stimulates children's critical-thinking skills. Here's what you would see if you look at a dust mite through an electron micro-scope. Children guess whether the "thing" they're looking at is animal, vegetable, or mineral. A pop-up window tells the correct answer with some added facts.

Search Together

Whenever you do a search of any kind with your child, you are modeling and teaching an appropriate way to use the personal computer. Be there to assist and encourage whenever your child gathers information.

When you search together, your child will be practicing how to use the PC and the Net in appropriate ways with your supervision, which is a pattern you want to put very firmly into place before your child becomes an adolescent.

e-Parenting doesn't just mean reading about something. e-Parents and children can take e-World information into everyday life and expand on it with new hands-on activities that nurture creative problem solving. Here are some examples:

- The information learned about clouds may inspire a school-age child to go outside to observe, draw, or paint the clouds—or to write a poem about them.

- The information learned on a science site may motivate an older child to make instruments that measure wind, rain, and air or to become a weather observer who calls in reports to the local television station.

- If your young child is afraid of thunderstorms, information from the Net may help desensitize the fears. Now your child may be better able to watch the sky with you during a storm and appreciate its beauty and power without the fear.

Spiders

Another easy way to get children to think and problem solve is to interest them in something that is all around us in nature—such as bugs and insects. We chose the simple natural science example of spiders because they seem to live everywhere, many children are afraid of them, and e-Parents usually want a way to deal with this fear.

Knowledge Is Power over Fear:
When a child learns more about something he or she is afraid of, the knowledge often helps neutralize the fear. You can use this example about spiders and apply it to other fears as well (such as a fear of snakes or bats).

On the other hand, your kid may not have any fears, but may have a real interest in bugs and spiders. You can find all sorts of good information about spiders on the Internet.

Do the searches together. Nurture problem solving by asking your child to talk about what he or she learns about spiders on one site and *compare* that to information from another site. Talk about the advantages of one or another site. Have your child print out favorite pages to reread.

Observing, comparing, and discussing together help your child learn and practice the skills of evaluating and making good choices on the Net.

The Right Search Engine for the Job

Searching the Internet can be overwhelming, tiring, and confusing. To make it easier, remember that the secret to getting the results you want are the *keywords* or *search words* you type in the search box. Expand your keywords into phrases, use plurals, and surround phrases with quotation marks.

The various search engines bring up different results for the same search because each engine uses different search criteria. Try any of these popular engines:

- Infoseek (*http://infoseek.go.com*)
- Yahoo! (*www.yahoo.com*)
- Excite (*www.excite.com*)
- AltaVista (*www.altavista.com*)

How would you begin a search about spiders? If you just use the word *spiders* or the phrase *"spider information,"* you will get thousands of results, many of which may not even be about spiders (such as the car, Alpha Romeo Spider). Instead, narrow your search with phrases in quotation marks, such as *"children's fear of spiders," "classroom insect experiments," "kids learn about spiders,"* and *"kids spider projects."*

We found the Spider Pages site at *www.powerup.com.au/ ~glen/spider.htm* with lots of information and pictures about spiders, interesting spider facts (researched by kids), an interactive spider anatomy info-picture, first-aid information, "Don't Be Afraid of Spiders" letters written by kids, and more. You can even obtain your own virtual pet spider and learn how to preserve a spider web! The site also has links (with descriptions) to related sites.

Result Sites Help Narrow a Search

Remember that the Web site links you find at a site are valuable tools in narrowing your searches and getting more of the information you want. Links are like shortcuts on the superhighway that other site owners recommend with give-quick directions...sort of a virtual word-of-mouth system.

Let's say your child is browsing the virtual arachnid world, develops an interest in tarantulas, and wants to get one. You suggest that he needs to learn lots more about them before you consider letting him have one. An e-Parent would remember to have the child check the links at the first spider site they had explored to see whether tarantulas are listed. Sure enough, there is a link to *tarantula tour* (*www.mindspring.com/ ~nlgray/ttour/index.htm*). You will learn about the care, feeding, housing, and dangers for tarantula owners—just what your child wants to know.

Using the information about spiders may spark an interest in insects. Armed with the information they find on the Net, e-Parents and kids can go on an insect safari, start a collection, or build a terrarium to study a spider or other creatures.

e-Parents and young children who are interested in more ways to experiment and problem solve with science should take a look at *www.cochran.com/theodore/beritsbest*. This excellent site is for kids up to age 12; it features a catalog of safe sites for kids to visit, rated for quality on a scale of 1 to 5, complete with links.

On the home page is a directory of categories: *Just for Fun*, *Holidays*, *Serious Stuff*, *Creatures Great and Small*, and *Kids on the Net*. The lists of links are extensive (for example, under the *Just for Fun* category is the *Crafts* subcategory, with links to more than 50 craft sites for kids up to age 12).

Under the *Serious Stuff* category is the *Science* subcategory, which lists about 40 links to which you can go in an instant to practice more creative thinking and problem solving. If you want to go straight to that science page, type *www.cochran.com/theodore/beritsbest/seriousstuff/science/index.html*.

For teen-age creative thinkers interested in the sciences, we suggest *www.chem4kids.com*. This site presents some great chem-istry-related information in an unusual way and includes other sciences (biology, physics, math, and so on) as well. Chem4kids is one piece of a growing community at *www.kapili.com*. Take a virtual tour of the beautiful Kapili Islands and be sure to visit the Research Labs area.

The home page at www.kapili.com shows the site's focus on science and technology. Artists, writers, politicians, philosophers, inventors, and judges come here to do research and to just think.

More Science Sites

We also found some really neat science sites for five- to eight-year-olds and would hate to miss sharing them with you.

• Science Made Simple (*http://waterw.com/~science*) is a site for both parents and children in which all the wonderful, difficult questions children ask from age 4 on are answered. (Why is the sky blue? Why do leaves change color?)

• Zoom Dinosaurs (*www.pbs.org/wgbh/zoom*) is a fun site that eight- to 10-year-olds will love, all about those mystic monsters of the past.

• The Space Place (*http://spaceplace.ipl.nasa.gov*) is (you guessed it) the NASA site.

• The Edible/Inedible Experiments site (*www.madsci.org/experiments*) is an archive where many unique experiments for ages 7 and up can be found.

• And last but not least, on The Yuckiest Site on the Internet is Worm World (*www.nj.com/yucky/worm*), where lots of great worm-science experiences can be found.

How to Use Open-Ended Media

Open-ended materials can be used successfully by any age or skill level. There is no right or wrong way to use blocks, music, clay, props, or art media such as paint, crayons, and markers. Open-ended materials are used for constructing, experimenting, and creating. They stimulate process thinking and help children practice creative problem solving.

Create a Picture

Children feel a sense of joyful power when they are given blank paper and media such as paint, crayons, or markers. They are in charge. They can fill that paper with any images and colors they choose.

The same sense of joy can fill children when they cover a blank monitor screen with colors and designs. Whenever they imagine, plan, experiment, and create with "paintbrush" software (or use low-tech marking pens on paper), children are having fun, doing problem solving, and using tools to implement what they have planned or imagined.

Observe your children as they create. You will see them *critique* what they have done and sometimes change it and try something new. When they assess, adjust, and modify their creation, they are evaluating it—and doing process thinking. (You'll see those wheels turning in their heads.)

Children will continue this process until they believe the work is complete. Do your best to encourage this type of activity. Children need lots of practice in evaluating and doing critical thinking.

Just Like Adults:

Even though the process is less complex and less detailed, when children play or create with open-ended media, they are using the same kinds of process thinking that adults use when they create or problem solve.

Now that you know what kinds of thinking skills are going on when your child creates a picture or design, we want you to help your child try to create a picture with the PC and its tools. Maybe you will even create it together.

There are many software programs for creative e-Parenting. They are based on creating pictures on the PC, using built-in tools such as scissors, paste, paint, crayons, erasers, and stamps, just to name a few.

In general, some sort of art software comes with your personal computer and is accessible from your desktop. For example, if you have a Windows PC, you get the Paint program with the Windows software. Any drawing application you use has a menu bar at the top of the screen that displays commands from which you can choose. (The drawing and painting programs available today vary in the skill levels they require.)

Your virtual tools will be icons or buttons that resemble scissors, glue, brushes, paint, and so on. You can help your child discover how to operate these icons to create an original picture. If your child can click and drag the mouse, he or she can use color palettes, different brush shapes, and special effects.

More Options for Advanced Users:

Advanced users have even more options for creating with art software. In addition, if you purchase a scanner, the device may come with a type of imaging software.

Even if the first picture the child makes on the PC is a scribble design bursting with different colors, the child is using tools to create a representation of his or her own ideas; the child is using the brain to do process thinking and problem solving. At the same time, you are both having fun together, doing a creative activity.

You can also search the Internet for software that allows you and your child to create pictures and designs. You can go to a shopping mall site or to a parenting site for recommendations on worthwhile graphics software.

We went to *www.smarterkids.com*, and there we found software, games, and packages for many learning skills. We found some interesting software that helps children make pictures. Kid Pix Studio Deluxe is software that helps kids draw, paint, animate, and showcase their work.

We also used the Yahoo! search engine to look for the categories *"computers and the Internet"*, *software*, and *children*. We found a list of reviews of children's software sites. At The Review Zone at *www.thereviewzone.com*, we clicked the Creativity-Art-Music link and located a review of the Disney's Magic Artist program. The Review Zone site has in-depth software reviews for parents and teachers. In just a few clicks, we found both Kid Pix Studio Deluxe and Disney's Magic Artist and read reviews that helped us make an informed choice about which one to purchase.

We found another game we like for kids age 8 and up called Simpark. Kids get to create and run their own virtual park complete with choices of plants, animals, and people stuff such as benches. Kids learn about different species, ecosystems, and the food chain. This game is good for critical-thinking skills and for nurturing an interest in the natural world. Also available is a teachers guide for using Simpark in class.

We hope that you will encourage your child to use both real-world and virtual-world tools for creating.

After your child has had several experiences in using the PC or software to create pictures, have the child do a real-world picture with paper and paint or crayons or pastels or markers. It can be a real-world version of a picture he or she already created on the PC, or something new and different.

Now talk with the child about these creations. How did he or she feel when creating the PC picture versus creating the real-world picture? Which was more fun to create and why? Is this always true? Again, if we want kids to learn the skills of comparing and critical thinking, we have to help them practice these skills.

The Global Children's Art Gallery found at *www.naturalchild.com* exhibits artwork created by children ages 1 to 12; art is in all mediums, including computer-generated art. Guidelines for submission include requirements that prohibit frightening images, messages of culture/country superiority, the entry of more than one picture a month, and a requirement that the art is the child's own initiative.

The Global Children's Art Gallery (www.naturalchild.com/gallery/) provides a venue you and your child can visit to see the kinds of graphics other kids are making. If you want, you can even submit one of your child's masterpieces for inclusion on a gallery page.

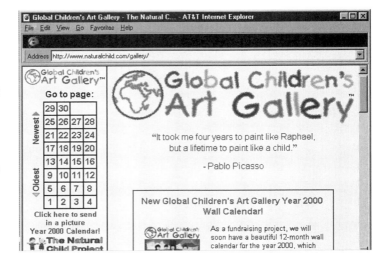

Directions for submitting art as an email attachment are clear; art sent by snail mail can be returned to the artist. The Art Gallery also includes information for parents, a painting site of the month, and a radio interview about the site's history and content. This site is a great place to encourage creativity and boost self-esteem.

Another interesting site is The Artroom, a site for older kids, at *www.arts.ufl.edu/art/rt_room/@rtroom_doorway.html*. This site presents ideas for art projects; examples of art for inspiration; a gallery of kids' projects; and ways to learn about artists through stories, scrabble, and trivia. The @rt Sparkers link is particular helpful if you don't know what you want to draw or do. The site also has a respectable book selection with books on mural painting, early cave art, art careers, painting techniques, and other subjects. The site's mission is to "provide a virtual learning environment for exploring the world of art."

Sculpting

Perhaps you have noticed a tactile and sensorial bent in your child's learning style or that your child loves to play with sand, mud, clay, or play dough. These types of yielding media are great tension and stress relievers, they increase finger strength and dexterity, they allow children to practice motor skills, and best of all—because they are open-ended materials—they help children do creative problem solving.

When a child creates something original with clay or play dough, a whole lot of process thinking is going on. To create something with any open-ended media, the child must imagine, plan, experiment, discover, critique, adjust or modify, make decisions, and complete the task. These are all great ways to exercise the brain!

Okay, you are convinced that sculpting is a great idea, but you don't want sand and mud in the house, and you would rather make your own play dough. (We heartily agree; why buy something that you can make in a few minutes for a few pennies?) But you and your child must first search to find a recipe for just the kind of play dough or clay you need.

Play Clay for Everyone:

All ages love play dough, and we have seen teens play with play dough or silly putty for hours, so if you make up a batch, always make enough for everyone to join in.

▼ **Try It Yourself**

1. Go directly to our site for parents and teachers, *www.askevelyn.com*. Click Resources and Reviews.

2. From the list at the top of the Resources and Reviews page, click the Creative Kids Studio link to open a page featuring information on creativity and things to do with kids.

3. Scroll down a bit to find the play dough recipe, with a blurb about its many advantages for learning. (You can also follow the Ev's Stuff link to see a list of pamphlets you can order, one of which contains the play dough recipe and other homemade art media recipes.)

4. Print the page (or write down the play dough recipe by hand) and take it and your child to the kitchen. Now that you've done your research, you can reward yourself with some more hands-on education in measuring and mixing.

▲

The EarlyChildhood site at *www.earlychildhood.com* (sponsored by Discount School Supply) has a good page explaining the benefits of arts and crafts for children. This site also includes projects you and your child can do together. At the Discount School Supply site (*www.classroomdirect.com*), click the Shop or Browse button at the top of the page, click the Arts & Crafts link, and then scroll down the supply list to find 14 products listed under *clay*. In your continuing search for a play dough recipe, go to *www.theideabox.com* and follow the Craft Recipes link to several good play dough and silly putty recipes.

About Money

Children are fascinated with money. They love the sound and feel of the coins, and they know at an early age that money is exchanged for many things that they like.

Money is also a perfect medium for sorting, matching, and categorizing. Letting your young child play sort-and-match games with money is a good way to introduce it. Understanding number quantity and the use of money as an exchange for goods is the next step. Again, playing or pretending with money is a way for a child to learn more about it and to practice problem solving at the same time.

Pretending with Money

Real Books about Money:

Here are two good books about money: *A Penny Saved*, by Neale Godfrey (Simon & Schuster, $18.95) and *Kids, Money and Values*, by Patricia Estess and Irving Barocas (Better Way Books, $10.95).

Using money, whether it is real or "play" money, will help children learn more about the values of different coins and will also help them learn about numbers and quantity. Using money also helps children learn the skills of sorting, matching, estimating, categorizing, classifying, and comparing—all skills that practice process thinking and problem solving. Pretending and using props (such as in a make-believe store) can add even more interest!

When children "dress up" or use props and take on adult roles in their pretending, they are experimenting with what they imagine or know about the grown-up world outside the home. e-Parents can take advantage of a child's interest in pretending to practice problem-solving skills.

Find a corner in your kitchen or dining area and use a small table or boxes to create a store. Give the child small cans and food packages; make some colored paper play money, use play money from the Monopoly game, or use single dollars. If the child is age 4 or older (and can be trusted not to swallow small objects) gather some pennies and nickels, and maybe some dimes and quarters, too.

Add a cash box, a toy cash register, or a silverware sorter for the money and give the child some bags for packing the groceries. Put up signs that state the prices or put sticky labels on the goods to price them, using simple prices like one dollar or 5, 10, or 25 cents (depending on the age of the child). Let your child sell groceries to you, friends, or siblings. Help your child count out the money and the change.

Play with Money

Young children who are just beginning to learn about money will want many opportunities to sort and match coins and group them to learn how many pennies make a nickel or a dime and how many nickels make a quarter. Even without a play store, they'll enjoy sorting and matching real money at the table. You can use fewer denominations to simplify the activity.

e-Parents will quickly realize that the entire process of planning the store and getting it ready involves problem solving. You can make play stores to sell anything—shoes, hats, jewelry, or stuffed animals. The planning, acting out, and exchanging of money for goods will help your child do process thinking.

When you ask open questions that nurture comparing and critiquing as you play store, you are helping the child practice critical thinking.

Purchasing with Money

You can take the idea of playing and practicing with money into the e-World with your child and purchase something simple and meaningful over the Internet together. If your child likes learning about coins and money, for example, you can look for that type of product.

▼ **Try It Yourself**

1. Start with the Yahoo! search engine at *www.yahoo.com* (we like the way categories are referenced on this site). Click *Toys Games and Hobbies*.

2. In the search box, type **children's math games**. A results page opens, listing all the products that match your search term and the stores in which they can be found. On the day we did this search, we found 168 products in 42 stores.

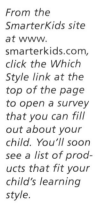

3. Scroll through the list of games until you see one you'd like more information about. For example, we clicked the *Primary Money Chase Game*; the description told us that it was a board game for levels K-3 in which children learn the equivalent combinations of pennies, nickels, dimes, and quarters. Directions for ordering were clear.

Some people are hesitant about purchasing online, but the online directions and information tell you how to do it and why it's safe. You also have the option to pay for purchases with more traditional methods (such as ordering by telephone with your credit card or requesting that a catalog and order form be sent to you).

Shopping for specific products online is much easier than doing so in the real world. You don't have to drive, put up with traffic, find a parking space, hunt through several stores, and sometimes purchase something you know nothing about or that does not even match your child's learning style or interests.

And there is lots of information on the Net about learning styles. The SmarterKids site at *www.smarterkids.com* can find products that match particular learning styles or learning goals and can also find matches for any interest your child has.

From the SmarterKids site at www.smarterkids.com, *click the Which Style link at the top of the page to open a survey that you can fill out about your child. You'll soon see a list of products that fit your child's learning style.*

With the Net, e-Parents can get information on products, compare values and prices, and read reviews about the products from teachers and real parents. You will also find shareware to download so that you can "try before you buy." How many nonvirtual stores allow you to do that? You can learn so much more about a potential purchase on the Net than you can by asking an 18-year-old store clerk!

Even more important, you can save all the wasted time that real-world shopping takes. You can spend that time much more effectively by e-Parenting your children.

Money Games

Sticking with the topic of money, perhaps your school-age kids like board games that use play money. Monopoly is a classic board game that practices the use of money and strategy. Kids love the playing pieces and the play money.

You can also purchase the Monopoly board game on the Internet (go to *www.hasbro.com*). The game is produced in many languages and is played all over the world. Playing family games in the real world teaches kids many skills and also strengthens that feel of "belonging" that kids need.

If you have a young child who wants to play Monopoly but cannot read, a sibling or parent can partner with him or her. Other ways to simplify the game are to use only the largest denominations of money and round off the costs of houses and hotels to even numbers. You can also set a time limit and stop play after one hour or so. Whoever has the most money at that point wins.

Online Versions of Old Favorites

Many of the best learning games online are actually based on the same good games we have played for years: online versions of Monopoly, Scrabble, Boggle, Mastermind, and so on. We are convinced that children prefer to play real-world board games rather than online games; nothing can replace the feeling of belonging to the family group, the excitement of social interaction, and the way the game pieces and boards look and feel. For more information about family games, go to *www.askevelyn.com* or to the Family Game Night site at *www.fgn.com*.

Encourage critical thinking when you play board games such as Monopoly with children. Should we buy that hotel, or should we wait and try for a railroad? What would happen if I traded this utility for that hotel? As the child begins to practice simple strategies, he or she begins to practice the kinds of thinking that will help in evaluating Web sites and making good online choices.

By playing games, children can also have fun and enjoy an activity with parents. "Together things" at early ages help set patterns for more "together things" online in later years!

An interesting site for e-Parents and older kids to explore is *www.littlejason.com/lemonade*. At this site, a computer whiz student is developing some online games. The Lemonade Stand game is about money management and how the weather can affect profit and loss.

This site linked us to some good interactive games that exercise brain and thinking processes. You can link from LittleJason to games such as Word Zap (an action word game), Webmind (a matching game based on Mastermind), a Sliding Puzzle Game, and more.

Creative Problem Solving in the Kitchen

Among the most overlooked opportunities for e-Parents to use to increase children's problem-solving skills are food experiences. We eat every day. We cook or make things to eat every day. We spend time in the kitchen every day. What an opportunity for e-Parenting!

One of the most basic ways to help your child practice matching, sorting, estimating, and categorizing (which are all problem-solving skills) is to encourage him or her to help put away the groceries. Get your child to think about the different types of groceries and where you store various items. Kids can sort the produce from the dry goods. They can learn about the differences between fruits and vegetables. You can talk about why some things need to be stored in the refrigerator and others elsewhere.

This activity can also lead to having children help make out a grocery list or note the things you may run out of. You can even have the kids help you shop, noting and talking about the ways stores display different categories of foods. You can give your child a few dollars and let the child purchase his or her choice of cereal, pay for it with cash, and get the change.

Poor Choices Are Learning Experiences

If a child makes a poor choice with the money in the store, talk about why that was a poor choice and how that choice could have been avoided by learning more about that product before buying it.

Sometimes a poor cereal choice is unavoidable, but if so, the child should still accept the consequences of the choice.

Ask open questions. What are some things you could do if you don't like the cereal you bought? Can you find a recipe (look at home and on the Net) to use that cereal as an ingredient in something else?

The point is to take every opportunity possible to get the child to do problem solving and critical thinking about choices. The little things e-Parents do to set patterns make a big difference later.

Let your child help you cook and bake. Food preparation requires children to engage in science activities and to practice many problem-solving skills. Think about it. Even when kids scrub veggies and make a dip, they are practicing motor skills and using tools to do problem solving.

When they help cook the carrots or make applesauce, chili, cookies, or a cake, kids estimate, count, measure, and combine. They will see "changes in matter"—the changes in the foods that happen because of the heat or cold we apply with the stove, microwave, oven, or refrigerator.

Let children make instant pudding and then make cooked pudding. Have children compare the tastes and textures. Which one tastes best? Which one took longer to make? You can repeat this experience in critical thinking with many food items you frequently use (such as instant and real mashed potatoes).

When children add spices to foods, they learn about new tastes. As they get older, they might try other spices or experiment with different food combinations—more creative problem solving.

When children help you in the kitchen, you have a great opportunity for conversation. Relaxed talking and listening while you prepare a salad, add toppings to pizza, or clean up after a meal strengthens the bonds of family and group feeling.

And don't forget that learning cooking skills is in children's best long-range interest. They will need to cook for themselves some-day and may also have to cook for the family occasionally when they are teens. Getting children interested in cooking and baking is good common sense.

The Internet has umpteen places where you can find recipes of all kinds. Many are on parenting sites or family fun activities sites. The *www.thefunplace.com* site has a great archive of recipes for families. (We actually found a long-lost recipe for tortilla soup on this site.)

Many sites on the Net provide young children's recipes and chil-dren's cookbooks. Earlier in this chapter, we mentioned the Idea Box site (*www.theideabox.com*), which has a recipe for play dough. This site also has many easy recipes for children's cooking (click the *Recipes* link)and recipes for children's crafts (click the *Craft Recipes* link).

Remember that young children need you with them in the kitchen, not only for safe supervision but also to encourage and enjoy their creative problem-solving efforts. The Idea Box recipes include fun ideas for snacks, which encourage the child to count and measure and to think of ways to use food items in new ways. Creative problem solving again!

For example, the Awesome Owl Snack requires banana slices, fruit loops, a cheese wedge, peanut butter, and a rice cake. The e-Parent can expand on the creative-thinking opportunities and ask open questions. What if we didn't have fruit loops? Could we use something else for eyebrows? What other birds can we make?

Another great kitchen idea that encourages critical thinking is to make "stone soup." You may know the folktale of the peddler who helps the town make soup from a stone...and a few other things. Make some stone soup with your child, starting with just the water in the pot and a very well-scrubbed stone. Your child can help add all the things you usually put into soup. When you serve and eat it, ask you child if it was the stone or the other ingredients that made the soup taste good.

Some projects and activities can take place around the kitchen table. Here are a few that help nurture creative problem solving:

- Give your child an old VCR and a short Phillips screwdriver—and let the discovery begin. When the child takes the VCR apart, you'll find many magnets. Experimenting with magnets can follow.

- Give your child a dry-cell battery, some copper wire, a switch, and a job for the electricity to do (such as an electric bell to ring or a tiny light bulb to turn on). Children from age 4 and up can experiment safely with these materials, discovering that when you break the path (circuit) back to home (battery) the electricity cannot do its job.

- Give your child some "junk" from the junk drawer and other odds and ends around the house (such as pipe cleaners, straws, golf tees, toilet paper tubes, plastic lids, and paper cups and plates). Using a sturdy paper plate or plastic meat tray as a base and masking tape to stick things together, your child and you can invent as you go. You can construct a three-dimensional creation that may look like it came from Dr. Seuss. Build up and out; have fun; go where you have never gone before!

After you have enjoyed it, take the "junk" creation apart and put it in a bag to use again another day. Each creation will be a new invention and a new way to enjoy your child as he or she practices creative problem solving.

Stone Soup Online:
You can get the stone soup folktale at your local library or order it online (start at *www.amazon.com* and type **Stone Soup** in the search box).

Kids Learn Differently

e-Parents must remember that each child is unique; each may have a particular learning style as well as special interests. Children practice problem solving in many different ways. Some enjoy creative problem solving with humor and language; others may prefer music and dance, building blocks, science or math experiments, cooking or foods experiences, or art media. Whatever the avenue, encourage it, nurture it by being involved, and praise all efforts.

What the "Experts" Say

In closing this chapter, we want to note that child development experts do not universally agree on the advantages of the PC and Net for teaching creative problem solving.

We believe that to use the Internet successfully as an educational tool, e-Parents must help the child by blending real-world creative problem-solving experiences and critical-thinking experiences with what is learned from the virtual world. Parent involvement is a must in teaching these skills.

In his book *Reinventing Childhood* (Modern Learning Press, 1998, $19.95), author David Elkind says that many psychologists fear that the capabilities of computers exercise the left (sequential) part of the brain at the expense of the right (creative) part. We believe that the best creative problem solving uses both sides of the brain at once.

Elkind believes that computers may eventually make significant improvements in the ways we educate children. For example, a virtual immersion experience in another country can help teach a foreign language.

More by Elkind:

David Elkind is the child development expert who brought us the bestsellers *The Hurried Child*, *All Dressed Up and No Place to Go*, *Parenting Your Teenager in the 90s*, *Grandparenting*, and *A Sympathetic Understanding of the Child: Birth to Sixteen*.

He says that human learning is a social activity and that there is no substitute for the magic of a competent, caring teacher. We agree, and we think that competent, caring teachers can also be e-Parents.

We also agree with Elkind's opinion that virtual learning experiences are symbolic and mediated with a keyboard; virtual learning experiences are not "hands-on" experiences in the truest sense. Young children up to about age 8 need to spend most of their time in direct, sensory, real-world learning experiences.

Summing Up

We hope you have learned some new e-Parenting techniques from this chapter. Teaching kids to be creative problem solvers and critical thinkers is a very big job. But we hope that now you see how this big job can be accomplished in many small but important ways.

When you understand that creative thinking means processing and evaluating information in order to create something, make choices, or solve a problem, you will be more adept at watching for opportunities in everyday life to help nurture this skill in your children.

We have discussed ways that parents can use real-world and virtual-world experiences with nature and science, art media, real and play money, and foods to nurture creative thinking and problem solving.

We have also stressed the importance of using the PC and Net *with* your children and of taking every possible opportunity to practice evaluation and critical thinking with your kids.

We hope that this chapter has provided the information you need to encourage your kids to become creative problem solvers. While you are trying out these ideas along with some of your own, remember to have fun with your kids, show an interest in what interests them, and teach them what you think they should know.

CHAPTER 4

Using the PC and Net to Nurture Self-Esteem

This chapter starts by talking about what self-esteem is and why children need to feel both capable and loveable. Then we'll go on with many ways to use the real and the virtual worlds to nurture self-esteem in children. For example, you can give a child special personal space both at home and on the PC.

We also want to talk a little about praise and the kind of praise that is meaningful to kids (as opposed to "good job" praise). The chapter closes with some thoughts on whether allowing children to risk, try, and fail helps or harms their self-esteem.

Why Is Self-Esteem Important to e-Parents and e-Kids?

Self-esteem is the way children really feel about themselves, deep inside. Self-confidence is an outer behavior and does not necessarily indicate inner self-esteem. (Sometimes people who seem overly self-confident actually have poor self-esteem. We have all met people like that.)

Sometimes children with poor self-esteem attempt to gain confidence by hanging out with peers who seem powerful or popular and who might actually be detrimental to a child's best interests. All the more reason for e-Parents to help build self-esteem in their children, the kind of confidence that counts.

What we want for our children is true self-esteem. We want them to feel good about just plain "being" as well as to feel good about the things they can do.

What You'll Learn in This Chapter:

- ▶ What is self-esteem and why is it important to e-Parents and e-Kids?
- ▶ How you can use real-world and virtual-world situations to help kids gain self-esteem
- ▶ How you can make the praise you give your kids more meaningful
- ▶ Whether you should allow your child to take a risk and have to deal with possible failure

But we also want our kids to recognize that they have capabilities as well as limitations. e-Children will be better able to cope successfully with stress, changes, relationships, and other challenges of adulthood if they develop positive *but realistic* attitudes about themselves.

Self-esteem is based on two things: feeling loveable or worthwhile and feeling capable or competent. e-Parents need to nurture both kinds of feelings in children.

- Feeling loveable has to do with the traits that are unique to your child's personality, such as a sense of humor, creativity, insight or perceptiveness, friendliness, and perseverance. Children feel loveable when e-Parents let them know they are appreciated for who they are, not just for what they have achieved.

- Feeling capable has more to do with behaviors that are specific skills and achievements, such as being able to follow directions, do chores well and independently, get good grades, achieve in sports, and so on. Children who feel capable often know both their capabilities and limitations and usually push themselves to increase their achievements.

Parents can help children feel capable and not stressed out by giving them the freedom and encouragement to develop at their own pace, make mistakes, learn from them, and achieve the goals they set for themselves.

Building self-esteem should be a daily awareness activity for parents. The process is made up of very simple things that mean a lot to kids, such as the following:

- Using children's names and nicknames

- Looking directly at them when you talk or listen

- Listening to what they have to say without interrupting

- Smiling, hugs, and loving touches

- Letting your face and voice show that you care

- Giving genuine compliments or descriptive praise

Behaviors like these, and the other specific activities we share in this chapter, may not seem important to adults when we look at each one separately, but over the course of a day or a week, they add up to a very big part of the way a child sees himself or herself.

The attitudes children have about life and about themselves are already pretty much in place by the time they are 8 or 9 years old. e-Parenting strategies to nurture self-esteem in the early years are vitally important because your child's self-esteem affects his or her success in school, with relationships, with jobs, and with life in general. So let's get started!

Tip:
Kids really don't care what you know—unless they know you care.

Teach Self-Esteem by Blending Real-World and Virtual-World Activities

In this section, we want to give you a few ideas that will help you teach and build your child's self-esteem. Some ideas are real-world ideas you can carry into the e-World (such as creating personal space for kids). Some ideas are Net ideas that may spark interests that build or reinforce self-esteem. And some ideas are very basic things that wise e-Parents will do in real time to nurture self-esteem.

Personal Space

Perhaps you never thought about this before, but all of us need the comfort and the "perk" of personal space; it is part of what makes us feel unique and special as individuals. The same holds true for children. e-Parents can help children build their self-esteem by creating special personal spaces for kids in both the real and virtual worlds.

Real-World Personal Space

At school, children have cubbies, coat hooks, or lockers that are their private and personal spaces. As they grow into the middle school years, they will decorate and individualize these spaces if they can.

If a child has his or her own room at home, it can be decorated or individualized as a personal space. Even helping the child to make a special name sign for the door is a way to personalize the space. Other options are a paper banner that can keep changing its look, a colored paper poster, or even a hand-carved wooden name sign.

Personal space for kids can be made in cupboards, closets, workrooms, and on personal computers. Even though the entire family probably shares the PC, you can easily create personal space on it for each child.

Virtual World Space

If you have a family Web site, include a page just for your young child—a photograph, some artwork, and other things just about him or her. Let the child decide what else to include. Encourage older children to make the page themselves. Many schools already teach kids how to make their own home page. Preteens or teens might like a page or even a Web site all their own. What an esteem builder!

You can also set up a folder on the family PC labeled with your child's name, just for things he or she wants to put in it (such as favorite scanned pictures and things the child has written or created). Teach your youngest children how to navigate around the computer to find their folders and help them learn how to put things inside the folders.

When you're surfing the Net with your child, you'll find sites that you particularly like and to which you'll want to return. You can make and organize Favorites folders for Web sites you want to save.

Tip
If your young child needs visual cues to find and open the folder, make a list of steps with accompanying drawings that help the child remember the sequence.

When you are online together, talk about the sites you find, compare them, talk about why you like them. Let your children decide which sites they like best and help them save their URLs in a Favorites folder of their own. This way, children can open the folder and go immediately to a favorite site.

A word of caution here. Remember to be an integral part of your child's online activities. You want to help children learn to find and enjoy their favorite safe sites independently, but you don't want them to go live there and become isolated from the family. Set time limits and be sure that your child balances PC time with active, enjoyable, hands-on activities.

The Benefits of Using the PC

When young children (2 to 5 years old) use the PC and Net with you, they are developing confidence. They are proud that they can use these tools just like grown-ups do. When preschoolers use the computer, they are cultivating new and unique interests of their own; they are not feeling jealous or left out when their older siblings use the PC for more sophisticated tasks. Young siblings will recognize their limitations and observe their older siblings' capabilities. And older kids will usually help the younger ones learn.

When parents use the PC and Net with their kids, they are implementing several e-Parenting strategies at the same time:

- They are helping children feel important and loved.
- They are helping children feel competent and capable.
- They are modeling and teaching kids appropriate ways to use these e-World tools.

Don't I Look Great?

Looking great makes most of us feel great. And feeling good usually makes us look good (as the song goes, "you're as beautiful as you feel"). There is no doubt that outer appearance plays a part in your child's self-esteem. We want to share a few real-world and virtual-world ideas about mirrors and photos that can enhance a child's self-esteem.

Mirrors

One of the things we take for granted is the mirror or mirrors we look into each day when we do personal grooming and try to look our best. Approving of how we look is a big part of our self-esteem. Many parents do not realize that mirrors in houses are usually at the adult's eye level; children have few, if any, mirrors to look into.

If they did have mirrors, even good hand mirrors, they could hear a parent say, "Look how pretty your smile is now that you brushed your teeth" or "That shirt makes your eyes look even bluer" or "I can see that you spent time brushing your hair" or "You picked just the right thing to wear today."

We miss many opportunities for esteem building when children do not have mirrors. e-Parents can take care of that easily.

Photos

Photos are another great self-esteem builder. Putting photos in family and individual albums—and leaving these albums out where people can look at them frequently—is a key strategy. Giving kids their own cameras and small, inexpensive albums for the pictures they take is a related idea. Putting framed photos up in your home is still another way to build a sense of belonging and family pride in your children.

Today the capabilities of the PC and Internet can really take the esteem-building opportunity of photos to new levels. e-Parents can scan photos of their children and add them to the child's page on the family Web site (or the child's own Web site). Photos can even be sent to friends and relatives using email.

If you do not have your own Web site, you can post your kids' photos on Web space that's made available for that purpose for free. A good place to start is My-Kids (*www.my-kids.com*).

A great place to post the photos your child takes is at www.my-kids.com.

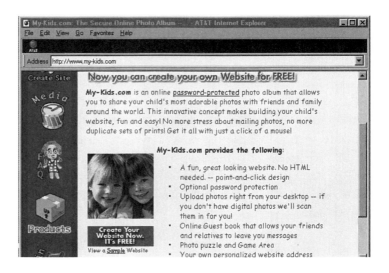

Family and friends can view your pictures from anywhere in the world and on any computer for free. You can create your own site and upload photos to the site through your browser. The site can be password protected if you want so that only selected family and friends can view it. (We strongly recommend this.) There is also a place for guest entries so that your family and friends can send messages about your children's pictures.

> **Digitizing Photos**
>
> If you don't have a digital camera that can feed photo images directly into your computer, scan your photos or have them scanned onto a floppy disk or a CD and then add them to your computer photo files. You can ask My-Kids to do this job for you by mailing the actual prints to them. For a fee, My-Kids will even build a Web site for you. My-Kids is one of several sites owned by My Website Inc. Others include *my-wedding.com*, *my-trip.com*, *my-party.com*, and *my-pets.com*.

"About Me" Books

We all know that kids like to hear stories about themselves. They especially like to hear about their birth and funny things they did as infants or toddlers. In the same vein, children like to create simple homemade books about themselves, which we could call "Me" books or journals. The e-World gives us some new options for creating these self-esteem builders.

Real-World "Me" Activities

In child care and preschool programs, making a "Me" book is a common activity, especially at the beginning of the school year. "Me" books are great esteem builders and are usually done in conjunction with other self-esteem activities, such as making full-body outlines of each child on newsprint paper to hang on the walls after the children color them with crayons.

e-Parents can easily make a "Me" book at home by using an unlined notebook or colored paper for each page and having the book spiral bound when it's completed (your local copy shop can bind the book for you). A "Me" book encourages your child to tell about his or her family, pets, favorite things to do, favorite foods, favorite colors, dislikes, fears, and so on.

Children usually draw and color the illustrations for the book topics, and the adult prints what the child says on each illustrated page. When an adult thinks the child's words are important enough to write down, that child is bound to feel proud.

Keep Your Photos Private:

Never post your child's photo on a public Web site or message board. Doing so would be the same as giving your personal information to the world. If you use a password-protected site, you ensure that only friends, relatives, and people you know personally can view photos of your children.

"Me" books are actually stepping stones to personal journals, and even preschoolers can enjoy a personal journal if they dictate and you do the writing. Getting children to feel comfortable about writing down ideas, events, and feelings in personal journals is a very good idea. It helps children release stress and express their feelings, dreams, and fears. Journals also improve written language skills.

Journals for Literacy:
Writing in a journal is a common activity encouraged in quality preschool centers that emphasize literacy activities.

Actually, the personal journal is yet another form of personal space, which is another reason it is a self-esteem builder. e-Parents should purchase notebooks and get young children started on the habit of writing journal notes.

At about age 4 or 5, children can be encouraged to tell their parents something they especially liked that day or thought was important. A parent can write the sentences the child dictates, and then the child may want to add some "invented writing" or a drawing. It's okay if the child wants to skip some days—journal writing should be fun, not a chore. When the child learns to print, he or she can take over journalizing.

Most schools begin requiring children to keep journals in middle school or junior high years. Your children will whiz through this assignment if you start them early, never pushing, but encouraging them to write notes in the journal at least a few times a week.

Virtual "Me" Activities

Try It Yourself ▼

And why not create a child's personal journal in the virtual world? A number of early education programs have found that some children are not interested in using markers or pencils to write down their ideas, but that they love typing words into the computer. Some children who won't attempt to make up a story on lined paper do it proudly and easily on the computer. If you want to try this approach with your child, here's how.

1. Do the actual writing of the journal entry together: let the child dictate while you type into a word processing program.

2. Print out the text on paper you can add to a three-ring binder or other easy-add type of folder.

3. In addition to daily personal notes and observations, you can print out computer-generated art and pictures your child likes that you have found together on the Internet. Add these pages to the journal notebook.

4. You can also add photos the child has taken and his or her original noncomputerized art.

5. Make a cover for the personal journal by using a laminated photo of the child. Your PC software can help you print the child's name and the title of the journal to place on the cover.

▲

"About Me" journals or books can be especially good for adopted children, special-needs children, or children of diverse cultures. As they learn more about themselves from their parents and from Net resources, they will be able to write in their journals about their personal history and heritage, their strengths, and their cultures.

Another idea is to have a custom book made about your child. At *www.custombooksandmore.com*, you can order a custom book printed with your child's name featured throughout the story in a standard or deluxe version. You can include up to four family members, include friends or pets, and have a special dedication or greeting put on the first page. The other characters in the book are well-known licensed characters such as Spiderman, the Flintstones, and Sesame Street characters. Each book is custom created at age-appropriate reading levels for ages 3 through 10.

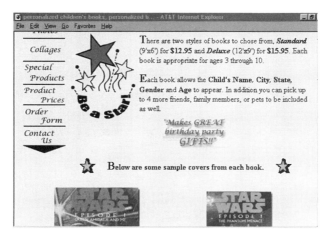

You can go to www.custombooksandmore.com to order a book in which your child and other important family members are star characters.

About typing and formatting those journal entries…. School-age kids learning about computers and keyboarding will already know the basics of using toolbars in a word processing program, but young children will need parental help with font style and point size. If a young child can't type, parents should help by typing what the child dictates. Otherwise, the typing process will take too long for the child, and the child will lose interest in the journal project.

New Interests Build Self-Esteem

Sometimes your kids need help finding an outside interest or hobby, but they don't know where to begin. Because new interests are likely to increase self-esteem—and also gain the child some new friends—they are important as self-image builders.

e-Parents really need to help out with this project. Sit next to your child and use the PC together to do some relaxed exploring on the Net. This kind of exploring can help your child find out more about his or her current interests and can spark brand new ones.

Explore Interests and Find New Ones

Expanding personal interests is much easier now than it was in the past. Now we have instant communication, interest-specific software, and Net resources to help.

e-Parents and kids with an interest or unusual hobby (which they may have discovered on the Net) now have resources for learning more, for taking online classes, for attending online seminars, for finding out about festivals, and for finding more people with the same interest to share ideas with. The more one learns, the better. A child can even develop an interest in a field that may lead to a lifelong career.

e-Parents need to show children how to investigate and cultivate a variety of interests. Not only does this activity encourage curiosity and a love of learning new things, it also helps children better cope with both the changes and the possibilities in life. As your children become adults, they will already be aware that when one door closes, many other doors are already open.

Start with the interests your child already has—horses, art, writing, dance, or taking pictures, to name a few—and build on any interest with the resources of the Net or software. You can start with general Web sites regarding that interest and narrow the search to a unique specific-interest Web site.

Equine Online

Lots of young people are interested in horses, so we tried a search with the word **horses** on the InfoSeek search engine. The results brought up an interesting site called Horsenet.com (*www.horsenet.com*), which is an entire Internet community for horse people. There were listings of shows and events, coverage of current events, discussion forums on many topics, chat rooms, editorials, classifieds, and a newsletter.

There are also over 1000 links (they say—we did not count) to sites that have anything to do with horses, such as riding camps (where your child can go "try out" working with horses for a week or two), horse clubs, horse products, horse racing, and more. We tried the link *Equestrian World Directory* at *www.countrybarn.com/pace/equestrian-search1.dbm* which is a database of over 1000 sites dedicated to horse people. There we found a category called *Computers and Software*. We searched this category for some horse-related software, and got many results.

One site was called Equivision (*www.equivision.net*), "the premier equestrian technology provider." There we found a huge variety of software, from screen savers to veterinary software. We found the World of Horse Multimedia CD-ROM, which is an interactive horse encyclopedia for ages 8 and up. Software ranges from high school reading-level information to games, including a virtual horse game you can play online with Macromedia Shockwave.

Just exploring a special interest in horses can keep e-Parents and their e-Kids very busy for weeks. This site at www.equivision.net *is a great place to start investigating an interest your child might have in horses.*

Electronic Discussions and Interests

e-Parents should also know how to connect their older children with kid-safe and teen-safe bulletin boards, chat rooms, and newsgroups. All these electronic discussion groups exist for the purpose of sharing ideas, information, and conversation. We'll give you more guidance for online safety regarding electronic discussion groups in Chapter 9, "Internet Safety for Online Kids."

- **Bulletin boards.** Bulletin boards are just that. People can read posted messages, reply to posted messages, or create their own message to be posted to a bulletin board about particular topic. Many Web sites include these boards for their users.

  You can find a bulletin board by typing **"bulletin boards"** along with some words describing the topic you are interested in into a search box. Home pages of search engines such as Yahoo! (at *www.yahoo.com*) often have bulletin-board areas, too.

- **Chat rooms.** Chat rooms are "live" interactive areas in which you communicate with other chatters by typing messages. These rooms, which are categorized by topics ranging from Persian kittens to cathouses of the more sleazy variety, are easy to find at many Web sites or with a search.

Links to Chats

Chapter 9 provides more information about safe sites, but if you want to look for some safe chat rooms for your kids now, start with *www.getnetwise.com*, a site known for its online safety resources. Go from the home page to their Web Sites for Kids pages. There you'll find many options. We scrolled down and clicked on the link to Cyber Angels and Cyber Mom's List of Sites (*www.cyberangels.com*) There were many sites listed, but we kept scrolling until we found Purple Moon, a site dedicated to girls ages 8 to 12, that sounded really neat. We clicked the link to that site (*www.purple-moon.com*) and were delighted to see many good categories, including *wannachat*.

Then we used the Back arrow and tried another CyberMom link to a site called FreeZone (*www.freezone.com*) where, again, we could go to chat from the home page. CyberMom's link page told us that Purple Moon's chat was monitored; it recommended supervision for the FreeZone chat, even though it is a safe site.

We used the Back arrow again and chose a different option, the link to Enough Is Enough (*www.enough.org*). Then we scrolled down the links to find KidsCom (*www.kidscom.com*), which we thought might have chats. Sure enough, chats and pen pals can be found on the home page in the *Make New Friends* category.

Suppose that you want to see whether another site suggests the same sites for safe chats. If you try *www.netmom.com*, you will see FreeZone listed as safe. If you try *www.safekids.com*, you will find KidsCom listed as safe. It is reassuring to see a safe site for chats come up more than once.

- **Newsgroups.** Newsgroups are like bulletin boards except that you can have the postings emailed directly to your e-mailbox. You select the topics you want to receive, and these newsgroup messages will be mailed to you.

  For a list of the bazillion newsgroups available, start at the Liszt Usenet Newsgroup Directory home page at *www.liszt.com/news.*

Special Interests

Let's look at a special interest, like a particular type of music. On the Internet, you can find inspiring stories about favorite artists, learn about all kinds of music, get information about writing lyrics, and (if your PC has sound capabilities), hear music from around the world.

The Club Scene Online

We started at Yahoo! and clicked *Clubs*, and then clicked *Music*, and finally clicked *Songwriting* to find a long list of clubs for aspiring poets, lyricists, musicians, and artists. We picked the Young Aspiring Artist club (*http://clubs.yahoo.com/clubs/youngaspiringartists*), a place where young songwriters and singers can discuss their dreams. You can join this club, which had 122 members on the day we visited, and read forums, see photos, read news and events calendars, and find contacts and links.

Then we went back to Yahoo Clubs and chose *Music* and then *Lyrics*. This time, we were intrigued by Lyrics R Us (*http://clubs.yahoo.com/clubs/aalllyricsclub*). This is a place where lyricists can collaborate with others of a like mind or give each other opinions and help.

When teens have a special interest in music, the Net can help them join a club or chat room to share and discuss their original song lyrics. Your teen can also be involved in a chat with a special musical guest on site—even though that person may be in a studio halfway across the world. Chat rooms, bulletin boards, and newsgroups can also be great places to exchange information or explore leads for finding more information.

e-Parents can even help teens research careers in music. Maybe your son is in band at school and likes music but doesn't know what part this interest should play in his life. He may find out about music therapy on the Net, learn more about it, and then decide to major in music therapy in college. (You can learn about the best colleges for this particular field on the Net, too.)

At the American Music Therapy Association (AMTA) Web site (*www.musictherapy.org*), you can learn what music therapy is, learn about careers in music therapy, and also find out about events and relevant news. You can join the discussion forum, find a therapist, order products, or become a member for more benefits. The site also presents a list of schools and colleges offering music therapy, complete with addresses, phone numbers, and contact persons.

When e-Parents involve teens in their own career searches and choices, teens become more motivated to do well in school and to attend college. The more you know about what your teens like and want to pursue, the more likely it is that they will attend college and not drop out!

Appearance and Fitness Build Self-Esteem

Online Cesspools:

It is easy for teens to stray into inappropriate sites and chats. We talk more about online safety in Chapter 9.

Fresh air, healthy foods, and regular exercise keep children fit. When they are healthy, they feel good about themselves. When they are overweight or underweight, they have less energy and feel far less loveable and capable than they would otherwise.

Your own modeling as e-Parents will make a big difference in the appearance and fitness of your child. It just doesn't work to tell children to eat right or exercise or comb their hair if parents don't also do these things. It is all too easy to get caught up in your work and forget your good modeling. But kids will do as you do, not as you say.

Encourage kids to take exercise breaks with you during the day, even if you can have only 10 or 20 minutes for this purpose. Take a walk, go out and toss a ball, or rake the yard together. When we stretch out or do exercises, the body releases endorphins that help keep us mentally alert and emotionally fit. A lifetime habit of daily exercise will help your child maintain flexibility, strengthen bones and muscles, increase immunity to infection, combat weight problems, and boost self-esteem.

Plant the seeds of healthy eating when children are young and keep building those seeds. Drink lots of water; avoid soft drinks. Avoid sugar cereals and snacks and eat lots of fresh fruits and veggies. Ask your kids to help make a fruit or vegetable dip; their participation really improves the way they gobble up those healthy snacks.

Appearance and fitness are big parts of self-esteem in older children. They can find sites that are geared to their special concerns, join clubs, or engage in chats to talk with other kids about things that make them feel different or unattractive. If they find the right resources on the Net (for example, safe sites for discussions), they will realize that they aren't so different after all.

Online Teen Advice

We used the HotBot search engine with the words *adolescent, teen,* *"self esteem"*, and *"teen issues and advice."*

We found a number of interesting sites. Your Turn at *http://www.courttv.com/choices/yourturn/stereotype* is Court TV's Beacon Award-winning public service program that works directly with local cable affiliates throughout the country to bring teenagers and community leaders together to discuss social issues.

New Moon at *www.newmoon.org* is actually a magazine for "girls and their dreams." This rather new but fast-growing site is dedicated to promoting self-esteem in girls.

Jennifer Esperante Gunter, who calls herself the "cha cha queen," is an author and expert on youth motivation and personal achievement. She has a site on these subjects at *www.chaqueen.com.*

Our favorite site, and one we believe would be very helpful to teens, is Mom, We Need To Talk: Serious Issues Facing Children and Teens. This site at Wide Smiles (*www.widesmiles.org/useful/serious.html*) is actually a list of links to sites for kids and parents covering such subjects as teen driving, health, fitness, emotions, eating disorders, grief, alcohol, bullies, and more.

e-Parents can help their kids by exploring the Net together and finding resources about appearance, fitness, and the way kids feel about themselves. Teens, for example, can find help on dating, fashions, puberty, driving, and more by doing a search for these words. Alternatively, they can go to an online teen magazine such as *Go, girl!*.

Online magazines (called 'zines) such as Go, girl! at www.gogirlmag. com can provide resources for your child's interest in his or her own health and fitness.

We would like to give you more resources concerning teens, but we believe that leading you straight to specific sites by giving you their URLs is a bit like giving you a meal instead of teaching you to cook. We want you to start thinking like an e-Parent; we want *you* to do a little problem solving. Remember that e-Parenting is a state of mind, an approach to parenting, a new way of thinking. Instead of giving you more URLs, we want to point you in some of the right directions and make you think and do on your own.

Try It Yourself ▼

For example, how would *you* go about finding resources for your teen about dating? or about being overweight? or about nutrition? Here's what we think you would do.

1. Now that you know the search engines (and probably have a favorite), you might do a search using some specific words (such as *teen dating*, *teen nutrition*, *teen fitness*, *teen sexual health*, *teen dating*, and so on).

2. You might also try checking some of the big parenting sites (such as Parent Soup at *www.parentsoup.com* or The Parents Place at *www.parentsplace.com* or The National Parenting Center at *www.tnpc.com*) and look for sections or categories about teens or problems with teens. You are sure to find articles on many topics from teen driving to dating, to fitness, to skin problems.

3. You might try a few health sites (such as *www.DrKoop.com* or *www.kidshealth.com*) and look at the sections or categories about teens (such as teen health, teen sexuality, teen nutrition, teen fitness, and more).

4. Then you should try browsing through lists of teen clubs (use the site-specific search engines; most have club sections). Here you can look for clubs that have key words in the titles, such as *overweight teens*, *teen good grooming clubs*, *teen fashion clubs*, and so on.

5. We hope you would also try teen forums. You know that forums are found at many Web sites, but you could also do searches for forums. You could try *bulimic teen forums* or *overweight teen forums* or *teen dating forums* or *teen fitness forums* and so on.

6. Ask your own teen for help finding sites or doing searches. Teens like to know more than you know and show you things—and they are really good at this particular thing. When you show your teens you're willing to learn from them, they are more willing to learn from you.

Many articles have been written about the correlation between fitness and self-esteem in girls (we bet you can find them online). Girls who participate in sports or are physically active and fit do better in school, in social activities, and in life.

Girls are much more active in sports these days, and the Net can help spark their interest in sports because there are so many ways to read about women athletes. Even though sports or fitness is a real-world activity, motivation can—and often does—come from the e-World.

For example, a competitive junior high gymnast can read about her gymnastics heroes on the Net, send email to some of them, or put up a home page about her own competitions, along with pictures. She can also look for a chat room for gymnasts—or for a more general one, such as Girls in Sports—and share stories with other female athletes.

As an e-Parent, you already know a lot about how to nurture self-esteem in their children. The hard part is just remembering to *do* those little things that mean so much and to *say* those things that mean a lot.

Descriptive Praise

When you say something general, such as "You are such a great kid" or "You are nice" or "You are wonderful," or when you repeat "Good job" many times a day, you may think you are praising your child and building self-esteem. However, those general remarks really mean very little to a child. After he or she hears those comments a few times, they lose their appeal. Your child really does not know what you mean by *nice*, *good*, or *wonderful*.

Look at it this way: If you prepare a special dinner for company, you don't appreciate the compliment "Good job" or "It was great" nearly as much as having your guests tell you they liked the way you added honey and dill sauce to the carrots or that the blue-cheese and poppy-seed dressing really complemented the salad.

Likewise, if your company asks how you marinated the chicken or whether you will share your dessert recipe, you would feel really good about the meal you had prepared. Comments that *describe* are much more meaningful than those that are nondescriptive and general.

Your child feels the same way about praise and compliments. Even a school-age child is unsure of what you mean when you say "you're great" or "good job." The child also wonders what *good* or *great* means when applied to him instead of to a celebrity and may even wonder whether you still love him when he is *not* "good" or "great."

At the end of a day, take some time to reflect about this issue. How many of your conversations with your child that day were about "taking care of business" or doing things you felt were important. Then think about how many times you gave your child genuine, descriptive praise of some kind. So often, we remember to tell kids what they should have done or did not do, and we forget to tell them about the things we appreciate.

e-Parenting means building self-esteem with descriptive praise and doing it through as many avenues as possible. It means showing your approval and appreciation of him or her with your face and body language and with your comments, whether spoken or written.

Nonverbal Praise

To children, actions usually speak louder than words. Kids are great at reading body language. When you nod, smile, or wink; give a child a pat on the back or a hug; or ruffle your kid's hair, he or she knows you care and that you are praising them, whether that praise is for being loveable or for being capable.

When your child is being extra polite at the table with company, you can let him or her know that you notice this effort by giving a meaningful smile or wink. When you are at a doctor's office full of people and have to wait a long time, you can let your child know you appreciate his or her patience with a gentle touch or an understanding or reassuring look.

Verbal Descriptive Praise

When the phrase *good job* is on the tip of your tongue, think first. What did your child do or say that you liked?

Describe it. It won't take long to get into this habit, and the expression on your children's faces will keep reminding you how much this kind of praise means to them.

> "I noticed that you remembered to put away the milk. I really appreciate that and am proud of you for remembering to do it."

> "You really got a lot of interesting information about kittens from the Net—especially about how to care for them. We'll be depending on you when we pick out one tomorrow."

It's Okay to Say No:

Saying *no* or sticking to your rules does *not* hurt a child's self-esteem! Children find security in knowing that your rules and expectations are consistent; security nurtures self-esteem.

"Your homework essay about bats was really well written and interesting. We were impressed with the way you searched for and found the information you needed on the Internet."

"Your teacher wrote a note to tell us what a good visual aid you made for that project about light. She wants to know what science software you used so that they can get it at school."

"Thanks for helping your little brother learn to use that new software for painting a picture. You explained it to him much better than I could have...and he was so happy that you worked with him."

"You have such a good sense of humor. You always notice the funny side of things and make me laugh. I would never have thought of it that way."

"We really admire what you did on that project about landfills. Your research on the Net made a big difference in the way people responded to the online petitions. We are proud that you used the Internet to make a stand on an environmental issue."

Written Descriptive Praise

Any of the preceding compliments can also be given to your child as little hand-written notes, tucked into a school lunch box or left as notes on the family bulletin board or the phone message machine. Some parents feel more comfortable when they can think out and write down what they want to say. Others have work schedules that make written praise a necessity.

You may also be able to send your child written messages by email. If you allow your child to go online by himself or herself at home, you can send an email surprise message from work addressed to the child. (If your child cannot go online alone, maybe one parent or another adult who is at home can know that the message is coming and get online with your child to read it.)

If your older child has a personal email account, you can send him or her personal messages and descriptive praise often. You may even want to send an electronic animated greeting, which we discuss in Chapter 10, "Saving Family Traditions in New Ways."

Be sure to give descriptive praise that nurtures both sides of the self-esteem coin. What you say should not only describe the child's achievements and competence but also describe those loveable things that are unique to your child's personality.

Risk and Failure: Can They Strengthen Self-Esteem?

We believe that there is no way to protect children from the disappointments they will encounter in life. We can actually help them most by teaching them that they have the strength to survive disappointments and become stronger.

We have to encourage kids to take appropriate risks and allow them to experience failure. By "taking a risk," we are talking about trying out for a sports team or a school play. We are talking about trying to make a new friend or trying out a new sport or game.

Experiencing small failures teaches kids that they become stronger by trying, even if they don't succeed.

It's like learning to ski. The first thing Jean Claude the ski instructor teaches you is how to get up—because *of course* you are definitely going to fall down. Kids need to fall down sometimes, too, so that they learn how to pick themselves up.

Don't discourage your children from trying, even if you think their chances of success are slim. They will learn many things from the experience of risking, not the least of which is that other people can do things better than they can. Kids need to keep testing their capabilities and rediscovering their limitations, even though these keep changing.

When your kids fail at something, fully acknowledge their disappointment. Don't gloss over their feelings. Saying "Oh, it doesn't matter" or "That's okay, because you can do such-and-such" or "I love you anyway" does not allow them to fully experience their pain and find out that they can get through it and go on.

Show you care and understand. Share some memories of times you tried and failed and felt devastated. Kids need to know that failures and disappointments are temporary. Don't overprotect them from failure; allow them to experiment with risk and learn from failure.

Feeling Bad About Yourself Can Be Good

One more thing, which is related to risk and failure and also to the ways you discipline your child: Healthy self-esteem does not mean that your child has to feel good about himself or herself *all* the time. Let's get real.

We don't feel good about ourselves all the time, and we have had lots of practice trying. It is not realistic to try to make your kids feel good all the time, and it is definitely not good for them to *expect* to feel good all the time, either.

When they make mistakes or do something hurtful to another person, feeling bad or guilty is very healthy and is part of normal development. The feelings of guilt also help them understand and accept themselves as human beings with both limitations and capabilities, which is part of strong self-esteem.

We found a site that may inspire your child to keep trying. Some of the children mentioned on the Amazing Kids site (at *www.amazing-kids.org*) have taken risks, but these kids have accomplished some special things.

Amazing Kids at www.amazing kids.org is dedicated to inspiring excellence in children.

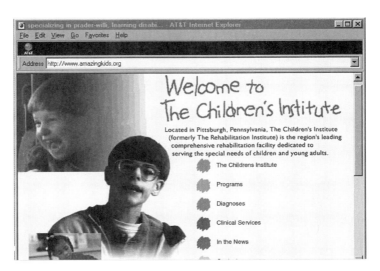

The Amazing Kids site also includes educational programs and projects, a television program under construction, pages featuring art and writing by children, a mentor program, and contests.

There is an Amazing Kid of the Month feature, as well as real-life stories about amazing kids in the news. The site also has an Amazing Kids scholarship fund. Definitely plan to visit this resource.

Summing Up

We hope you have enjoyed this chapter about self-esteem and how you can nurture it with activities in both the real world and the virtual world. To get you started with your own ideas, we have given you suggestions ranging from creating personal space to using Net resources for appearance and fitness. You know how to use meaningful praise, and you know that self-esteem can be stronger and healthier when it's forged in some fires of risk and failure.

We hope you and your children are having fun together with the PC and Net and that you are just as interested in these activities as the kids are. Through these experiences, you can help establish good behavior patterns and provide lots of guidance.

CHAPTER 5

Using the PC and Net to Enhance People Skills

This chapter focuses on the people skills that e-Parents want to nurture in their children. The most important of these skills is communication in all of its many forms. Their own ability to communicate is the main tool e-Parents will use in teaching communication and people skills to their children.

The chapter covers how parents lay the foundations and how they build on communication and people skills. It emphasizes the importance of putting in place positive, open communication patterns when kids are young, not only to prevent problems in the teen years but also to help ensure ongoing, positive interactions with kids as they become online users.

We'll share tips and strategies for nurturing people skills and communication, including real-world and virtual-world activities. We'll talk about building people skills by using family games, as well as how to nurture the ability to make friends and maintain both real and online global friendships.

What You'll Learn in This Chapter:

▶ Why people skills are important

▶ How to nurture people skills in your kids (and yourself) by using both real-world and virtual-world activities

▶ How to develop and maintain both virtual-world and real-world relationships

Why Are People Skills Important to e-Parents and e-Kids?

People skills are the ways we get along with the other people in our lives. Getting along well with others depends a lot on our attitudes about them and on the ways we communicate with them. The kinds of e-Parenting you do to nurture people skills in your kids will affect the ways they communicate, cooperate, and work with others for their entire lives.

Communication—the way we listen, talk, and interact with others—is our most important people skill. It affects *all* the ways we get along with others, whether we are engaged in "live" or online or written interactions.

The kinds of communication skills e-Parents nurture in e-World kids is vitally important to their children's well-being and success. Communication will affect their success in school and on the job, help them prevent and solve problems, and give them opportunities to make their lives more meaningful.

The e-World gives us and our kids unlimited access to knowledge and information, but that privilege also comes with the responsibility of using our communication tools and information wisely.

In the e-World, kids have to do more than talk, listen, and interact; they have to do critical thinking to make choices about who they talk with, what they listen to, and why information is being presented to them.

It won't do our e-Children much good to have super self-esteem and excellent problem-solving skills if they can't communicate or get along with others.

It won't do our e-Children much good to be able to gather and evaluate information if they can't do critical thinking to sort the junk from the good stuff or don't feel okay about asking their parents for help when they need it.

We can't write about communication and people skills without saying that Internet communication is limitless. Your kids can access the world, and the world can access them. Therefore, your kids must understand the importance of using the Net purposefully and safely. That's your job, but we will try to help.

In Chapter 9, "Internet Safety for Online Kids," and in Appendix B, "e-Parenting Web Site Directory," we give you more online safety information as well as leads to other resources. You will have to make your own decisions about what you think are the best ways to cope with potential e-World dangers to your children.

In this chapter, however, we present what we think is the best tool to prevent problems in the first place: good interpersonal communication with your own children.

Online Safety

We have to be realistic about e-World communication. There are thousands and thousands of sites. Some contain great information, some contain mediocre information, and some contain poor information. Remember, too, that just about anyone can launch a Web site.

Fortunately, the Net also contains plenty of information about censorship, information on safe sites and chats, ways to prevent kids from entering chat rooms, and ways to filter information coming into your PC. e-Parents can get information on current or proposed legislation to regulate kids' online communications, read transcripts of hearings, and read about or take sides on issues such as whether public libraries should have Internet censorship and filtering systems in place.

All this online activity tells is us that the issue of e-World safety and censorship is a communication issue that will not go away and that it will still be here for our kids to live with when we are long gone.

e-Parents have to see the forest on this one, not just the trees. Keeping kids safe and teaching them to use their communication skills wisely in the real and virtual world will do more than teach kids to cope with or avoid dangerous chat rooms or bad language. Using the Net wisely will also help kids practice critical thinking. It will help them practice making informed choices in their own best interest in the real and the virtual worlds, whether they are choices about personal health or choices about environmental issues.

We must also remember that even though the e-World has its exploiters and predators, those types of people exist in the real world, too.

Both the virtual and the real world are home to people who can be mean or ugly, who can hurt your child's self-esteem, who can harass you and invade your privacy, or who can give false information that may encourage inappropriate purchases or bad choices. We can't make these societal problems go away; we have to teach kids to deal with them.

Instead of focusing on Internet safety as a problem, we should see it as an opportunity! We have to teach e-Kids to take advantage of the wonderful options for fun and learning that the Net offers to families.

We can use it to teach our kids how to communicate wisely, use critical thinking, use defensive surfing, and learn ways to avoid dangerous situations. These skills will serve them well in coping with real-life situations—from the kinds of friends they choose to the kinds of political issues they support.

e-Parenting is about teaching kids to do the kind of communicating in the real and virtual worlds that helps them make choices in their best interests. And it's about kids being able to communicate with *you*, their parents, about how to choose and use online information wisely. It's about feeling free enough and safe enough to discuss anything with you—good stuff as well as bad stuff.

The most powerful tools for keeping kids safe when they listen and talk online are your parenting skills. The parenting skill that will make the biggest difference in your child's well-being is your parent-child communication and the ways you nurture that important people skill to build a strong relationship between you and your kids.

Open, honest, positive communication *within* the family is the best way to get kids safely and successfully into adulthood in the e-World. Research indicates that positive communication and relationships between e-Parents and kids can prevent many problems in the adolescent and teen years, including inappropriate use of e-World technology.

Another Thing:
The e-World doesn't just give us the opportunity to communicate with the whole world; it beats on our doors and demands that we pay attention.

The ironic thing is that the e-World gives us limitless communication with the virtual world, but does not teach us real-world interpersonal communication skills. The first, ongoing, and most important teachers of these skills are e-Parents.

In the e-World, it may become easier and easier to distance oneself from face-to-face contact and choose only to use online written communication. As a result, we may lose some of our people skills just because we aren't using them. A world full of competent technology users without good people skills doesn't sound very appealing.

Even if online communication becomes a major part of daily life, the most successful adults will use face-to-face interactions and real-world people skills as effectively as they use technology.

e-Parents want to raise children who are healthy, happy adults as well as competent technology users. They want their kids to be able to make friends and have good relationships. Therefore, e-Parents will nurture real-world communication skills and teach their kids to use their people skills wisely in both the real and the virtual world.

How e-Parents Can Nurture People Skills with Real-World and Virtual-World Activities

Children begin to learn people skills, including communication, from almost the moment they are born. Parents lay strong foundations for these skills with their own modeling and in the ways they interact with their children. This kind of parental teaching continues from the very early years into the teen years, when children become more skillful with language, interactions, and relationships. Some of the ways parents build these skills in their kids are with everyday behaviors such as modeling, manners, playing games, cooperating, sharing, and resolving conflicts.

Building People Skills

Building people skills starts earlier than you may think. The infant's brain is programmed to begin learning language (a most important people skill) at birth. Babies recognize and show preference (using body language) to their significant others within two weeks. Parents start building people skills from day one.

How e-Parents Can Lay the Foundations

If you have an infant, think ahead a few years. Do you want this baby to grow into a child who trusts you and will come to you with any problem, even when the child thinks he or she has made a mistake? If so, you need to start doing certain things *now*.

During the first year of life, an infant's main goals are to survive and to begin to trust others (pretty impressive goals). Learning to trust in significant others is actually the foundation of a child's self-esteem, communication, and people skills.

Parents model their own people skills for their infants as soon as the babies are born. The ways parents look at infants, the way their voices sound as they talk to them, the ways parents copy the infants' sounds, and the ways parents handle them teaches infants that it is okay to trust other people.

Do you want to raise a child who is sociable, and who can talk easily to others (even adults), and who enjoys being part of a group? Toddlers are quick to learn even more about people skills, social skills, and communication. One important—and very ordinary—place they learn these things is at the dinner table. A family meal is the child's first "social" group situation; lots of people skills are demonstrated there.

Your child will see people sharing food, eating, passing food, smiling, and nodding. The child will hear people talk, hear them take turns talking, and hear them say "please" and "thank you."

Your child will note how people talk to each other and what kinds of sounds their voices make. Your child will be a part of the group and feel that he or she "belongs" in the group.

To learn more about the baby's development, you may want to explore some of these Web sites:

- I Am Your Child at *www.iamyourchild.org* includes information on health and development. We found some excellent summaries and articles about brain development at this site very easily and quickly.

- Babyhood at *www.babyhood.com* is another site that focuses on development from birth to age 2. The site has some good links to further resources.

- At Parent Time (*www.parenttime.com*) you can choose the category *Behavior and Development*. Within that section, choose *Verbal Skills*, which will give you some excellent articles about language development in infants.

How e-Parents Keep Building People Skills

Teach Them Young:

By the way, the human brain is programmed to map and to begin to process sounds and language information from birth on. Toddlers exposed to two languages will probably learn and use both easily.

And the beat goes on. e-Parents keep building communication and people skills with their own modeling and by encouraging children to copy it. You teach good parent-child communication by using it yourself. The way you communicate with your child makes a huge difference in the ways your child gets along with other people and the way your kids get along with *you*.

The *way* you say things is always more important than the exact words you use. But all the patterns you put in place during the child's early years are important because those patterns will still be there as children grow into the school years and beyond.

The kinds of modeling you do, the kinds of parent-child interactions you have, and the kinds of things you say will all be part of the pattern for the child's own people skills. Moreover, the kind of relationship you develop with your young child will be a major part of the pattern for his or her future relationships.

Tips on Positive Communication

Another question: Do you want your children to be able to talk to you about anything and come to you whenever they have questions, are worried about something, or when feel unsure about an e-World activity or online communication? If so, here are some e-Parenting tips on everyday ways to build your child's people skills--and to build positive communication between you and your child:

1. Really look into your child's face when you are listening or talking. Let a caring touch or your facial expression tell your child that you are listening or that you understand.

2. Use a calm voice, especially when you are being firm about something you are explaining. Speak slowly and clearly, but do not patronize. Be straightforward.

3. At your house, get each family member involved when you are brainstorming or discussing something. One person talks at a time while others listen, and everyone has a turn. Get all the kids' input, make them a part of the decision making, even if you, as the parent, make the final decision.

4. Listen attentively when your child is talking; show your genuine interest, and wait…do not interrupt. If you can't stop and listen just then, take the time to look at your child and explain, tell him or her when you *can* listen—and follow through.

5. Older kids may want to talk to you at odd or inconvenient times. Stop and listen, no matter what time it is, no matter what you are doing! If you don't want to talk to your kids, there are lots of people online who do—and some are dangerous.

6. Be sure that your face and body language match what you are saying. Children pick up more on face and body language than on words. Be honest when you talk to your children; they know when you are holding something back.

7. Teach kids by your modeling and action how to use words to express needs, wants, and feelings. Show your children how to use words to negotiate, compromise, and problem solve.

When children practice this kind of talking and listening with the
family in normal, everyday ways, they are building good lifetime
habits for both the real and virtual worlds.

Tips on Conflict Resolution

Sometimes kids need a little extra e-Parenting guidance when
they fight with a sibling or with friends. e-Parents can teach their
kids the basics of conflict resolution. When kids have arguments,
teach them to use words and these five steps to compromise and
solve the problem.

1. Ask the kids to stop arguing for a minute, think about what
   they are doing, and then tell each other how they feel.

2. Ask each child to explain, one at a time, what he or she
   thinks the problem is.

3. Encourage the children to think of as many different ways to
   solve the problem as possible.

4. After several possible solutions are discussed, have the children choose one and try it.

5. Discuss whether or not that solution was successful. If it did
   not work, have them choose another option and try it.
   Continue until they reach a compromise and find a solution.

When children use language as a tool to negotiate and compromise, they are also doing creative problem solving.

> **You Are Not the Referee**
>
> Parents with more than one child who fight: Try to stay out of the argu-
> ment. Realize that your home is a safe place for children to learn lots of
> good stuff while they are bickering. They'll learn about things they can
> do and things others may do better. They will learn to share space and
> work with someone they may not agree with. They will learn about
> negotiation, compromise, winning, and losing. Look at your home as a
> practice ground for life, not as a battleground for personalities.

As kids get older, e-Parents can help them find new ways to practice communication and people skills at home, in public, and in
the e-World. The more they practice, the more kids learn about
cooperation, sharing, and communicating.

Practicing People Skills with Family Games

All real-world family games teach people skills and help kids practice getting along in a group. Family games also give kids a sense of belonging—a feeling that they are connected to the family. Games also help shy children enjoy a group situation more easily and naturally.

When a family does regular family group activities and socializing together, children are less likely to look elsewhere to find a group to belong to (such as an online group you might not approve of). Kids are also less likely to look for a fantasy escape online or with television.

Games help kids learn to be sociable and to have fun. When kids and parents or friends are talking and laughing and enjoying a game together face to face, they are communicating, cooperating, and having a good time. Family games help parents and kids have fun together, and that's one of the three basics of good e-Parenting.

In addition, when you really think about the things games teach children without them even knowing it, you will see that playing games together is a way you can teach children what you believe and what you think they should know.

Here are some people skills that kids practice every time they play games with their parents:

- Sharing and taking turns

- Being patient when you have to wait

- Negotiating and learning to compromise

- Being honest; playing fair

- Winning and losing gracefully

- Cooperating and working as a team

We believe that the best games to teach cooperation and communication are real-world family games that require interaction and conversation (and that sometimes include loud vocalizing and laughter, depending on the players).

Some of the family games we recommend are classics such as charades, in which you make up the puzzlers for the opposing team. Others are standards like Monopoly, Clue, Scrabble, Jenga, Yahtzee, Password, Pictionary, Gestures, Sorry, and Outburst—all of which you can buy (of course) online. Try *www.hasbro.com* to browse for games.

Something you may want to try is the new CD-ROM version of one of the most popular games of all time: Monopoly. Hasbro Interactive has redesigned Monopoly so that you can choose from ten city versions, customize the board to your own town, or scan in pictures to personalize the properties. Cool!

You can play against computerized players; if you want to play against real people online you can (to do so, however, you have to register at a special Web site and join a Monopoly chat room).

Try It Yourself ▼   Hasbro Interactive also offers CD-ROM versions of several other popular games—Yahtzee, Scrabble, and Boggle. And Hasbro has started a new way to play games by email with an Em@il Games series. People we know who tried Scrabble this way enjoyed it and said it was easy to use.

1. Go to the Hasbro home page at *www.hasbro.com*; click Enter to open the site. Click the *Click and Play* link to open a page with descriptions of game options.

   One of the drawback of downloading the free version of an Em@il game is that you can only be Player two. Player Two can only join a game initiated by Player One (whoever that might be). To be Player One, you have to purchase the game software (which is easy to do from the Hasbro site). If you have a friend who has sprung for the full-featured version of the game, you can join any game that friend initiates by using your free downloaded software.

2. Click the link for a free download of Em@il software. Choose the game you want to download (Upwords is a kind of crossword-puzzle version of Scrabble). Click the *Download Now* link.

3. Fill out the short registration form and download the program (it's a relatively small file). Install the program on your computer. (You can find instructions for these tasks by following the *More Information* links for the program you want to download.)

4. Open your email program and look for a message sent by Player One. Open the message, check out the move your friend has made, click and type to take your turn. Then click *Send* to mail your message back to your friend.

5. You can wait around for your friend to email you back with his or her next move, or you can sign off and continue the game the next time you check your mail. What a cool way to keep the little letter tiles from spilling out all over the floor!

All this online game playing is great, but we still want to play at least some of our board games the old-fashioned way—at the kitchen table.

As e-Parents can see, there are increasing opportunities to play games with your children in the e-World. To get started with family games on the Net, check out sites such as these:

- *www.kidscom.com*—KidsCom is a great family site that includes games for different age groups, family fun activities, recipes, chats, and ways to get pen pals.

- *www.familyplay.com*—Familyplay, sponsored by Crayola, is an interesting site containing many activities for families; you can search by topics and age groups, as well as indoor/outdoor games.

- *www.Nickjr.com*—The Nick Jr. site contains games for preschoolers as well as older school children. It is easy to use and navigate.

- *www.theideabox.com*— The Idea Box was one of our favorite sites for games and interesting activities for all age groups.

- *www.randomhouse.com/seussville/games*—At the Dr. Seuss game site, you can play a Lorax Save the Trees game or a Cat in the Hat concentration game. This game site was also recommended by Jean Armour Polly (*www.netmom.com*), who writes the famous and annually updated *The Internet Kids & Family Yellow Pages*, now in its Fourth and Millennium Edition. This paperback book contains recommended sites for online families.

- *www.funbrain.com*—For games to play with your school-age kids, try the FunBrain site. Lots of the games featured here are fun ways to practice many math skills, including making change with money.

- *www.kidsdomain.com*—Kids Domain is another good site for family fun because the family activities have so much variety, ranging from coloring and clip art to software for helping develop computer skills.

- *www.ysn.com/gameroom*—The Youth Sports Network (YSN) Game Room presents lots of good games with really creative quirks. Older kids should like this site, which includes games you can play outdoors in the real world with your friends. (Net-mom Jean Armour Polly at *www.netmom.com* recommends this site.)

Games with a Seal of Approval:

The National Parenting Center site at *www.tnpc.com* lists games that have been tested by parents and kids and that have won the National Parenting Center Seal of Approval.

- *www.thefunplace.com*—The F.U.N. Place and the Family Fun Network (at *www.ffn.org*) are both good family activity sites, but we were actually more impressed with the Chats and Boards at these sites than the current games that are up for play.

Visit Net-mom

Visit Net-mom Jean Polly's site, *www.netmom.com*, where you will find sample "hotlists" of sites from the *Yellow Pages* book. These sites are continually updated and are listed with interesting and thoughtful reviews in many different categories (such as games, parenting, and homework). Although the site is at *www.netmom.com*, when you're talking about *her*, she's Net-mom (with a capital *N* and a small *m*).

The Dr. Seuss games at the Random House site (www. randomhouse.com/ seussville) are great for e-Parents to play with younger kids—the graphics are delightful.

Older kids might enjoy game clubs where they can play online chess, sports games, crosswords, or action computer games.

We did a simple search in Yahoo! with the words *"online game clubs"* and found more than 300 Web pages for online game clubs of all kinds, from golf to chess. We decided to go to some of the sites listed to learn more.

We tried *www.brushstrokes.com/games/intro038.htm* and were pleasantly surprised at the variety of games that could be down-loaded for free. Categories included action, adventure, sports, board games, card games, arcade games, and even flight simulator games.

Then we looked at *www.links2go.com/topic/chess_clubs*, which was a well-organized and interesting chess club site. There were chats and ongoing discussions about chess, chess resources, and chess clubs that included listings from all over the world. We sug-gest that you try to find online and software games you can play *with* your child or games that are played with more than one per-son. This way, your children can not only enjoy new technologies but also reap the benefits of the people-to-people interaction that family games provide.

For example, a software program for first graders called *Jump Start First Grade* from Knowledge Adventure (Mac/Windows $20) includes treasure hunts, simple reading games, and singing and dancing animals. Older siblings might enjoy playing with younger ones.

Another possibility for family fun software is Broderbund's Carmen Sandiego series of games, which help kids (and parents) learn lots of U.S. history and geography while tracking down the villains.

> **Try Before You Buy:**
> Preview any game your child wants you to purchase. Read online reviews of games or try shareware or free downloads of limited versions of the games you're interested in.

Other Ways e-Parents Help Kids Practice People Skills

We do a little people watching. In that mode, we have seen parents who talk to complete strangers with friendly, polite voices—and then turn around and shout, bark, or growl at their own children. We think you know what we mean.

We are our children's most important teachers. We really have to stop and think about what we are teaching them about manners, cooperation, and communication with our own modeling.

Manners

Monkey See:

It's a funny thing.... When parents forget to use the *please* and *thank-you* words in everyday situations, you don't hear kids say them either.

When kids are young, everyone remembers to say "please" and "thank you" to help the little ones learn to say these magic words. However, when kids reach the school years, sometimes the please and thank-you manners disappear. Everyone gets busier, we spend less time eating together as a group, and children have fewer opportunities to practice good manners at home.

Saying *please*, *thank you*, or *pardon me* are basic good manners that show respect of others. These phrases are used all over the world; e-Children will work and communicate with the entire world, so these words should be part of their vocabulary (and ours).

Using positive social language is a people skill that spills over to the ways kids behave in public, on family travels, in e-World communication, and with other adults. e-Parents will not want the people skill of manners to die from lack of use. Model good manners, encourage kids to keep practicing good manners, and praise them for doing so.

Cooperation and Sharing

e-Parents can teach kids cooperation in many ways, such as working together on a family project and helping each other with chores at home. Older kids may learn and practice teamwork and cooperation in sports activities. But parents can also use ordinary everyday activities to help kids learn to get along well with others. Here are some tips:

- Point out some of the ways that adults have to cooperate, share, and take turns every day. When you're in the car with the kids, talk about how adults share parking space, office space, library books, and the foods in a restaurant. We take turns at the stop streets when we drive and in the lines at the grocery store, the car wash, the library, and the bank. We share space on roads and highways in the real world, and we share the information highway of the Internet in the virtual world.

  Part of getting along well with others is being able to do those things comfortably, without frustration. If you tell your kids to "be nice and take turns," and then they see you mutter (or worse) when you have to wait your turn at the stoplight or at the store or to get online, your credibility is definitely damaged.

- Another way e-Parents can teach people skills is by taking their children to public places and providing clear rules or expectations beforehand about ways to behave. When e-Parents take children to the library, a movie, or a restaurant, parents can point out the kinds of behaviors that other people are using—and the kinds of behavior people are expected to use—in public spaces.

- e-Parents model sharing and taking turns with plain old everyday activities at home. e-Parents can talk to kids about how we share appliances such as toasters and telephones, space in the closets, and space in the refrigerator. Family members also take turns in choosing what to watch on television, what to listen to on the radio, or which video to rent. In addition, e-Parents and kids share the personal computer and take turns using it.

Most importantly, e-Parents and their e-Kids will be sharing the personal computer and taking turns using it.

Put the PC Where Everyone Can Use It:

Position the PC so that it is always accessible to all family members. Keeping your PC in a central location encourages sharing and provides accountability for appropriate use.

Whenever e-Parents and their children sit down together to discuss the priorities—and to figure out who gets to use the PC first and next and for how long—everyone is practicing the people skills of communication and problem solving.

Virtual-World and Real-World Relationships

Human beings are social animals, and e-Kids, like their parents, need to learn about relationships and how to make and keep friends. The e-World provides kids with the option of having both real-world and virtual-world friends.

Making Friends

Knowing how to make friends is a people skill that children are not born with; it's a learned skill. Some children watch the ways their parents and other children make friends and learn this skill quickly and naturally. Other kids need help in knowing what friendships are, how to make friends, and how to keep them. When children need help, e-Parents should begin by talking with their child about what a friend really is.

To Have a Friend, Be a Friend

When kids understand what a friend is, it is easier for them to see that they can *initiate* the kinds of friendships they want, instead of being in a "needy" position. When kids are desperately looking for just any kind of friend, they put themselves in a vulnerable position, tempted perhaps to follow anyone who seems "popular." Kids who are desperate for a friend may try to be friends with a less-than-ideal person at all costs—or worse, may find an online friend who may actually be a stranger or predator.

A friend is someone who listens to you and cares about you and your ideas and feelings. Friends are people who do things with you and enjoy being with you. You have fun together. Friends are there for you and understand when you are happy or sad. Friends don't say mean things to you or about you. They stick up for you. They don't try to get you to do things you don't feel good about.

e-Parents should point out that sometimes friends are people in our own family. Friends might be your own age, or they might be much, much older—as are aunts and uncles and grandparents. Whatever their age, friends are always your friends, every day (not just on some days), and they show that they are your friends by the ways they act with you. e-Parents must explain that a child has to *be* a friend, not just have a friend, which means treating a friend in all the same ways you want to be treated yourself.

If your child needs more help in making friends, teach him or her how by actually practicing these "friend-making skills" at home until he or she feels completely comfortable doing them. Relax and have fun with this exercise; make it a game, not a chore.

- Try to find at least one thing you can admire or like about every person even if that person is not a friend.

- Think of something you like about another person and tell that person; give at least one sincere compliment to someone every day. (The child can even send compliments by email.)

- Always smile and greet people by name when you see them. (Computer video cameras allow us to communicate face to face; someday soon we will be able to see the people we're exchanging email with.)

- Think of questions to ask people about things you really want to know. Questions are a form of compliment. Give your full attention when you listen to the answers.

Chats and Clubs

The good thing about chat rooms, especially for kids who are not outgoing, is that kids can go there to find other kids like themselves. However, e-Parents must help their children find safe chat rooms that fit particular hobbies or interests.

Friends Not Only by Email:
Don't let your children retreat into "email only" friendships. This type of activity can put your child at risk. Encourage face-to-face friendships as well.

Chats Are Good Practice for the Real World

The interaction and communication in these chat rooms might be good for kids who are a little reserved or shy in social situations. You can help your child start out by just sitting together and watching the conversations in the chat. Simply being a part of an appropriate chat room might give a shy child enough confidence to participate in the chat.

e-Parents can help kids find chat rooms categorized by various topics, by age groups, by cultures, and by issues. Search engine home pages have chat sections organized by categories. You and your child can go to one of your favorite family fun sites to see whether it already has a chat room, or you can search for a specific chat room topic.

Perhaps one of the best ideas is to use a kid-safe search engine with your child to find an appropriate chat. Choose from any of these search engines:

- Yahooligans (*www.Yahooligans.com*)
- Ask Jeeves for Kids (*www.ajkids.com*)
- Zeeks (*www.zeeks.com*)
- Alfy (*www.alfy.com*)

You can also check a kid-safe directory service such as Lycos Kids or Disney Dig Internet Guide.

A special chat event may spark a child's interest to interact or communicate more with others—even if the communication is on a virtual level. Many chats have events calendars that list the time when a special guest, such as a TV star or sports celebrity, will be in the chat room to talk and answer questions. Kids like that.

Here's how we found our favorite kid-safe chat Web site. We watched for kids' sites that were recommended by credible reviewers (such as Net-mom or the Association of Childhood Education International) or by respected safe sites (such as Web Wise Kids at *www.webwisekids.com*, GetNetWise at *www.getnetwise.com*, and SafeKids at *www.safekids.com*). Then we visited these sites to see which ones offered chats.

The site we liked best for chats was *www.kidscom.com*.
It includes many family fun activities as well as options for
worldwide communication with pen pals and "Graffiti Wall
Chats." One Graffiti Wall is for kids up to age 11, and another is
for ages 12 to 15. The walls are open for chat from 3:00 to 10:00
p.m. (Central Time) seven days a week—and staff members monitor the chats! Sounds really exciting!

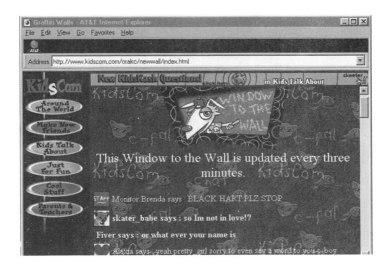

The Graffiti Wall chat (follow the link from www.kidscom.com/orakc/Friends/new friends.html) may be just the thing to encourage a shy child to participate in a conversation without the perceived risks of a face-to-face conversation.

Some parents will not allow kids to chat at all; some parents let
kids chat with close supervision. The ongoing debates about chat
room safety extend into complex issues about online safety and
censorship. We talk more about these issues in Chapter 9.

One more important note: It's not what they read or listen to
online, but what kids say online that might be dangerous to them.
Even though kids often know not to give out personal information
online (for example, in a chat room), they may not understand
exactly what "personal information" *means*. e-Parents must give
their kids lots of examples of what *not* to say online.

What You Type May Stalk You

A few months ago, an email story was circulating on the Net about a teenage girl who had frequent email conversations with a "boy" who said he lived hundreds of miles away from her. In the course of their message exchanges, she told him about her baseball team, its name, what position she played, what time their games were, what school she attended, and so on. The boy told her about his life in the distant state.

However, the "boy" actually turned out to be a *man* who lived in the girl's home town. One day, he followed her home from school, attended her baseball game, and in effect, "stalked her." You don't need any help imagining what could happen at this point in the story.

Fortunately for the girl in the story, the man turned out to be a cop who was making a point about what not to say in email exchanges and what can happen as the result of loose fingers on the keyboard. The cop talked to the girl and her parents, and the story ends happily. But....

As you know, there's no easy way to verify that what someone tells you in an email message is actually true. And unless you're really savvy, you probably won't know how to track the domain portion of the email address (the *@Company.com* part) to a particular city. These facts made it possible for the man in this story to convincingly pretend to be a boy in a city miles away. What your child may think of as innocuous details of a boring life may be just the clues a predator needs to strike.

We don't want to scare you into unplugging the computer and forbidding your kids from using email. What we want to underscore here is that you—and your kids—should treat online email friendships with caution. Most email friendships are above board and can be taken at face value. It's the "what if it's not?" factor that should be your filter as you and your kids type email messages.

Joining clubs on the Net may also be a good stepping stone in the development of social skills for those who find it easier to write (type) their thoughts than to talk. Clubs give kids unlimited topics to "talk about" online.

On the other hand, parents should closely supervise the clubs their children are interested in. We consider clubs a viable option for kids who show that they are responsible, who are very open about their online activities, and who are relaxed in talking about their clubs and online friends.

It is wise for e-Parents to make a rule that the child *not* put up an online profile (a form that lists pertinent facts about the Internet account holder, such as name, home town, and so on); profiles tend to attract predators who may even pose as another child in the club.

The Yahoo! club area is a good starting place for considering different clubs to join. You'll find health clubs, support clubs, religion clubs, collectors clubs, and just about any club you can think of. For example, in the teens interest group of clubs available through Yahoo!, you can find Teens Against Suicide, Teen Writers Coffee Shop, Overweight Teens, and Teen Parents clubs.

You can join an existing club or start your own club. Then you can post messages, chat, see photos, read news, find out about events, learn about other members, and get contacts and related links.

Your best bet for helping kids find safe clubs is to first check on a search engine's home page for a kid-safe zone and for links to kid-safe sites. Search for clubs from the kid-safe sites, just as you do for kid-safe chats.

Watch the Club:
e-Parents have to stay on top of their kids' involvement in clubs; there are some clubs you won't want your kids to join.

Global Friendships

Wow! Kids today are lucky to be living in a world that keeps getting smaller. They can travel on the Net to any place on our planet, learn about other cultures, and have pen pal friends all over the world.

Learning About Other Cultures

Today's e-Children will live in a global community and interact constantly with people from other cultures. We believe that e-Parents should expose their children to other cultures whenever possible. We also believe that kids learn many good things when they can observe and practice social skills with different kinds of people in different situations.

Kids Only on AOL:
AOL Netfind has its own safe zone for kids called Kids Only. Select the Kids Only channel. Then choose a topic: art, homework help, clubs, chat, games, news and sports, or movies, TV, and music.

One way to help your children learn about another culture is to host an exchange student for a few months. Just having a exchange student in your home will help kids have more open and flexible attitudes about others, a people skill they will certainly need as e-World adults.

Hosting an exchange student lets your kids understand, firsthand, that people in different places have different languages, customs, and ways of doing things. And your kids will see that *different* is just *different*—not better or worse. *Different* is not only okay; it is often very interesting.

If you do decide to host an exchange student, the PC and Net will help you get acquainted, let you see each other's photographs, and allow you to exchange many letters before the student arrives. You can learn about the student's country, the kinds of music or foods he or she likes—anything you want to know. Knowing more about each other will make for an easier adjustment all around.

If you are interested in hosting a student, you can learn more about it with a simple search on the Net. We used the Yahoo! search engine and looked for *"exchange student programs."* The search quickly brought up several categories and more than a hundred sites about student exchange programs. On the first page of results listed many programs, but we investigated two we are personally familiar with. Both the American Field Service (*www.afs.org*) and Youth for Understanding (*www.yfu.org*) had interesting sites and many country options. You'll find this site quite interesting, and you'll also find many different options in the exchange program list.

Even if you decide that hosting an exchange student is not your cup of tea, you can help your children learn about other cultures and countries with real-world and virtual-world resources. Often, something your child sees on television—such as an African photo safari or a Barrier Reef scuba dive—will pique a child's interest in another culture or country.

e-Parents can take advantage of this interest to help kids learn more. You can start with an online search; use the encyclopedia that is part of your PC's software package; or go to the local library to borrow books, videos, or CD-ROMs (such as Explorerpedia) about other cultures or countries.

The national forum on people's differences at *www.yforum.com* is dedicated to exploring differences in cultures and getting people to interact and learn more about each other. At this site, experts may lend a hand where needed, and you'll find guidelines for posting questions and replies. People can talk about anything including race, occupation, sexual orientation, age, and religion. The forum is "a place to exchange information on the more basic, time-honored facets of everyday human behavior and customs that make us different from each other." Here are the site's goals: "Our hope is that this sharing, done in an atmosphere of curiosity and mutual respect, can help us deepen and broaden our understanding of one another—and perhaps help us discover some of the ways in which we are alike."

A site like this might really interest teens who want to learn more about other cultures and other viewpoints. The site might also enhance their social awareness skills and their understanding of global issues.

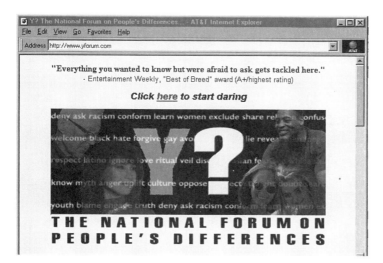

The Y? site at www.yforum.com is a nonconfrontational forum for discussing the differences among peoples and cultures—around the world and in your own backyard.

Having a Virtual Pen Pal

Formal pen pal programs began after World War II as way to try to heal animosities that existed between counties. The programs were promoted through school systems, and kids had to wait about two months for a roundtrip letter to come back from abroad. In the e-World, the process is faster. Today's kids can use email to correspond with their pen pals whenever they wish; letters can come and go in a matter of hours.

Children from about age 8 to 13 really enjoy pen pals and global friendships. The "one-on-oneness" of a pen pal friend may be just the outlet your child needs to develop his or her people and communication skills.

Pen pals can be a real help to shy children; when these kids start enjoying and having reasons to interact with another person, their people skills start to blossom. The topics of discussion and types of people children interact with, both online and in the real world, play a big part in their people skill participation and their ability to make real, online, and global friends.

The Net provides plenty of opportunities to find virtual pen pals. Start out at a search engine home page such as *www.yahoo.com* or *www.altavista.com*. From there, just type the search words **pen pals** along with a country of interest. Narrow your search and sift through the various pen-pal options that best match your child's interests. You can also use the search engine to check for pen pal clubs. Yahoo's pen pal clubs include a variety of countries and ages.

The Kidscom Web site at *www.kidscom.com* (mentioned earlier as a safe site for chats) has several pages devoted to pen pals. Many of the family fun and games safe sites also have pen pal options.

Summing Up

e-Parents can teach people skills in everyday life, enhance these lessons with e-World experiences, and find e-World resources to help kids develop people skills. e-Parents have the opportunity to use many resources to nurture communication and people skills in their children. From real family games to virtual games, from family conversation to global chats, clubs, and email, the possibilities have never been so varied.

But whatever resources you use, the most important e-Parenting tool you have is your *own* communication and modeling! You model people skills when you show an interest, provide guidance, and have fun with your kids. Keep using the PC and Net together and keep your kids talking to you about their feelings, friends, and activities.

CHAPTER 6

Using the PC and Net to Teach Discipline and Responsibility

In this chapter we felt it necessary to limit our guidance and discipline discussion to those topics we believe will make the biggest difference to parents and kids in the e-World.

Of course, we always hope as parents that our kids will *want* to do the right thing and be responsible. The kind of e-Parent–child relationship you have and the kinds of communication you have in place will make the biggest difference in motivating children to do the right thing.

The e-Parenting basics we have talked about throughout this book will help develop the kinds of relationship and communication that are needed in e-World families. But e-Parents will also need to use several important strategies to teach self- iscipline and responsibility.

e-Parents will need to use critical thinking and the major strategies of modeling, setting limits and expectations, and using logical consequences to raise children who will have the self-discipline to make responsible choices and accept the consequences of their choices.

To teach responsibility to kids, you *give* kids responsibilities. This chapter offers some ways to use real-world and Net experiences to enhance and motivate responsibility in children from toddlers to teens. The chapter also explains some of the ways that advocacy and "causes" can help children demonstrate responsibility at home and responsibility to our world.

Why Is Self-Discipline Important to e-Parents and Kids?

Children don't learn self-discipline and responsibility overnight or because they reach a certain age. They learn it little by little, bit by bit, every single day, from the time they are toddlers until they are adults. They learn self-discipline and responsibility from their parents, caregivers, and families, and also from their culture or the community in which they live.

True responsibility and self-discipline mean that we are motivated from the *inside* to do things or follow rules that help us and help others. Self-discipline is choosing what you are going to do or how you will behave, based on what you think is right. e-Parenting is about self-discipline.

Responsibility kicks in when you accept the consequences of the behavior you choose. You don't run away from it or avoid it or blame it on someone else. Taking responsibility for our own behavior and accepting the consequences is part of self-discipline.

e-Parenting means raising kids who are not just "obedient" to rules or who take responsibility for their behavior only when they are forced to do so. e-Parenting means raising kids who have the self-discipline and responsibility to do what they believe is the right thing to do. They choose what they are going to do and follow through. If they've made a mistake, they accept the consequences of that mistake.

Self-disciplined children understand the need for rules, help make the rules, and *want* to follow them. These are children who not only accept responsibility for their own behavior but also accept other responsibilities that have to do with the family, community, and the world they live in.

You may think that's a tall order, but remember: *It is the little things you do with children every day (especially in their early years) that make these big things happen.* e-Parenting means using parenting basics and commonsense strategies to help kids learn the self-discipline and responsibility they will need in both the real and virtual world.

e-Parenting and Self-Discipline

You can find hundreds of good parenting books and lots of online information about discipline and responsibility. But this chapter focuses on the aspects of discipline and responsibility that we think are the most relevant to e-Parenting. Let's start with self-discipline.

The biggest challenge of the e-World is making choices. We want e-Children to think carefully about their choices. What information do I want? How do I get it? How can I know whether what I chose was good information? What will I do with the information? What are the consequences of my choice? How might this action affect me and others? Is it in my best interest? Is this what I want to do?

We want kids to have the self-discipline to do this kind of critical thinking so that they can make choices in their best long-term interest. We are not talking about *discipline* as in "punishment," but as self-discipline that helps kids make the right choices in the first place.

Discipline Is Not the Same as Punishment:

The word *discipline* comes from the word *disciple*, which means "to learn." Discipline means that you learn not only what behavior is expected, but why it is expected and why it is appropriate. This motivates learners to discipline themselves because they *want* to do the right thing. Self-discipline prevents problems from happening in the first place.

Punishment as a way of teaching appropriate behavior to children is a quick fix based only on fear. Punishment does not help a child learn what is appropriate or why, nor does it motivate children to *want* to behave appropriately or to learn to do this independently. Instead of *preventing* problems, punishment occurs *after* the problem has happened.

What motivates kids to be self-disciplined? Their relationship with you makes the biggest difference, and the kind of communication you have with your children is the foundation of that relationship. If you are nurturing the kind of communication discussed in Chapter 5, "Using the PC and the Net to Enhance People Skills," you are doing one of the most important things you can to motivate your kids to be self-disciplined.

There are other things e-Parents can do to teach kids self-discipline. Some of these strategies are e-Parenting basics:

- If you consistently "show a genuine interest" in your kids, they will be motivated to do things you approve of.

- If you "provide guidance" by sharing the things you believe in and the things you think your kids should know, they are likely to know what you think is right and try to do it.

- If you "have fun" with your kids but know when to provide them the security of your parent role, they will respect you and want to make good choices. And if they are confused or unsure, they will come to you because you are a friend as well as a parent.

The other aspects of self-discipline that we believe are most important to e-Parenting are your modeling, your ability to set limits and expectations, your ability to teach critical thinking by using logical consequences, and your encouragement of responsibility. e-Parents will often reinforce these strategies with constructive comments and with descriptive praise.

It is most important to note that the patterns of guidance you put in place during the early and the elementary school years will be there in the teen years when the challenges will be greater. Start today to do smart e-Parenting that teaches self-discipline and responsibility; don't wait.

Modeling

Modeling teaches more than words can teach. Children learn more from what you do than what you tell them to do. Let them see you using self-control, taking responsibility for your own actions, and treating others with respect and good manners.

Let them see that you love learning new things and let them see you using the PC and Net in appropriate ways. And don't just use it; help kids see the *ways* you use it!

Use the following checklist to assess yourself in how you teach the Internet; the more Yes boxes you check, the better!

Yes	No	Question
☐	☐	Do you tell kids any of the ways the Internet helps you in your work or with your finances, or in household matters, or in planning family events?
☐	☐	Do you share interesting things you learn from the Net?
☐	☐	Do you show kids ways to have fun on the Net as they're learning something new?
☐	☐	Do you use the PC and the Internet with your kids as a way to spend quality time together and have fun?
☐	☐	Do you explain ways you save time by using the PC and Net so that you have more time to spend with the family?
☐	☐	Do you show them how to save time with schoolwork by using the Net?
☐	☐	Your PC and Net modeling can also teach kids critical thinking and get them to practice it. Do you model how to use the Net as a tool for gathering information?
☐	☐	Do you show your kids how to use more than one source in gathering information?
☐	☐	Do you help kids learn to evaluate Internet information, that is, to ask themselves questions about the source of the information, how old it is, or how it compares to other materials they find?

Learning to assess and evaluate information is critical thinking! Critical thinking helps kids make self-disciplined and responsible choices.

Limits and Expectations

Children feel more secure and more responsible when they know what is expected of them and when they know and understand the rules.

Let your children help make family rules, even if you lead the discussion. Let them help set the consequences for breaking rules, too. Your rules should say what you want, not what you don't want. ("We put away toys before bedtime," not "Don't leave toys on the floor." Or "We hang up our jackets," not "Don't leave

Adults Have Rules, Too:

Rules are a part of life. In case your kids don't believe this, give them some examples of the rules adults follow every day.

jackets on the floor or furniture.") Remember, too, that children of any age keep rules much better when they help make them. When kids have some input, they feel invested in the rule-making process.

You can and should have fun with your kids, but remember that you're much more than a pal: You are the parent.

Be a Parent First:

Kids have lots of friends, but they have only one parent or set of parents: *you.* They need to see you first as a parent, then as a friend.

Children need limits. They do not run the house or make family decisions—you do. They can give input on rules and consequences, but *you* make the rules and enforce the consequences. Saying no and explaining why is one way to show kids how you take responsibility as a parent. Saying nothing confuses children—or worse, they take your silence as a yes.

Kids do lots better at self-discipline if you explain the reasons for your nos. (Keep explanations simple to prevent tuning out.) When you explain logical reasons for a no, you are *modeling* critical thinking.

When kids understand your reasons for saying no or your rules well enough to explain them, they are *practicing* critical thinking. If you just repeat a rule to a child, the child does not really have to think or attend to you. If you ask them to tell you the rule and why we have it, they need to do lots of thinking. Ask them the whys for rules frequently, to see whether they can explain them clearly.

What's an "I Message"?

An "I" message given by the parent starts with the word *I* not the word *You.* For example, "I feel really upset and disappointed when you leave the table and forget to clear your place or rinse your plate." Or "I would feel less anxious and stressed in the morning if you could get dressed for school a little faster. Let's think of ways to make this happen."

One more thing about limits. If you expect the worst from your children, whether out in public or at home, they will give it to you. If you expect their best, you are much more likely to get it. Always expect their best, *and praise them for giving it.*

Logical Consequences

You will never teach self-discipline or responsibility if you make excuses or "clean up" after your child. When you need to address a behavior problem, first describe why you see it as a problem. (Use an "I" message.)

Then explain how the problem behavior affects others, and ask the child to think of ways to solve the problem or change the behavior. Be sure to praise them for any good ideas they come up with. (Use critical thinking and be prepared to give suggestions.)

Use logical consequences for inappropriate behavior. Here are some examples of what we mean by "logical consequences":

- Dirty clothes not in the hamper don't get washed.

- Toys not picked up get stored and are unavailable for play.

- Homework that kids forget to take to school will be late.

- Chores not finished mean less time with friends.

- Abuse of phone privileges and rudeness in answering the phone mean temporary removal of phone privileges.

- Inappropriate use of the PC results in a serious discussion and a temporary loss of privileges.

- Having the use of the car means working to help pay the extra insurance costs.

- Being late for the curfew means taking the consequences that the teen helped to decide when the curfew was set.

- Using up one's allowance means delaying gratification for purchasing something else right now.

Here are a couple of examples that show why imposing logical consequences for poor choices works and how this practice helps teach self-discipline and responsibility.

When kids use up their allowance and want an advance—and cannot have one—they will manage their money better on the next go around. If they use their money and buy something that falls apart, they will learn to make a more informed choice the next time. Furthermore, in this situation, they may also have the opportunity to learn about guarantees, warranties, and care of the product.

On the other side of this coin, if you notice that children have learned and improved their behaviors in any way, *praise them.* Children repeat behaviors for which they receive praise. (See Chapter 4 "Using the PC and Net to Nurture Self-Esteem," for examples of descriptive praise. Praise not only nurtures self-esteem, it modifies behavior.)

Immediate Gratification Is Not Reality

Giving kids what they want when they want it teaches kids to be demanding. It does not help children learn that they cannot have every-thing they want—which is reality. It does not help them to learn that most good things in life are earned—which is responsibility. And it does not teach them that we need to wait for some of the things we want—which is delayed gratification. Kids need to experience reality, responsi-bility, and delayed gratification.

When we never make a child take responsibility and accept the conse-quences of his or her behavior, when we look the other way, or when we say, "Oh well, that's just a little thing," we are raising another irre-sponsible adult.

We spoil kids (that is, we do not allow them to mature) when we make constant excuses for them, believe that they are never at fault, and res-cue them from all difficulties. We also spoil them when we expect them to never make mistakes; in this case we are not allowing them to learn that real life is not perfect and that everyone can learn and grow from their mistakes.

When kids make mistakes, e-Parenting consequences should be logical. For example, don't overreact if the child makes a mistake; the consequences should match the misbehavior.

Tip:
If you are overreact-ing, it may be because you are thinking of all the "bad" things the child ever did and all the "bad" things the child might possibly do in the future. Stop. Think only about the current situation.

Improper use of the PC should *not* mean that you pull the plug or never let the kids use it, because they can always find another PC to use. A more sensible response on your part is to make the PC off limits for a short time while you and your child have a serious conversation that includes critical thinking.

Talk about why the behavior was not a choice in their best inter-ests and how it could affect them and others. Also talk about what they could be doing with the PC and Net that would be more appropriate in terms of their long-range best interest.

Think about the long-range consequences of your own e-Parenting. Which is more important: pleasing your child and giving him or her whatever he or she wants to avoid a fuss, or let-ting kids experience the consequences of inappropriate choices, as they will in the real world of adulthood?

e-Parenting and Responsibility at Home

Children learn responsibility through the everyday family experi-ences of daily life. e-Parents can watch for ways to take advan-tage of these day-to-day activities to give children experience in taking responsibility. Responsibilities should grow as children grow and mature, starting with simple things such as helping out at home in many ways to more complex responsibilities such as volunteering or advocacy in the community.

The Help-out Habit

Teaching young children responsibility means giving them simple responsibilities and letting them practice self-discipline in carrying them out. Start early to establish the "help out" habit, when children love to help and are eager to do so on a daily basis. Rewards and praise will make them proud and motivate the self-discipline they need to keep the help-out habit going.

Some of the child's first daily "jobs" will relate to personal self-help, like dressing, undressing, hygiene, picking up toys, hanging up coats, and putting dirty clothes where they belong. You'll have to be close by at first and provide reminders to help children stay on task. Reminders are normal and necessary during this first step in the children's learning process.

When they can do these things with just a few reminders, you'll know they are at step 2 in the process—that is, that they are learning both self-discipline and responsibility. When they can do their chores with no reminders, they've really got it! If you want them to keep on doing it, don't forget to praise them.

e-Parents build discipline and responsibility skills by moving kids from personal responsibilities into household ones as soon as they are old enough.

Not Just for Kids: All the daily personal responsibilities you expect of your kids should be modeled by all family members (dads and moms, too).

Kids can set and clear the table, help with food preparation, put away groceries, and help sort laundry and put it away. They can make their own beds, water plants, and take care of pets. They can help vacuum, dust, and sweep the sidewalk; help rake and bag leaves; and help wash the car.

All family members should share these kinds of responsibilities. Help kids think about the reasons for doing their share. Talk about it. Praise children for helping out.

Do we all live together and share the space? Can jobs get done faster when more people help? Is it fair for older kids to do harder jobs than little kids have to do? This kind of conversation exercises logical and critical thinking. Help your kids practice critical thinking every chance you get! It will help them in the e-World.

But remember that the *habit* of helping out (not how perfectly the child does the job) is the focus of e-Parenting. Your goal is to nurture the habits of responsibility and self-discipline in your kids. Just ask that they try to do their best. Descriptive praise and rewards (such as playing a game together or getting to go somewhere special) will help keep the help-out habit going.

Chore Lists

One good e-Parenting strategy is to use the PC to print a weekly Family Chore List to post on the bulletin board or refrigerator. Kids still like using gold stars to show that the job or chore was completed. e-Parents can also use PC programs to print up special praise certificates or humorous awards. Help kids to feel pride in their responsible behavior.

Caring for a Pet

Another way children can learn self-discipline and responsibility is to have a pet to care for. All too often, parents buy pets for children who make promises about care that they don't keep. Then the parents—who probably love the pet by this time—take on all the responsibility for the animal, and the child learns nothing.

One way to find out whether the child is ready for a pet is to go to an electronics store and buy a virtual pet first. The child will get a good workout as the virtual pet simulates the demands of pet care. After a week or so, talk about the ways real-world pets need care and see whether your child is still willing to take on the responsibility.

Where to Find a Virtual Pet

Electronic virtual pets are electronic devices that are programmed to tell their owners when they need care. You can still purchase them (they cost about $6 to $8) at stores such as Radio Shack, where currently the most popular virtual pet is the Radio Shack dinosaur for $4.97.

We found an even more interesting option at *www.pfmagic.com*. PF Magic is a company that sells "computer petz" that live and romp about on your computer, do tricks, and require owner care such as grooming, training, petting, and feeding. You may choose from Dogz, Catz, or Oddballz for about $20. Free demos can be found at the site, and your purchase can be downloaded.

If your kids seem ready for the responsibility of a real pet, talk about the kind of pet your child might want and can handle. Suppose that you decide on a small dog but are not sure what breed you want. You and the child can go to the Internet and do a search about dogs. You will find out about the characteristics and temperaments of the breeds, see pictures of them, and see the advantages or disadvantages of owning or caring for each one.

You and your child can learn about training, health, and pet care products—everything you want to know. You will also be modeling how to use the Net to get information and evaluate it so that you can make an informed choice about a pet. When you involve your child this thoroughly in preparation and thinking, you have an excellent chance of being successful in buying a pet to teach your child more about self-discipline and responsibility.

▼ **Try It Yourself**

1. Go to the *www.altavista.com* search engine to start looking for help in choosing a dog. Choose **Hobbies & Interests** and then choose **Pets & Animals**; finally choose **Dogs**. From the information in this section, choose **Getting a Dog** to see a list of sites to visit.

2. At *www.waltham.com/pets/select/f1.htm*, you can find an interactive questionnaire of 17 multiple-choice questions. Based on your answers, you'll see a list of suggestions in priority order of "the best dog for you." You can click any of the suggestions for a picture and description of that particular breed.

3. Go back to the AltaVista list of results for the topic, **Getting a Dog** (use the Back button). If you click the title **Finding the Right Dog**, you'll go to *www.canismajor.com/dog/topic1.html#choosing*.

   This page is loaded with information about all kinds of dogs and dog issues.

▲

Both the Waltham.com site and the CanisMajor.com site demonstrate that responsibility in dog ownership is more than having a dog and taking "pretty good" care of it. Kids should be informed and prepared and asked to decide whether they can follow through with ownership responsibilities.

Net resources and software about breeds of dogs, as well as simple experiences with dogs in the real world, can help parents and kids make good pet choices. We found the information we needed in about 20 minutes on the Internet. In the real world, we would have needed considerably more time!

More About Dogs

One site on the AltaVista Dogs list—called How to Love Your Dog—really piqued our interest. The description below the link reads "just for kids." This excellent site explains the importance of caring for a dog, training, the needs of special dogs, and keeping safe around dogs; this site also includes tons of other great stuff.

One reason this site may be so well suited to kids and families is that the site author has a degree in early childhood education. She developed this site modeled after her humane education program in which dogs are used to teach children kindness, commitment, and responsibility.

This site even has an I Love My Dog responsibility contract for kids to print out and sign. Another page lists all the other kids who have signed the contract and made the commitment to their dogs. The How to Love Your Dog site also has interactive quizzes, kids' stories and poetry, a message board, birthday listings, information about careers with animals, and information about losing a pet (which includes a dedication page).

Of course, you'll also find information about getting a dog—questions to consider, needs of a dog, different breed characteristics, special needs, training, and the overpopulation issue (still a problem with irresponsible adults who don't spay or neuter their pets). This site's address is *www.howtoloveyourdog.com*. Go there; you'll love it.

At www. howtoloveyour dog.com, a site designed specifically for kids, visitors can learn about dogs, post dog stories and poems, and take "tours" of doggie information pages.

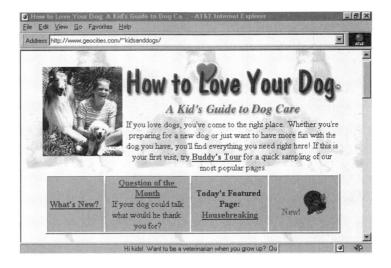

Rescue Leagues Are Another Resource for Your New Family Pet

Almost every major dog breed (and some cats) have national rescue leagues that find unwanted or abandoned animals and make them available for placement with new families. And of course, many of these leagues have an Internet presence. Our editor shared this related story with us, and we thought you'd like to consider its possibilities in your online search for pets. She went online and did a search for **keeshond** (the dog breed she favors) and **rescue**. She wound up on a very cool site that listed all the Keeshonden available through the Keeshond Rescue Railroad—complete with photos and biographies. She and her family got their second Keesie through that site, communicating with the woman in charge almost exclusively through email. Although the rescue league can arrange to get your new animal to you, our editor and her family made the two-hour car trip to visit with all the dogs that were available for rescue. On a money-saving note, the rescue league charged only $150 for the dog; a Keesie puppy in the pet store was priced at $695.

Being a New Big Brother or Big Sister

Some older children are excited about the impending birth of a new baby in the family; some are worried about their new role as big brother or big sister. Some hospitals have special programs where e-Parents can prepare their kids and make it easier for them to adjust to the growing family.

But the e-World gives parents and kids even more opportunities to learn about new arrivals. e-Parents can help children do searches on the Internet about newborns to help the older siblings understand more about how helpless babies are, how they develop, what things babies need, and ways to interact or "play" with the baby.

When children know more about babies, they are usually more excited and involved in the planning—and more likely to anticipate their new "helper" roles with pride. Let siblings help; they have the self-discipline to do lots of things, and taking responsibility will make them proud.

Help Prevent Jealousy

As parents and children explore Net information and plan together, parents can talk to their children about "when they were little" and get out photos and baby books. Kids need to know that, when they were babies, all this attention and more was lavished on *them*.

Preparing for a new sibling is a big responsibility for the parent as well as the child. e-Parents can find material on the Net or discuss many issues about new arrivals with other parents in chats or on electronic message boards. A few searches can bring you lots of material about introducing another baby to the family.

For example, at *www.storknet.org/articles/sibs.htm* we found 12 brief letters from parents about preparing children for the arrival of a new sibling. In a short time, we came across about a dozen pages with information or articles, as well as information about a book called *Baby Science* that we highly recommend. This book contains hands-on activities presented in age-appropriate ways that help children learn more about babies.

e-Parents can also go to virtual bookstores or malls to find children's books and videos for learning about babies and about becoming an older brother or sister. The more the child learns about the baby, the more prepared the child will be for new responsibilities as a big brother or sister.

e-Parenting and Responsibility Beyond the Home

When children are accustomed to taking responsibility at home, the next logical step is to accept growing responsibilities beyond the home in the neighborhood and community. When children see parents being socially responsible or volunteering and promoting good things in their communities, it helps kids see that all of us are part of an increasingly global society. Because e-Children will live and work in a global e-World, e-Parents should help kids understand that virtual-world responsibilities come hand in hand with its privileges.

Volunteering

We think that the more children practice responsibility through different activities, the more pride they take in being responsible individuals. Being responsible extends beyond the home into one's neighborhood and community. Sometimes families teach their kids about taking responsibility by volunteering.

e-Parents need to take the lead in sharing with their children the family's belief in the importance of helping out in the world beyond the home. Whether it is volunteering to clean up a stream or park or volunteering at a church soup kitchen, e-Parents and kids with the desire to do so can always find opportunities to volunteer in their communities.

Almost every community has a humane society or an animal adoption program. If your child is interested in animals, you can take him or her to give TLC attention to prospective pets once a week, help put up posters of pets that need adoption, or help with a fundraiser. The child will feel proud that he or she is helping and will be learning about self-discipline and responsibility in a way that is meaningful and fun.

When e-Parents make volunteering a regular part of children's lives when they are young, even if it is a monthly or occasional occurrence, kids may continue volunteering as young teens and adults.

Preteens and teens who are too young to have jobs have lots of energy as well as some free time. And volunteering of any kind tells prospective employers that a teen is self-disciplined and responsible. Volunteer work looks great on a resume when a teen is ready to look for a job!

Kids can volunteer at parks, the zoo, the fire station, the hospital, the library, a gymnastics club, the YMCA, a child care center, the church, the recycling center, or at a nursing home that needs someone to play music once in a while. A volunteer activity that is encouraged by e-Parents can even become a hobby or lead to a career.

Sometimes volunteering sparks an interest in a cause, leading an older child or teen to explore advocacy on the Internet. Sometimes the process works the other way around. A preteen might discover an environmental or social cause on the Internet that spurs him or her to do related volunteering in the community.

Volunteer Opportunities

At the Traverse City Area District Library in Grand Traverse County, Michigan, the library does not use filtering programs to censor information. In an effort to satisfy the concerns of some of its constituents, the library is considering a plan to use volunteers—including responsible teenagers—in the computer area to help and to supervise school-age children using the PCs.

At the Freeman Memorial Branch of the Harris County Library in Houston, Texas, (*www.hcpl.lib.tx.us*), senior high school teen volunteers provide help with shelving books, community events, and performing bibliography maintenance of the PC systems. During the school year, the library uses teen National Honor Society students who are required to do community service. In the summer, any local seventh to ninth grader can apply to participate in the Youth Volunteer Program. During the summer, these preteens shelve books, prepare crafts, help with community events, and man the reading tables for the summer reading program. In this program, these kids help younger children choose books, enjoy books, and earn reading incentive rewards.

Responsibility to the World

When children are preteens or teens—and at an age and maturity level to see ways to help out in their communities—e-Parents can also show their kids ways they can be more involved as responsible global citizens. Many teens are interested in causes such as anti-bias, cultural diversity, substance abuse prevention, natural health practices, animals, population growth, world hunger, and endangered species. The Net is a perfect vehicle for them to learn more about these global issues and find ways to take on personal responsibilities that match their interests.

Advocacy: Why It's Good for e-Parents and e-Kids

Children today are becoming more involved with special causes because online technology can bring out the issues so much more easily and so continuously. The e-World enables kids to find out about issues such as air and water pollution, car design safety, the use of animals for medical research, protecting reefs and marine life, and online safety.

On the Net children can gather plenty of information on almost any issue; they can even follow both sides of any debate. If you have put patterns in place that encourage your kids to talk to you about anything—including their online activities—you can have some great workouts in critical thinking as you discuss a cause your kids have learned about on the Net.

Encourage this kind of exploring and discovery. Kids have lots of energy and enthusiasm, and they can make a difference as advocates. Young teens are tireless in their efforts if they believe in a cause. e-Parents should keep their eyes and ears open for children's potential advocacy interests for several reasons:

- Getting involved is good for kids; it's a positive and constructive use of their time.

- The process of evaluating information, discussion, and action is good practice in critical thinking that will help your child learn even more about wise and responsible choices.

- It takes both self-discipline and perseverance to be involved in advocacy efforts; getting practice in both of these skills is in your child's best interest.

- Advocacy experiences include responsibilities.

Your child might see a show on TV about an endangered animal or about a wildlife preserve, or your child might learn at school about how recycling helps the environment. Any of these interests could lead to more online research and/or finding advocacy organizations. One experience will lead to others, and your child might learn ways to further a cause in his or her own community or at school.

Paying attention, listening, and learning more about your child's interests by exploring software or the Internet can help you lead your children to discover special advocacy groups for just about any topic or interest. Some advocacy sites are geared specifically toward child involvement, and they include resources, online petitions, activities, career information, and more.

Advocacy "Causes"

Kids Can Make a Difference (at *www.kids.maine.org*) is a site devoted to ending hunger and poverty. The site offers an educational program that teaches middle school and high school kids what they can do to fight poverty.

The 4-H site, *www.areyouintoit.com*, is about kids who volunteer for various causes. The site gives information on how parents can help children get involved. You'll find stories about volunteering, information about why kids should volunteer, advice on supporting different causes, and links to other sites.

The Youth in Action Network at *www.mightymedia.com/youth.asp* is part of the Mighty Media Network where kids are the focus for change in a variety of causes. One section is designed and operated by youth, and another is educator oriented.

The Youth in Action Network site includes learning activities for environmental and human rights education, discussions on important issues, and information on how to make use of the media (including the Net) for support. Also included on this site are forums, surveys, petitions, government information, a calendar of pertinent events, a place to voice your opinion on issues, and more.

e-Kids who combine these e-World strategies with traditional methods of social action are not only doing critical thinking and taking responsibility but also making a difference that no previous generation could ever have made!

We have shown you just a few examples of e-Avenues for your child's advocacy in action. Real-world hands-on organizations are also using the Net for spreading the word, making contacts, and signing petitions. Visitors and members of these sites are getting educated about the issues online and then participating—virtually or actively in the real world.

Children who get involved with advocacy experiences will learn a great deal about dedication and self-discipline as well as responsibility.

Advocacy in Your Own Back Yard
The National Wildlife Federation's Web site at *www.nwf.org* is a great example of a hands-on, real-world, advocacy activity. Environmentally conscious kids can have their backyard certified as an Official Backyard Habitat by the federation. All kids need to do is use information from the National Wildlife Federation (NWF) site and exercise some muscle and self-discipline by working outside in the yard.

From the home page of the National Wildlife Federation (www.nwf.org), click the Backyard Wildlife Habitat link to see how you can register your backyard as a wildlife habitat.

The site has an application to register your yard as a wildlife habitat and provides habitat hints and project ideas. (You can use your own ideas, too.) When your child completes the habitat, he or she gets a personalized certificate proclaiming an official backyard wildlife habitat, a free *Habitats* quarterly newsletter, and the option to have this achievement recognized in your community by NWF. Your child is eligible to get NWF's Backyard Wildlife Habitat sign for your yard. Many schools, workplaces, and even communities are involved in this program.

Also listed in the NWF site are magazines and publications for kids (even a magazine for toddlers), environmental education resources, news about the environment, real-life outdoor activities for youth groups and teens, a section called Just for Kids, an "Earthsavers" club for kids, plus much more.

Adopt an Animal

Adopt a real animal through a virtual adoption! We did a search with words such as **wildlife animal and adoption** and got a long list of animal-adoption programs. Some of the titles that came up were Adopt a Lemur, Adopt a Bat, and Adopt a Big Cat. e-Parents and kids can also look up specific animals of interest, such as manatees. We searched for **manatee** and found a great site.

Would your child like to adopt a manatee? The Save the Manatee Club at *www.savethemanatee.org* has an adoption program. You can choose a manatee and visit some of them by taking an underwater Web cam tour. When you adopt, you get a photo, an adoption certificate, a biography of "your" manatee, and a 28-page handbook with information on manatees.

You can search the Net for adopt-an-animal programs like this one at www. savethemanitee. org. *Adopting an animal is a great way to learn more about unusual or endangered species and to take an active role in their preservation.*

Your child can also receive a quarterly *Save the Manatees* club newsletter featuring updates on adoptees. Some adoptees need to be rescued and rehabilitated. You can apply online or with snail mail, and you can even visit the animals in person. Your contribution to the Save the Manatee Club helps research, conservation, rehabilitation, and education.

Adopt a Tree

e-Parents can plant trees with the kids and can also help the environment by joining the National Arbor Day Foundation. A $10 donation entitles you to 10 Colorado blue spruces or other conifers, as well as a subscription to *Arbor Day*, the bimonthly publication. Find out more about trees and the Arbor Day Foundation at *www.arborday.org*.

Sometimes young children who cannot plant a tree "adopt" a tree in their neighborhood or a nearby park. e-Parents can help them observe their tree in different seasons, see what animals live in or under the tree, have picnics, or read stories there.

e-Parents can help their children learn more about trees on the Internet. You can learn how trees grow, how they help improve the air we breathe, and how trees are used; you can investigate related topics such as forests, tropical rain forests, and advocacy for saving the rain forests. It's not hard to see that a real tree can be a catalyst for many new learning activities.

Another activity your child might enjoy, especially if he or she likes creative activities, is to enter the Arbor Day poster contest. Entering contests of various kinds to help a good cause may even be a possibility in your own hometown. If your community does not sponsor this type of contest, you can find many opportunities online.

More Tree Sites:

Another option is a fairly new site with similar goals called *www.american-forests.org.* Take a new look at an old tree-planting campaign called Global Releaf.

Here is one of the contest winners you can see at the National Arbor Days Foundation Web site at http://www.arborday.org/teaching/oklahoma_winner.asp?event=.

From little things (such as taking care of a pet or separating recyclable trash every day) to big things (such as organizing a petition to transform a vacant lot into a park or saving the gray whales), the rewards of advocacy are great, and the e-World makes advocacy possible for everyone.

Tip:

You can show kids how you are helping various causes simply by doing your online shopping at sites such as the iGivemall that donates part of its proceeds to non-profit organizations.

Summing Up

Remember that self-discipline and responsibility go hand in hand. The more responsibilities kids take, the more self-disciplined they will be. An interest in advocacy may inspire kids to take more responsibility.

Advocacy helps kids learn about being able to take a stand and to be proud of it. Advocacy helps them learn about the responsibility of taking their places as members in society and teaches them that the work and discipline it takes to make a difference are worth the effort.

As children grow, expand your e-Parenting basics to help them do more critical thinking so that they learn about the kinds of choices you want them to be able to make on their own. The earlier you put positive patterns in place, the stronger they will be.

To teach self-discipline and responsibility, remember to model the behavior you want from your children, set clear limits, use logical consequences, and help kids use the PC and Net to practice making informed, responsible choices.

PART III

Web Resources
for Parents

CHAPTER 7

Online Resources for Schooling

In this chapter we share some tips on Internet resources for parents and kids as well as some of the good Web sites we found as we explored the topics in this chapter. We start with software and move into resources for homework and networking for school children.

Then we take a look at home schooling resources for parents and children. The Net, with its vast educational resources and many ways to share ideas and strategies, has been an enormous help to e-Parents who are home schooling their children.

Online Resources for School Children

Online resources for school children include many things from software to resources and homework help. In the next sections, we want to share some thoughts about finding and choosing educational software, and also give you some tips on how to help your kids network with others and find homework resources. We'll also share tips on ways to support your school-age child in his or her learning endeavors.

Software for Fun and Learning

Before we talk about software sites or how to get children's educational software, we'd like to mention a few things about quality that e-Parents should keep in mind when they're shopping for educational software.

- It should be age appropriate and should vary in difficulty and challenge so that it matches children's changing skills.

- It should be free of bias, stereotypes, and violence.

What You'll Learn in This Chapter:

▸ How to use the plethora of online resources to further your child's primary and secondary school learning experiences— and get information about colleges and universities as well

▸ How to find home schooling resources for home school parents and children

▸ How to find educational help for kids with special needs

- It should be fun and should integrate creativity and play with learning.

- It should encourage experimenting and discovery, but should not become frustrating.

- It should encourage pride in accomplishment.

- It should allow for open-ended questions.

- It should have graphics that are clean and well defined.

Although these may seem to be lofty goals, parents can use them as a guide in searching for good software. Parents can also try to use demos or software samples that allow them to try out software before purchasing. Parents can also ask the opinions of teachers and other parents they respect, read reviews of products on the Net whenever possible, and check the recommendations of The National Parenting Center (*www.tnpc.com*) or their libraries and school media centers. In addition, parents should take advantage of product guarantees. Observe your child's reaction as you try out new software together. If software products are not what you expect, or if they seem to frustrate your children, return them.

Remember that no matter how interesting the software is, the experience will be even better if an e-Parent is involved. Now let's look around.

We started with a simple search for **learning software for kids** and found tons of Web sites that sell software. If you are in the market for software and are doing a similar search, remember how important it is to model the appropriate use of the PC and Net. As you shop online with your kids, show them how to gather information and how to make informed choices.

The best approach is to do some software searches with your child. Visiting software sites is like window shopping at the stores: Discuss what you find and compare your options before making your choices.

Talk together about what software would be the most useful or why one might be the best buy. (Keep practicing that critical thinking!) Sit next to your child to assist him or her but let the child do the searching if at all possible.

To avoid being overwhelmed by the options and succumbing to impulse buying, e-Parents should use Internet resources to read reviews and consumer reports about software before making a choice; remember that you can also try out shareware.

Software sites will lead you to age-specific software, learning-specific software, and other options listed by subject within the site, so you should try to have some idea about what you are looking for when you start the search.

Here are some more tips about finding software for fun and learning. Use the techniques that work best for you.

- Do simple searches for learning software for kids. Use words like **homework**, **educational**, **software**, **CD-ROMs**, **math**, **elementary school**, and **special needs kids' software**.

- Read reviews and consumer reports about software and try out shareware (try before you buy).

- Home schooling sites often recommend or include lists of educational software or links to software product sites.

- You can go straight to the Web site of a software company such as Microsoft and check the categories there.

- Check parenting sites such as *www.parentsoup.com* for pages on software or links to software sites.

- Check the National Parenting Center at *www.tnpc.com* for the current and the archived Seal of Approval recommendations for children's software.

- Go to a bulletin board or newsgroup for either parents or education to ask about finding specific learning software for children; see what others recommend.

Here are some of the software sites we explored.

School House Software Review at *www.worldvillage.com/wv/school/html/scholrev.htm* has a long list of categorized educational software with reviews. It also includes links to articles, games, and downloads. The site is useful for both parents and teachers. Smart Kids Software at *www.smartkidssoftware.com* is loaded with software and reviews for educational and entertainment

Tip:
Kids really don't care what you know— unless they know you care.

software. There are also specials in the Bargains section, and articles, links, and more in the Features section. We liked the reviews and found them useful; the bargains were helpful, too.

Houghton Mifflin Interactive makes multimedia CD-ROMs and Web sites for schools and families. You can see demonstrations of products at this site, too. This site's demonstrations of products were particularly helpful.

Edmark.com at *www.edmark.com* has a wide variety of learning software plus technology support pages, a section for teachers, and a section for parents. The site is easy to navigate and includes topics such as learning styles, home schooling special-needs and gifted children, as well as all the academic areas. You can download free samples, too. Edmark has been well respected as a learning software publisher for many years; we found their site particularly helpful.

The Edmark home page is easy to navigate: Click any labeled image to access valuable information, products, and more.

The parents' pages (click the **Dear Parents** link) include thoughtful advice that is well grounded in child development and education but is very practical and readable—both friendly and professional. You can reach these pages another way, by using the URL *www.dearparents.com*. A click will take you from there to Edmark.com.

Children's Software Review at *www2.childrenssoftware.com* is a review site of children's software in which the reviews are written by teachers. These reviews can give you the real scoop on the value of the products! We felt that these reviews were particularly helpful.

Check out MindPlay at *www.mindplay.com*, which specializes in educational software for schools including many curriculum-based programs for special-needs students. MindPlay offers 30 titles of reading, math, and science software for special-needs kids.

We also like the children's learning software from Sunburst Communications. The company does other things too, but one of its specialties is software that teaches math and literacy concepts to young children as well as school-age children. Find it at *www.sunburst.com*.

Don't forget to check out Broderbund at *www.Broderbund.com* and its online partnerships with Mindscape, American Greetings, and The Learning Company (*www.learningco.com*). Software options here emphasize creative activities and games, and parents will find a wide variety of options for this kind of playful learning.

Congratulations on a Sensitive Site!

In our opinion, MindPlay deserves kudos for its attention to special-needs kids and its software for this group.

Parent Reviews Are Valuable, Too

Here are excerpts from one parenting newspaper's review of the Treasure Math Storm software (published by The Learning Company): "A great way to develop math skills.... As your child finds treasures, s/he will learn about counting, time, money…addition, subtraction, multiplication, and more. …gradually introduces concepts so that your child is constantly challenged yet not frustrated."

"Includes six math levels that automatically adjust to your child's abilities. …arcade action encourages fast thinking, lots of laughs, and hours of fun. …nine charming, speaking characters provide feedback, helpful hints, and messages. …my son has played this for over a year, learned a lot, and still has lots of fun with it."

From "Computer Kids" by Karen Dillon, *Omaha Family*, November 1999.

Several other publishing companies that have been around a long time and that also publish learning software for children are Scholastic, World Book, and Random House.

Sites for Homework and School Projects

Think about all the real-world resources you would ordinarily use for homework and school projects: libraries, museums, encyclopedias, dictionaries, and atlases. Today, these resources are all online! So, think like an e-Parent before buying books or driving kids to the library.

When we were in school, we spent hours in libraries, finding magazine articles and books, making copies, filling out index cards, and so on so that we could put together reports for school. Worse, we couldn't pick the brains of anyone who could really help, such as professionals or people with first-hand information (people who were at the Woodstock concert event, for example). Online resources take a fraction of time of the old paper-bound editions. Today children can even get pictures of an event from the Net and can often communicate with people who participated in a historic event.

The Electric Library is at *www.elibrary.com*, and it has thousands of sources for homework help. Included are newspapers, encyclopedias, articles, radio reports, TV reports, maps, pictures, and more. This site is easy for school-age kids to use, too. However, you should know that this site requires you to pay a fee of $9.95 a month. You may decide it is worth it when you use the 30-day free trial.

Speaking of libraries, have you seen KidsConnect (at *www.ala. org/ICONN/kidsconn.html*)? It's a question-answering, help, and referral service for kids in grades K through 12, and its goal is to help kids access and use Net information effectively. School library media specialists all over the world are cooperating on KidsConnect. Through email, students can ask questions and receive feedback from a library media specialist within two school days.

KidsConnect is a component of ICONnect, an initiative of the American Association of School Librarians and the American Library Association.

One way to find help with homework is to do a simple search with keywords such as **homework** or **science**. Another technique is to start at an education section of a search engine home page;

you should be able to find a homework link to bring up many options.

We started to look for homework help sites by checking in at *www.netmom.com*. Netmom Jean Armour Polly has an Emergency Homework Help hotlist of nine sites. This list, like her hotlists on other topics, is taken from her book *The Internet Kids & Family Yellow Pages*, Fourth Edition (Osborne McGraw-Hill).

The hotlists are continually updated, and Jean Polly's reviews are fun to read; they give good information in a friendly, interesting way. Many e-Parents check the *www.netmom.com* site often.

One recommended site, B. J. Pinchbeck's Homework Helper site, seems to target elementary kids with its useful homework resources. The site, at *www.bjpinchbeck.com*, is published by a 12-year-old boy and his dad.

All the sites recommended by Net-mom sounded interesting, but Jean Polly's review of *www.mtsu.edu/studskllhsindex.html* was so intriguing that we took a look. This site would really help older kids and teens with their study habits and study skills. Lots of good tips!

On Kids Web at *www.npac.syr.edu/textbook/kidsweb*, e-Parents and kids can find all kinds of links organized by subject, such as math, geography, geology, history, and so on. Kids Web is not an information or homework site in itself, but it gives links and points you in the right direction.

Another comprehensive homework site covering many angles is the virtual schoolhouse at *www.metalab.unc.edu/cisco/schoolhouse*. This site also links you to educational sites on various subjects. Here you can get homework help on specific subjects; you can also access libraries, art museums, colleges, and more. This site is well organized and easy to navigate. It should be helpful to your kids.

Fun Brain, at *www.funbrain.com*, is a site we mentioned briefly in Chapter 5, "Using the PC and Net to Enhance People Skills," in the section on games. You and the kids should check out this site for its schoolwork help. Fun Brain is a place for teachers, students, and parents. Teachers can use or submit online quizzes and

can use a curriculum guide designed for collective participation
by parents and teachers at the bulletin board.

*The FunBrain
home page at
www.funbrain.
com is easy to
navigate and has
links to lots of
intriguing, inter-
active activities.
Parents and
teachers will find
as many resources
here as the kids
will!*

Besides playing the games found here, children can practice skills
in math, grammar, spelling, science, history, or logic. For example, in the Shape Surveyor activity, each time a correct math
answer is given, a piece of the picture is revealed.

In addition to these sites, *www.schooltime.com* and
www.familyeducation.com are good sites for homework and
general research covering many topics.

Of course, older children who are better at searching (or who are
getting help from search savvy e-Parents) can find very specific
sites for homework assignments by using a phrase in quotation
marks, such as **"battle of Gettysburg"**.

Today the e-World gives kids some great virtual tools—sites
devoted to research tools such as encyclopedias, dictionaries, and
thesauruses. Well-known reference-book publishers such as
Britannica (*www.eb.com*), Compton's (*www.comptons.com*), and
Merriam-Webster (*www.m-w.com*) are online. World Book is also
online at *www.worldbook.com* and includes special pages for
homework and current events.

Some resources and encyclopedias are "virtual only" sites, meaning they only exist in cyberspace. For example, the Electronic Library, which we mentioned earlier in this chapter, is a virtual-only site, at *www.elibrary.com*. Also, the Internet Public Library at *http://ipl.org* is a virtual-only site.

The massive New York public library is online at *www.nypl.org*. The Library of Congress is online. If you still can't find what you're looking for, try the Internet public library at *http://ipl.org*.

Up-to-Date and Online:

An online reference book is probably more current than a real book; updating online books is easier and cheaper than updating printed books.

There's Nothing Like the Real Thing

Surely you and your child will sometimes want real books to read, to use for research, or to just plain enjoy looking at. Nothing can replace the sensory experience of touching books, turning the pages, looking at fine illustration details, or holding a book and a child on your lap. And your kids may want particular real books for a specific homework assignment.

Many local libraries are online. Find out about yours. Kids can find out online whether a book they want is in; if the book is out, they can find out when it will be back. An online search can save an unnecessary phone call or trip to the library. Kids can also put in their requests for books and know exactly how many people are ahead of them. (If your library is not yet up on the Net, it won't be long.)

One of the most exciting things about the Net is that kids and parents canonline;museums;visiting visit museums and galleries online for enjoyment or research. Try the Smithsonian Institution or the Berkeley Museum of Paleontology. Or you can go to the Virtual Library Museum Page, which is a guide to all types of museums on the Internet. You can access all these museums from *www.comlab.ox.ac.uk/archive/other/museums.html*. (You may have to exercise patience when visiting these pages; the main server is in the United Kingdom; even with a speedy modem, connection times can seem sluggish.)

There is even a site about the White House. It is geared to kids ages 5 through 12 and is called White House for Kids at *www.whitehouse.gov/WH/kids/html/home.html*.

Safe Surfing:

Be sure that your kids know and make use of these safe surf engines when they do homework searches: Alfy, Yahooligans, and Zeeks. Two other helpful sites are Ask Jeeves for Kids (*www.askJeevesforkids.com*) and Study Web (*www.studyweb.com*).

The First Dog and First Cat will take you on a tour of the most famous house in the nation if you visit the White House for Kids at www.whitehouse.gov/WH/kids/html/home.html.

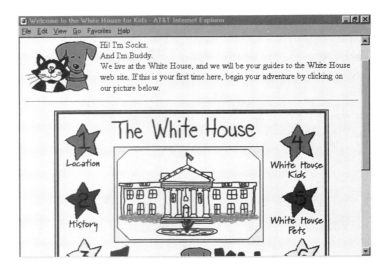

Support Your Resident School Child

In closing this section on homework, e-Parents should remember that kids need ample and comfortable space for doing their homework or school projects. They need good light, a table or desk, comfortable seating, and no distractions (that is, no phone calls, television, or loud music).

Kids should also do their homework at a regular time each day, but not immediately after school. They need some time for physical activities and fresh air or just for chilling out and talking to you about their day. One more thing: They should prioritize their homework tasks and focus on just one task at a time. (Some kids look at the whole pile, and if it seems too overwhelming, they don't even get started.)

It's not just making sure that the homework gets done that shows you support your child's school efforts. Even if both e-Parents work, there are still ways to stay involved with your child's school.

Studies have shown that if you show an interest, the teacher will *expect* your child to do well. Guess what? When teachers have this expectation, it almost always influences the child's grades and achievements for the better. Here are things you can do to make sure that your child knows you support his or her efforts in school:

- Make sure that the teachers know your faces; drop by before school starts (possibly on your way to work) just to say hello.

- If your child is ill, get his or her books and daily assignments from the teacher so that your child won't get behind.

- Arrange time with your employer to go to parent conferences and be sure to attend events or open houses. Take turns with your spouse, a friend, or a family member if that will make it easier.

- Ask teachers to send notes or email to let you know if there are any problems, or if there are things you can do at home. Email saves time and puts proof of your support in writing.

- School friends are very important to kids. Make time to get to know your kids' friends and their parents. Invite them to your home or go to an event or movie together. Making sure that your child feels comfortable about having his or her friends hang out at your house will be very important in the preteen and teen years.

- Praise your kids for just being themselves, as well as for their responsible school and at-home behaviors. Put little notes in their lunch boxes or coat pockets to let them know you are thinking about them.

- Make a special time each evening, even if it's for 15 minutes, to listen to your child tell about the school day. Really listen and also make positive comments or ask casual questions to encourage conversations that will give you more information.

Schoolwork and Networking

Every kind of group and every individual has the Internet resources to network with others while working on homework, research, or projects.

Just like sports clubs, teen chats, or hobbyists' newsgroups, groups are forming homework clubs where kids (and teachers and parents) can interact, helping each other to find information and learn.

Talk Is Good:

Putting in place a pattern of listening to your child talk about his or her day will also help your child talk to you about online activities.

- Check homework sites, such as the ones listed in the preceding sections, for chat rooms and bulletin boards or links.

- Show your child how to use newsgroups to find other students who are working on the same things he or she is working on.

Many e-Parents help their kids form "classroom help clubs"; teachers and schools can often help you get started. These clubs are interactive ways for kids to get more information, more opinions, and do more brainstorming on school projects. (More brainstorming equals more critical thinking.) When parents are involved in the clubs, they can keep the kids from drifting off track.

This kind of networking is a way for kids to choose their own time for getting together to interact and learn. Kids are usually more invested and motivated when they set the time and do the planning. Most kids learn faster and do schoolwork more efficiently when they work in small groups on specific subjects or projects.

One networking resource that school kids can use is ICQ at *www.icq.com*. ICQ, which stands for "I Seek You," is a huge site with extensive service options for its millions of users, who are adults as well as school-age students. The site has won numerous awards its free downloads, shareware, global chat capacities, and tools. ICQ is a user-friendly universal platform in which you can engage in a variety of peer-to-peer activities such as email, chats, file transfers, interest groups, and Net meetings.

ICQ offers free email and many networks (including those for Family, Students, Games, Sports, Site Creators, Travel, Finances, Romance, and more). The site boasts its own strong search engine to help people find friends by age or by topic of interest.

Go to ICQ for PenPal Help

By the way, ICQ won the Best of the Net award for pen pals for kids in 1998, its first year online.

Because of its many adult options for finding new friends and its vast public chat rooms and message boards, we suggest that parents closely supervise their kids' ICQ activities and stay consistently involved as team members in children's online communications through this site.

We do not suggest this site for immature kids or kids who are just beginning to use the Net. It might work well for older kids who have proven themselves responsible and who keep you fully aware of their online activities.

Having said that, we also must say that ICQ can be quite useful for parents who want to help their kids set up a special chat or interest group in which kids can discuss and work on school projects together.

When users register with ICQ, they get a special universal Internet number (UIN) that identifies them and lets other ICQ users know every time they log on. If your child registers, he or she can compile a selected list of friends to join in chats about assignments or do homework or school projects. Your child will be alerted when the other members of the selected group log on; the kids can then click icons to chat, exchange files, and so on.

AOL recently bought Mirabilis Ltd., the company that started and continues to operate this site as a free Web-based service; this move should improve AOL's existing chat features.

Homework Help from AOL

America Online has a homework help site that combines reference tools and live assistance including tutoring rooms, student-teacher chats, message boards, and teacher-response email.

If you're an AOL member, go to **Keyword** in **Favorite Places** and type **homework**. From there, you can go to the **Ask a Teacher** page, which has several options. You can go to a database called **Homework Helpers** to see whether your question has already been posted in a topic folder; find out about becoming a peer tutor; see the e-Library; or go to pages for elementary school, middle school, high school, or college students.

For example, if you click the link to elementary school pages, AOL takes you to **Kids Only Homework Help** pages for grades K through 6. Here you will find a knowledge database, a thesaurus, a dictionary, and an encyclopedia, as well as live chat tutoring rooms for subjects such as math, science, English and reading, and social studies.

AOL has developed a system for teacher-student interactions. If you click a tutoring room subject, you will find posted the hours for live chats with teachers. If the room is not currently open for chat, you can post an email question for the teacher. Answers are not emailed to you; you must check back to the posted question list to get your answer.

continues

continued

On AOL you can also enter the keyword **charter** to see the files about charter schools and read the monthly charter school forum.

Or you can enter the keywords **home schooling**, which will start an AOL search that leads to general information on home schooling, general and specific information on teaching middle school to senior high students at home, and information about online home school tutorials.

If you enter the keyword **preschool**, the returned options include parental controls; current feature articles; and pages on health and wellness, chats, and child development. Links to more preschool resources are also listed.

Entering the keywords **road to college** will bring you to AOL's information options about choosing a college, SAT tests, testing preparation, online college applications, and financial aid information.

About College

e-Parents can use the Net to help teens get ready for college or begin to decide what they may study in college. Various sites have information about preparing for college and for finding out about different types of student grants and loans. You can do searches for specific schools or possible careers. You can help your teen prepare for SATs online, use career guides online and even do career testing online.

The U.S. Department of Education site at *www.ed.gov* has lots of useful information and links. You can find free publications and information on financial assistance, disabilities education, technology in schools, and research statistics, to name just a few.

At the *www.CollegeNET.com* site, applicants can complete, file, and pay for their admissions applications entirely over the Internet. This site has an excellent search engine just for cataloging and searching education-related pages. You can search for your ideal college by region, major study, tuition, or other criteria. *College.NET.com* has a recruiting system that works with your student profile, bringing universities to you. On CollegeNET you will also see resource links about preparing for college, as well as a bookstore.

Check out the FishNet College Guide at *www.jayi.com* for another great site with a good all-around variety of college topics. Read about college life, go to financial aid resources, and request college information. Here, too, you can create a student profile to email to particular colleges. You can even download the common application, meet an admissions guru, and ask questions or read his or her previous advice on a variety of questions.

The FishNet home page at www.jayi.com is an excellent resource for investigating colleges and financial aid.

Another site is *www.Embark.com*, a wide-ranging college guide site with forums and advice, links for getting online applications, and more. You can sign up for a recruiter service at this site.

Maybe you and your teen just want a site devoted to finding general information on colleges and universities. The *www. universities.com* site lets you find the home pages of thousands of schools by typing in the name or part of the name of a college; alternatively, you can do a search by region. This site has a link for financial aid and a link to message boards where you may find additional information.

You'll also find sites for SAT preparation. *www.testprep.com* sells SAT study guides and publishes an online guide for improving SAT scores. More guides and courses are in the works for other tests. Also on this site are a newsletter, online support, an online store, and a parents corner. e-Parents can get a better understanding of the partnerships between education and technology by reading the TestPrep.com page on distance learning technology and Internet-based training (IBT).

www.Kaplan.com contains a variety of online courses and test preparation materials and has an extensive careers section. In the large parents and kids section teens can improve study skills, learn about financial aid, find college information, get books, purchase software, and more.

The Best of Both Worlds:

Students can take a variety of online classes for college credit, a possible option for kids who want to live at home for a year and work but still earn college credit.

www.jobprofiles.com is just what the name suggests. This site is not about job skill requirements or resume posting; it's about real people in different professions sharing their real-life experiences. It explores the personal side of careers by giving advice on entering a field, future challenges of that field, its rewards and stresses, and the skills needed to succeed in that field. The site also has links to career guides and interactive quizzes to help students who have not decided on a particular field.

Try It Yourself ▼

Of course, you and your teen can always do your own search for information about a specific career (for example, you can search for **medical career advice** or **chiropractic assistant**) or you can search for sites on **career and interests testing**.

1. Start with the search engine Lycos.com and type **career self assessment**. Then click the title **Monster.com: tools and quizzes**, which will take you to *http://www.content.monster.com/tools*.

2. At Monster.com, you'll find links to quizzes; click **Self Assessment Links**. From the additional list of self-assessment links, chose **The Career Key**.

3. When the Career Key page comes up, start the quiz by clicking **Take the Career Key**. Enter your name, age, sex, and years of education and click the **Begin** button.

4. A list of careers is presented; choose the ones that interest you by checking boxes. Then click the **Enter** button.

5. For the next several pages of questions, answer True, Mostly True, or Not True. The questions deal with things you like to do, your abilities, how you see yourself, and what you value.

6. When you're done answering questions, a page shows your "score" (from 1 to 10) and personality types: Artistic, Realistic, Enterprising, Social, Investigative, and

Conventional. Choose your highest ranking personality type from the pop-up menu and click **Next**.

A page displays jobs that fit your personality type. Click any entry to learn more (such as nature of the work, conditions, employment, training, job outlook, earnings, related occupations, and sources of additional information).

This search and test combined took all of ten minutes. A decade ago, we would have had to find a professional for this kind of advice and career testing—and pay handsomely for it.

Home Schooling

While teachers and students are taking advantage of the available technology in the classroom, many parents are beginning to educate their kids at home with software, home school Web sites, Web-based classrooms, and curricula available on the Internet.

Home school parents who are online have some unique advantages. They can provide exactly the real, hands-on experiences they think their kids need and they can also use the PC and the Net to enhance the learning of any subject.

Doing home schooling is a very individual family decision, and much depends on the family's location, the kinds of public or alternative schools available to them, the education of the parents (states must approve parents who do home schooling), and the lifestyle of the family. A critical prerequisite to the home schooling decision is a parent who has a flexible work schedule or who can (or can choose to) stay home to do the teaching.

Two advantages to home schooling are the flexibility of the curriculum the family uses and the ways teaching and learning times can be scheduled. One family we know took a year off and traveled across the United States in their RV while the parents home schooled their three children. The parents said there was no better way to teach U.S. history and geography than by having this kind of hands-on experience. (And yes, they took the PC with them.)

Well over one million American kids are being home schooled by their parents these days, and the number is growing partly because of the resources of the PC and Net for home schoolers.

Home Schooling in Your State:

Each state has different rules and regulations about home schooling. If you are interested in home schooling, contact your state department of education for information. Your local school may be able to provide a state contact person.

Home Schooling Resources

To learn more about home schooling, check out the National Center for Home Education, a division of the Home School Legal Defense Association (HSLDA), at *www.hslda.com*. Here you can learn about the home school laws that exist in your state and find out how to get a list of home school organizations in your area.

You will also be able to read news, articles, and legislation concerning home schooling; read statistics on home school performance and achievement; and read articles by parents and students about their experiences. Through this site you can become a member and get direct email access to your state's HSLDA staff members.

To learn more, you will have to do some searching. Try searching with the words **home schooling** to get started or try the education sections of search engines. In AltaVista, for example, we clicked the link to reference and education. This link gave us many main topics and subtopics, but it was easy to click Back and Forward to navigate through the information.

When we clicked **Home Schooling**, we got lists of sites, organizations, curricula, and lesson plans. From there, we started to explore some sites.

The site at *http://members.tripod.com/maaja* offers planners, worksheets, maps, and other downloads for home schoolers. In addition, a support page lists organizations, newsletters, email lists, and message boards. The materials section contains a long list of resources for buying curriculum, including some curricula that is free and some that has been used by other home school parents. The site also has links to good articles about special education programming and lists of home school sites for children with disabilities.

At *www.n-h-a.org* you will find advocacy and support for home schooling and some good reading material that explains what home schooling is all about. This organization offers a Home School Information resource packet for $4.

In case you are just getting started or are interested in home schooling and want to meet other home schoolers face to face, the site at *www.sound.net/~ejcol/confer.html* has a list of home schooling conferences by state.

At *http://www.computerage.net/homeschool/findit/*, you can use an internal search engine to search through a database of home school information and resources. There are sections for curriculum suppliers, getting started, information on why you might choose to home school, a fun page, and a products page. This site also has a section called Home School Community, which lists events, reviews, legislative news, magazines, and newsletters. There you will also find lists of places to interact with other home schoolers through chats, bulletin boards, and newsgroups. Networking and interacting with other home schoolers are very important activities that put what the kids are learning into a real-world perspective.

We found one site that's geared not only to home school issues but also to dads. Look at *www.homeschooldad.com* for articles, activities, links to fatherhood and home schooling sites, and links to lots of related sponsors.

We also found a wonderful site devoted to art in home schooling: *www.homeschoolarts.com* has lessons in different mediums, lessons on perspective, and a gallery for student and teacher work. The site also includes a list of sites for home school art resources.

We agree with what Net-mom Jean Armour Polly says about the *www.dimensional.com/~janf/homeschoolinfo/html* site in her excellent review (see the **Book Samples-Hot Lists for Parents** section at *www.netmom.com*):

> Visit this excellent selection of home schooling resources for an overview of what's current and what's useful. You'll find thoughtful, briefly annotated links to home schooling associations, magazines, newsgroups, and more. Some of the most interesting are a site started by a teenager about how to "do high school" at home, and real audio files with interviews of interest to home schooling families…. Don't miss the links to selected high-energy home schooling families, and scroll to the bottom to find some great software….

At *www.waymarks.com/homeschool* you can find links galore on specific home school issues. There are magazines and articles, laws and regulations, support, online lesson plans, information on

Teacher Dads Online:

For e-Parents who are at-home dads, check out *www. athomedad.com* for great (often funny) articles, a newsletter, and an established at-home dad network. The Fall 1999 newsletter featured an article on home schooling that listed these sites: Midnight Beach (*www. midnightbeach.com*), Home School (*www.hsc.com*), Learning Freedom (*http:// learningfreedom. org*), and Home Schooling (*http:// homeschooling. miningcp.com*).

learning styles, curriculum packages, and a special section on gifted children.

The site at *www.childu.com* offers interactive and comprehensive curriculums for grades K through 6, a tutoring enrichment program, and more. You can find another virtual school to enhance the home schooling experience at *www.academyonline.org*. Read "A Day in the Life of a Student, Parent, and Teacher at Academy Online." You will find an outline of the technologies used by the school, QuickTime movies of the school, and a slideshow presentation made by the staff.

If you're a home schooler, you'll find invaluable resources at ChildU (www.childu.com). The Learning Odyssey is an enrichment program you can pay for if you want to broaden your kids' education even more.

When home school parents need help with a specific subject or are not satisfied with a curriculum they are using, the Net can help. e-Parents can do searches on that subject; search in their own home school reading forums; or check out chats, bulletin boards, or newsgroups on a search engine for help.

We want to share one other resource for online families who want good links to topics such as homework; home schooling; and kid, parent, and teacher resources. The Net Family News site, *www.netfamilynews.org*, is worth looking at for just the links! This site also offers up-to-date news and articles of interest to online families.

At Net Family News, we found a really neat home schooling site called Kaleidoscapes, which is a networking and support site for home school parents. It offers discussions on curriculum as well as bulletin boards and other resources.

Find a Real-World Peer Group

Socialization with other children is sometimes an issue or a challenge for home schoolers. Parents of home schooled children need to recognize—as most do—that kids need peer groups and friends outside the family and online friends. After age 8 or 9, this need to belong to a real-world peer group increases.

Many home school families get together with other home school families for fun, potlucks, and other activities, including field trips for expanded learning about a topic of study. And often home school kids maintain friendships from the local school system and continue to attend school and sports events.

A fairly new trend in schools is to support home school families by actually including them in school activities and in sports, as well as by making them welcome at events.

Other home school parents say their kids are in clubs related to their interests, such as 4H, gymnastics, scouts, swimming, and crafts. Still others attend regular church activities to fill their children's needs for peer relationships.

The parents admit that the socializing is an extra effort but well worth it. They believe that their kids are getting the best education possible through home schooling and Net resources without sacrificing the friendships and extra curricular activities they choose.

Special-Needs Children

Some parents choose to home school their children with special needs and disabilities and have found the PC and Net very useful in finding resources specific to their unique situations. Computer-adaptive devices have also been an enormous help for many children.

For example, if a child is visually impaired, a large size monitor can enlarge everything on the screen; software magnification lenses can also enlarge screen images. When a child is severely vision impaired, sometimes speech synthesizers, along with speakers, can help the child read images on the screen.

When children have fine-motor impairments, key guards help prevent them from hitting the wrong keys; voice-recognition systems can accept voice commands as input so that they don't have to type; a head pointer and mouth stick or a head-controlled mouse can also used by some children.

Sometimes an expanded keyboard (where there is more space for keys and where keys are positioned in easy-to-reach locations) is all a child needs to be a very successful and proud PC and Net user.

Many special-education experts are finding that the PC is an effective learning and teaching tool for kids with disabilities. The PC presents small bits of information in a planned sequence, provides lots of repetition, and offers positive reinforcement. Teachers have observed that even kids with attention problems respond well to using the computer and can stick with a PC activity as long as others do.

Just Like You:

What special-needs kids want most is to be "just like everyone else" and do the things other kids do. Personal computers certainly help fill that need.

The sites we found will be useful for all parents of special-needs kids, whether they are home schoolers or not:

- *www.iser.com/nps.html* is a page with many links to information on special-needs nonprofit resources, both national and regional.

- *www.iser.com/nps.html* lists links to special-education programming and home school disability Web sites.

- *www.mindplay.com* lists 30 titles of software covering math, science, and reading for special-needs children.

- *http://www2.edc.org/NCIP/* is the National Center to Improve Practice in Special Education through Technology, Media, and Materials. On this site you can read about voice-recognition technology, visit classrooms, and see video clips of students using adaptive and instructional technologies. You can hear about workshops and events, use a library with resources about technology and special education, and read a What's New page that includes information and some good links.

- There's some "funtastic" learning at *www.funtasticlearning.com*, a site offering games, toys, and tools for helping special-needs kids develop particular skills.

- Dreams for Kids Inc. at *www.dreams.org/index/html* specializes in assistive and adaptive technology. It was founded by the parents of a child with Down's syndrome. The site has a newsletter, *Directions: Technology and Special Education*, and can help parents find products and other resources.

Remember that gifted children have special needs, too. We searched AltaVista for the search term **"gifted children"** and quickly found three topics for the gifted: guides, schools, and organizations. Under **organizations**, 50 sites were listed (and we had barely begun to search). e-Parents of gifted children will have no trouble finding resources.

Summing Up

Let's reflect a bit on how e-World resources can help motivate children's learning. We know that a virtual encyclopedia (with its interactive tools, images, sound, and video) contains much more information than a regular encyclopedia contains. So which type of encyclopedia do you think will best motivate your child for learning: real or virtual? Which type do you want your child to use—and know how to use effectively—in the world we live in?

Although e-Parents may realize that the PC and Net technology gives children an edge and provides them with tools for learning, nothing will help children more than parents who use these tools *with* them.

As you can see, the Internet offers endless possibilities for assisting kids of any age with their schooling. Kids in home schools, charter schools, private schools, and public schools can all benefit from these resources for learning, but the kids who will make the most of these resources will be those who are encouraged by informed and involved parents.

Let's look at our e-Parenting basics in terms of this chapter. Kids who are the most successful will have e-Parents who are part of the team and part of the fun! These e-Parents not only show an ongoing interest in their children's schooling but also provide the kinds of guidance and resources for schooling that their children need.

You can also see that it continues to be vitally important for e-Parents to show an interest in, provide guidance for, and have fun with their children.

CHAPTER 8

Online Resources for Parenting

In this chapter you'll learn a lot about parenting resources. First you get a detailed eight-point checklist that will help you evaluate parenting sites and that you can use to help teach your kids how to use critical-thinking skills to evaluate other sites.

Next we give you some good e-Parent resources, ranging from general parenting sites to special sites about parenting, child development, and special-needs children. We hope you enjoy this chapter and find it useful.

If you go to your search engine and just type **parenting**, you will get thousands of listings. Many good parenting resources are available on the Net, and more are added every day. We think this is great, because today's e-Parents are information seekers; they are always looking for advice or information about kids or about ways to be better parents.

With the loss of the extended family and the increasing numbers of single parents, being able to turn to the Internet for information is a lifesaver.

It's a good thing that so many parenting resources are available because parents who are looking for advice or information on a specific topic may actually be looking for different answers, depending on their needs or values. This situation is especially true in the United States, with its diversity of family structures, lifestyles, and cultural backgrounds.

Each parent who searches the Net for parenting information may be looking for something different. When you are doing a search for parenting information, you may need to keep narrowing the search, using very specific words or phrases in quotes to find

What You'll Learn in This Chapter:

► How to use an eight-point checklist to evaluate a Web site

► How to use the recommended parenting sites

► How to find support and advice online

► How to find online help for kids with special needs, for kids in nontraditional families, and for health-related issues

exactly the advice you need. Remember to use several search engines; also make use of the links from one site to other sites.

We also suggest that e-Parents should always find more than one source for the information they are researching. For example, if your topic is spanking as a form of discipline, you are going to find many different opinions and kinds of advice. What the American Association of Pediatrics recommends may not be what a television ministry recommends.

Here's where your own values enter the picture. For example, if you have already decided that spanking is what you want to do, you will certainly be able to find opinions on the Net that agree with you. But you will find just as many or more that disagree!

Our hope is that you will gather information from *many* good sources when you make your parenting choices. We want you to find enough Internet parenting information to make an *informed* choice. What you do as a parent will always be your decision, but try to get comprehensive information before making important choices.

How to Spot Good Sites: Use a Checklist

We think that everyone should have some sort of framework for evaluating Web sites, whether they are parenting sites or any other type of site. We hope that the following checklist will help e-Parents choose and evaluate appropriate parenting sites.

You can easily modify this checklist and use it to evaluate other kinds of Web sites. Using this checklist as a starter, you can make a simple checklist for your kids and help them use it to evaluate some of the sites they visit. Using questions in a checklist helps kids practice their critical-thinking skills.

You will quickly internalize this eight-point list as you explore and evaluate sites with your children. Here are the eight points in short form:

1. Approach

2. Child development

3. Credentials

4. Sponsor

5. Content

6. Navigation

7. Links

8. Contact

Now let's look at these points one at a time.

What's the Approach?

What we mean by *approach* is the style of writing and how it makes you feel as the reader. Is the style rigid and didactic or patronizing? If so, you may feel like you are a little kid getting scolded. We haven't seen many of those kinds of sites ourselves—and are glad of it.

Does the approach or style of writing make you feel like you're in college reading a textbook? Are you seeing lots of big words, long sentences, and educational jargon? Some parenting sites are like this, and they may or may not be what you want.

Does the approach make you feel comfortable, and does what you are reading seem like practical, commonsense information? Those are the kinds of parenting sites that most parents like best and use often.

However, to evaluate a site critically, you have to look beyond its style and approach.

Child Development Knowledge

We think that parenting information should be based on knowledge of what children are like and how they learn. Sometimes a parent with lots of experience can share information with others on a Web site but still have no knowledge of child development other than his or her own personal experience and observation.

We believe that personal parenting experience is important; it adds the practical commonsense elements that people need if they are to apply the information to real life. However, we also believe that the information should be rooted in the child development knowledge available in the early childhood or child development/ family life fields.

You Can Always Go Back to School:
If you appreciate academic content but are distracted by the educational jargon, you may want something more practical and easy to read. Find a different site; you can always come back to an "academic" site for more information or confirmation.

For example, we would hope that particular advice would not be based only on one person's experience but on what we know works because of thousands of other cases in which it has worked.

When professionals in the field of parenting offer advice, they base it not only on their own experiences with children but also on the experiences of hundreds of parents with whom they have worked.

In addition, professionals base their advice on what the profession has learned in more than 50 years of study and research about children and how they grow. As you read through a site, look for clues that the person giving you parenting information has a child or human development background as well as actual experience.

How Will You Know?

In this example, information about how children grow and develop is worked into the advice:

If parents are worried because their 3-year-old child has an imaginary friend, a person with professional child development knowledge would tell them that this behavior is very normal for threes, who are really into practicing language and are also beginning to use their imaginations along with language.

Threes usually play alone or *next to* another child, but don't really interact with that child (parallel play). So pretend friends are very comfortable for threes.

The pretend friend usually disappears gradually and naturally around the age of 4 or 5, when the child begins to develop more complex cooperative play skills and has more real friends.

Credentials of Experts

We always use credentials as one of our criteria in evaluating a parenting site (or any other site). You need to ask yourself whether the person, persons, or entity giving you information is qualified to do that. You need to ask yourself where that information is really coming from.

Most good parenting sites have a section or page about themselves and pages about their experts or advisors. Click **About Us** or **Expert Bios**. Sometimes you have to click the pictures of the experts to read their biographies. See what kinds of degrees or credentials they have. The experts should show training or experience in human or child development/family life, parent education, early childhood education, psychology, or related fields.

The best parenting sites rely on a panel of experts with different but related expertise. For example, the National Parenting Center (TNPC) has professionals with degrees and experience who have written several books as well as people from different parenting fields such as parent education, child development, health and nutrition, psychology, and public education.

When a parent emails a question, TNPC forwards it to the person best qualified to respond. Often the parent gets an email answer as well as suggestions for further resources or contacts.

Sponsor or Source

This one is pretty obvious, but be sure to take it into consideration. The sponsor of the site can certainly affect the kinds of information you will get. You are going to get very different information about "kids and guns" from the NRA than from a nonprofit gun control organization or a children's hospital site.

Some parenting sites may be heavily sponsored by one large corporation, by a coalition of several corporations or companies, by a branch of the government, or even by nonprofit groups. You should at least consider the ways a profit or a nonprofit sponsor may influence the information on a site.

The sponsor's influence does not necessarily mean the information you get will be incorrect; it just might be limited. For example, a soap company sponsor may have hired good parenting professionals, but the information on the site might be mostly about health and hygiene instead of child behavior or study habits.

Content and Updating

When e-Parents are gathering information, they want it to be comprehensive and up-to-date. The content should be interesting and varied.

How much of the content is fluff (bells and whistles, extensive flashing banners, horoscopes, and so on)? You should not have to dig through irrelevant, overstimulating stuff to find practical information. Useful content should be the emphasis.

The home page at www.askevelyn. com is an example of how content should be the focus of a parenting site.

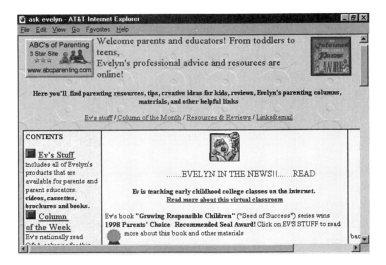

For example, our parenting site, *www.askevelyn.com*, emphasizes content. The site wouldn't be very useful to parents if it contained only a list of our own books, tapes, and brochures, or just one parenting column. The content on this site includes pages on family humor, lists of early childhood conferences, lists of recommended consultants, reviews of books and articles (of course, with Amazon.com links), a creative kids activity section, tips for teachers as well as parents, information on Internet child care training courses, information on Family Game Night, archives of past tips and past columns, and many links to other sites for parents.

When you go to a parenting site, check not only the content but also how often new information is added. A site that is not updated is one to which you may not return (you've already read the pages of that book).

Navigation

Parents aren't the only ones who get frustrated when a site is hard to navigate. Kids get frustrated, too. Help your children see what *makes* a site easy to navigate and help them understand the clues to look for in navigation.

Does the site have clear headings or icons for each section, and are they listed on the home page as well as at the top and bottom of the other pages? Does the site just start out by overwhelming you with information, or does it tell you something about its mission? Are contents consistent, or are the contents so inconsistent and confusing that you get lost?

Can you click to learn about who founded the site and about their credentials? What about the site's "experts"; can you find them quickly? Does the home page start out by trying to sell you something? Does advertising detract from the information and navigation?

Referrals and Links

You can tell a lot about the credibility of a site by the kinds of referrals it gives or the links it has with other sites. Are the links useful, and do they link you to other parenting information? Or are they merely long lists of national organizations and their Web sites?

It is good to see some national nonprofit organizations listed with their URLs, but the site should also have links or referrals to practical parenting information sites, such as Parents Place or The National Parenting Center TNPC.

If you have some surfing experience on the subject of parenting, certain parenting sites are already familiar to you because you have seen links to them at other parenting sites.

If the site you are looking at is recommended by other parenting sites or is listed in a real-world publication you respect, that's a good sign, too. For example, *www.askevelyn.com* is not as large or well-known a parenting site as *www.parentsplace.com*, but it is linked to *www.earlychildhood.com*, *www.women.com*, *www.tnpc.com*, and others.

Contact

We believe that it is very important for a parenting site to maintain contact with its users. Parents and professionals should always be able to contact or email someone at the parenting site who can forward the message to the right person, be it a manager, Web master, author, or publisher.

Contacting a Web site is one way to investigate or check on its information; having to respond to users helps site owners maintain accountability for the site and the information it presents. The current trend is for most Web sites to contain privacy statements that assure the reader or user that information they send to the site will not be misused or sold.

Another Resource for Evaluation

www.quick.org.uk is a London-based Health Education Authority that puts out a Quality Information Checklist to help kids evaluate quality on health sites, but the checklist can also be used to evaluate other sites. This site was a little hard to navigate when we last looked, but don't give up. Also check the **Teachers** section of the site, which gives links to more sites with guidance about evaluating Net information.

When we were there, the site included a quiz kids can take to help them learn more about the Net and analyzing Web sites.

Here are some of the questions in the Quality Information Checklist; they are good questions to ask yourself, especially about parenting sites:

- Who wrote the information?
- Are the aims of the site clear?
- Does the site achieve its aims?
- Is the site relevant to me or my problem?
- Can the information be checked?
- When was the site produced?
- Is the information biased in any way?
- Does the site tell about other choices?

Good e-Parenting Sites

As you know, there are hundreds of parenting sites, and we will certainly not attempt to list them all or prioritize them. However, we do want to give you some examples of good parenting sites that have met the criteria in our eight-point list. We hope you will do some exploring of these examples to find the sites most useful to you. You should also do some surfing to find even more options and information. We are dividing our general e-Parenting information sites into two groups: child development resources and general parenting resources.

General Information Sites

When we were choosing sites for these sections, we decided to give you a mix of both theory and practicum, as well as examples of well-respected sites. e-Parents need to know what to expect of children at various ages, and they also need to have practical, commonsense ideas about guiding, teaching, enjoying, and working with their kids. First up are parenting sites that focus on child development, or the "whys" of child behavior. The next group of general parenting resources include sites that focus more on the practical and hands-on aspects of parenting.

Child Development Resources

The National Maternal and Child Health Clearinghouse (NMCHC) site at *www.nmchc.org* is a huge library of digital resources for new moms and pregnant women. The development of the baby is something new moms always want to know about, and the research on infant development and learning is changing rapidly. The NMCHC site is a very good place to stay up-to-date. Information packets can also be ordered.

Baby Center at *www.babycenter.com* is a site dedicated to helping new and expectant parents find information, support, and reassurance. It is packed with reference information, links, hints, checklists, and ways to connect with other parents. There is also a special page for dads called (appropriately), The Dad's Page.

The BabyCenter home page at www. babycenter.com is a good example of a site with lots of information in an easy-to-access presentation.

www.babyhood.com is dedicated to providing information on growth and development in babies from birth through 24 months. There are many useful links as well.

The Pampers Parenting Institute at *www.totalbabycare.com* provides advice from a panel of experts including T. Berry Brazelton; advice is arranged chronologically by the age of the baby. You can write to the experts, access a library of articles and archives, and sign up for a customized newsletter.

Parent Time at *www.parenttime.com* focuses on parenting children from birth to age 6. Here you can "ask an expert" and communicate with chat and message boards. The site includes material on behavior and development, health, and other special topics.

Parent Partners.com is sporting a new name and expanded services as *www.escore.com*. The original Parent Partners site was completely devoted to information and resources on child development from birth through age 13. This site, with its comprehensive database on growth and development, was purchased by Kaplan Educational Centers and is now called eScore. *www.escore.com* now offers information categorized not only by topic or the child's age but also by the child's interest or needs. The site has a very credible panel of experts. Although some advice/information is free, quick turnaround personal advice will cost you a few dollars.

General Parenting Resources

In addition to a wealth of information on parenting, the Parents Place at *www.parentsplace.com* features an "Ask the Expert" section and lots of message boards. You will also find sections devoted to dads, as well as good links to other sites.

At *www.earlychildhood.com* you can get advice from experts in early childhood, see collections of creative projects, see current articles about various topics, share ideas, and ask questions of early childhood professionals.

The *www.askevelyn.com* site features advice and tips for both parents and teachers, archives of Evelyn Petersen's columns, creative ideas for kids, information on online courses, a Family Game Night section, resources, reviews, and links.

The National Association for the Education of Young Children at *www.naeyc.org* develops programs and policies on behalf of young children. The site has an extensive list of publications covering child care, child development, parent involvement, and all aspects of children's learning. It also offers full-length position papers on issues such as standards of quality, cultural diversity, developmentally appropriate practices, and teacher training and certification.

ERIC, the Early Childhood and Elementary Education Resources and Information Clearinghouse at *http://ericeece.org* is a government clearinghouse for education and research information with access to vast ERIC databases. **AskERIC** and **PARENTSaskERIC** are two links at this site where parents and educators can ask questions about education, child development, and parenting.

The I Am Your Child site at *www.iamyourchild.org* includes descriptions of child development; answers to common questions; suggested parenting practices; summaries of brain research; and video clips of T. Berry Brazelton, C. Everett Koop, and other experts.

TNPC site at *www.tnpc.com* is dedicated to providing parents with comprehensive and responsible guidance about parenting from some of the nation's most renowned child-rearing authorities. The TNPC site is the oldest parenting site on the and has a vast database of information categorized by age group. If a question or topic has been raised online, it's probably here.

Kidsource Online at *www.kidsource.com* has up-to-date news and articles, product-recall information, books and software reviews, and a free newsletter. The information on health and education is especially comprehensive. Sections are categorized by age groups: newborn, toddler, preschool, and K–12. Other related sites and forums are also listed. Another section worth mentioning is called **computing edge**, where people can donate and educators can apply for computer equipment.

www.parenthoodweb.com has a panel of experts, articles, and email as well as a pregnancy section, a page on sleep, a baby store, message boards, chats, and more. You can select information by topic (all listed on the topics page) or use the internal search engine. You'll find lots of good parenting material here.

Parent Soup at *www.parentsoup.com* is well organized with a vast amount of material. The Education Central section has lots of material arranged by age/grade, a variety of other features and articles, expert advice, chats, message boards, and other resources.

The Parent Soup home page at www. parentsoup.com has links to vast amounts of material, organized handily by topic.

www.women.com is a large and growing site with many resources and sections. You can choose activities for your child by age group, by type, and even by outdoor or indoor activity. You can find advice in the Family Channel, either by the topic or by the child's age (which includes teens). You can email questions to the experts at this site and receive answers by return mail.

www.kidshealth.org focuses on children's health but also has many resources in its sections for parents and professionals. For example, you will find guidance on expressing feelings, divorce, children's diseases, and ADHD (Attention Deficit Hyperactivity Disorder).

Information by Age Group or by Topic

You will find that at *any* large parenting site (most of which have their own internal search engines or internal links) information is arranged by age group and topic.

At the Parent Soup, Parent Time, Parents Place, TNPC, Women.com, Parent Partners, and other sites, you can find both advice and activities for children by age group and topic.

Suppose that you have a problem with your teenager about a curfew. In Women.com, you can find the section called Family Channel. Then choose the topic Raising Teens for a fistful of professional columns and advice about teens. If you want more information on teens, try other large parenting sites such as TNPC. You can also use a search engine to search for sites specifically about teens or to find information about your particular teen problem. Try **"teen behavior and curfews"** or **"teen curfews and discipline"**.

If your 3-year-old child is biting other kids, you can start with a large parenting site and search for information on problem behavior in this age group. You can use the age and topic list choices to find advice about biting. You can also email an expert with your question about biting, or you can do a separate Web search with words such as **"preschool problem behavior and biting"**.

Tip:

The *www. virtuescalendar.com* site has an extensive list of general parenting Web site links. We would like to see this site annotated and organized by category.

Other e-Parent Resources

In this section, we wanted to give you some examples of what you might do if you need to go a step beyond general parenting sites. For example, if you are looking for special parent support resources or for some type of particular professional advice, would you know where to look? This section gives you some assistance in finding additional e-Parent resources.

Parenting Support Sources

We believe that the Internet itself is a gigantic support group, connecting parents to a worldwide community of support resources. With the Net, you can find information, advice, reassurance, and someone to talk with who has the same kinds of problems you have.

If you have special support needs—perhaps you are the parent of a child with learning disabilities—you can go to *www.ldonline.com* and find out about online and real-world support groups for parents of learning disabled kids. Links at this site may also lead you to other kinds of support groups or information.

Search engines also can lead you to support groups. Start with a search engine home page and look for a section on support groups or simply type **"support groups"** in the search box. You will get lots of options to choose from.

If jumping into the entire World Wide Web to find support is too overwhelming, e-Parents can also find support by using large parenting sites, which are like smaller communities or villages in that greater e-World.

All the large parenting sites have chat rooms where you can talk with other parents, message boards where you can ask for or exchange information, forums where you can read and learn new things about parenting, and experts to whom you can write for free reassurance or advice. And you can do all this while the baby is napping or while the kids are in school or in bed sleeping.

Before the Internet, how many people could you go to for advice in a matter of minutes? How quickly could you find professional *free* advice?

www.parentsplace.com has lots of departments and experts. It is a great place to go to interact with other parents because it has a *huge* list of bulletin boards and chats.

Don't forget about newsgroups, which can also give you support-ive information. Lots of leads to interaction, information, and recommendations come from newsgroups.

▼ **Try It Yourself**

1. To get more information about newsgroups, go to *www.lycos.com*, type **"newsgroups parenting"** and press Enter. You'll find groups on lots of topics, such as parenting twins, grandparenting, spanking, elementary school, adop-tion, and parenting mistakes.

2. Choose the newsgroup *alt.parenting*. Under that heading, you'll see many parenting subjects—many concerns were listed along with the advice.

3. You can be as active in a newsgroup as you want to be. For example, a parent of an ADD (Attention Deficit Disorder) child may read and post messages daily at an ADD news-group such as *alt.support.attn-deficit*. It isn't unusual to see 20 new postings in a day at a newsgroup.

4. If you want to get more active with newsgroups, simply search for **"about newsgroups"**, **"how to subscribe to newsgroups"**, and so on. You may not find an entire Web site devoted to newsgroups, but you will find lots of pages from sites. We have often seen computer/Internet guide sites and university sites that include newsgroup information.

   The Usenet Newsgroups via Netscape page at *www.gcccd.cc.ca.us/grossmont/internet_guides/ newsgroups.html* describes newsgroups and how to subscribe. You can also read about newsgroups at *www. primocomputers.com/public/ learn/23nwsgrp.htm*. This page has some information describing newsgroups and their his-tory, how to subscribe to them, how to search for them, and how to start your own newsgroup.

▲

Professional Advice

Sites that have "experts" available often let you email questions to them. The length of time you have to wait for a response usually depends on the volume of mail the expert gets. Sometimes your question, if it is pertinent to the needs of many parents, will appear as part of an article or column on the site. (If that happens, the article will be written so that your anonymity will be protected.)

You already know a little about evaluating the credibility and credentials of experts. And you also know how to contact them through large parenting sites and links to smaller parenting sites. You can check the biographies of individuals on an expert panel and contact the panel member you think best meets your needs.

If you want to contact an expert in a special field (such as someone who works with emotionally disturbed children or special problem behaviors) and you cannot find what you need in a resource list or link, you'll have to do a search. Or you can post a question on a bulletin board or newsgroup asking, Where can I find....

James Windell's site at *www.jameswindell.com*, for example, focuses on child behavior and, in particular, problem behavior. Windell is the author of four books on discipline and behavior; his experience in working with parents and with children who have behavior disorders makes him an excellent resource for parents with questions about special behavior problems.

At his Web site, you can learn more about James Windell, his background and awards, his books, and the classes and lectures he offers. You can also email him for a personal response or read some of his parenting columns. You may also want to read excerpts from his books and view the calendar of his courses, lectures, workshops, and book signings.

James Windell on AOL

James Windell offers his parenting class called 8 Weeks to a Well-Behaved Child on AOL. Another class, based on 8 Weeks to a Well-Behaved Child, is for parent educators. This two-day class is called Training the Trainers.

The AOL online course consists of 8 one-hour sessions at $40 and includes a class bulletin board, a class library for downloading material, and a way to contact James Windell outside of class.

Find the information by typing **Online Campus** in AOL's search engine or click the **Research & Learn** channel and go to **Courses Online**. Go to **Course Catalog** and then to **Health & Personal**. There you will see Discipline That Works, which is James Windell's class.

Parents may also want to do searches to find out about parenting courses, lectures, and forums online. Community colleges may be good leads for finding out about such courses or classes. AOL has a section that lists online courses; other online communities or search engines may also list them.

Special Resources

We've all heard that every child is unique, which means that every *person* is also unique. When a number of these unique individuals live together as a family, it is logical that more than one parenting approach will be needed. What works with one child in the family may not work with another child, and what works one year might not work at all the next year.

This is why good e-Parenting tends to be a somewhat eclectic process that needs occasional rejuvenation and insight from other resources. As the family raises its children, many types of resources may be needed or explored. The Internet can be very helpful to today's e-Parents in locating resources for special-needs children, for stepfamilies and blended families, for grandparents, for at-home dads, and for children with special problems or health needs.

Special-Needs Children

Here are a few special sites for exceptional parents…parents of children who have special needs. We know that you have to be advocates for your children every day. We know that you have a tough job trying to protect your children while encouraging them to risk and to try. You have to treat them just like everyone else (which is what they want most), even if there are some differences. So you have special needs, too. The Net can help.

Ability Online Support Network at *www.ablelink.org* brings together kids with special needs through an email system. Kids with or without disabilities or illnesses can log in and share stories and information. Great idea! This site also has lots of links to both parenting and special-needs sites and includes a page with relevant news items.

If you go to *www.chadd.org*, you will find one of the best, most established, and most used resources for parents of children with ADD or ADHD. CHADD (which stands for children and adults with attention-deficit/hyperactivity disorder) was founded in 1987 by a group of parents. It has grown into an internationally known resource for education, advocacy, and support of children and adults with ADD. On this site you can find links to research, special-needs legislation, conferences, a magazine, and more. You can find a local CHADD chapter and meet other CHADD parents and kids.

CHADD is a national nonprofit organization representing children and adults with attention-deficit/hyperactivity disorder. Its home page at www.chadd.com opens the door to a wealth of information on attention disorder/hyperactivity disorder.

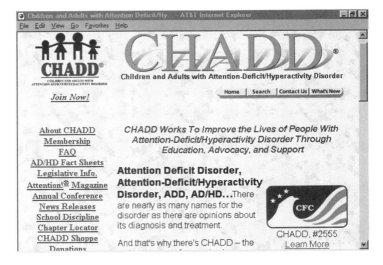

The National Information Center for Children and Youth with Disabilities site at *www.nichcy.org* is the information and referral center on all disabilities issues for families, educators, and professionals.

The Disabilities Studies and Services Center site at *www.dssc.org* provides legal information for parents and educators. The Federal Resource Center for Special Education section gives links to more organizations, sites, and resources for specific disabilities.

www.eparent.com is the site of the national magazine called *Exceptional Parent*. This site is full of interesting and up-to-date articles about children's disabilities and children's health care, including new research findings and real-life stories.

Learning Disabilities Online at *www.ldonline.org*, is a guide to learning disabilities for parents, children, and teachers, is loaded with information. There is a Kids Zone, an electronic newsletter, first-hand accounts of experiences, expert advice, an extensive calendar of events, articles, and information on assistive technology. From this site you can also find out about particular learning disabilities, such as dyslexia, and about a well-established resource for dyslexics, the International Dyslexia Association (*www.interdys.org*).

Dyslexia Is Fairly Common

According to some estimates, nearly 15% of our population is dyslexic to the degree that requires intervention and another 10% has mild dyslexic tendencies. Both adults and children can have dyslexia, which is a learning disability that interferes mainly with written language skills (writing, spelling, reading words, and reading sheet music).

Researchers tell us that dyslexics are usually average or well above average in intelligence and may excel in science and the creative arts. Both Thomas Edison and Albert Einstein were dyslexics. You can find a simple explanation of dyslexia at *www.DrKoop.com*. You can also learn more at the International Dyslexia Association, formerly the Orton Dyslexia Society, at *www.interdys.org*. This site offers many resources, as well as 50 years of research data about dyslexia.

Remember to search for sections on special needs within large parenting sites. For example, the *www.families.com* site has information on special needs, and you can also ask an expert or visit a bulletin board for this information.

Stepfamilies, Blended Families, Grandparents, and At-Home Dads

Our world is home to many different kinds of families and many differing lifestyles within families. At the same time that single moms head many families, fathers are more involved than ever before in raising kids.

More and more grandparents are raising children, too, and in many cases uncles, aunts, or other relatives are taking on the roles of parents and caregivers. The Internet community seems to be responding to this need; more alternative-family resources keep appearing.

Today's alternative families looking for information can start a search by trying categories in various search engine home pages or by using specific search words. They can also try large general parenting sites, check bulletin boards, check links, and use the newsgroups that fit their needs.

We opened the search engine *www.go.com* and did a search for **"blended families"**; we found many pages containing articles from a variety of sites. We also saw a Web site called the Ring of Blended Families at *www.blendedfamily.com/blendedfamily/blendring.html*. This site is one of a series on blended families, linked together in something called a *webring*. You can click to view all the member sites or visit them one at a time.

You can also be more specific regarding blended families and search for **stepmoms** or **"adoptive family"** or **"foster parents"**.

We found resources quickly and easily for grandparents who are raising kids. We started at the search engine *www.go.com* and clicked the **Family** link under the **Topics** tab. That brought us a list of sites—and still more topics to choose from. We clicked on **grandparents**, which brought up a lot more sites and more topics. We were happy to see a topic called **Grandparents Caregivers**. Clicking that link brought up seven sites devoted to grandparents as caregivers…just what we wanted in less than a minute.

One site in the list was *www.grandsplace.com*. Here we saw legal help for grandparent caregivers, as well as a Connections page with bulletin boards, chats, an ICQ connection, and email lists.

The site also offered interesting articles (some by grandparents) and other resources, including some good links. Links are always a good way to stretch out or narrow your search. This site is a good resource for grandparents who are either raising children or are heavily involved in that challenge. You will find support, legal information about custody and visiting rights, and also many good ideas for ways grandparents can help support and nurture children and provide both fun and reassurance.

www.daddyshome.com has articles and resources for stay-at-home dads and for dads who just want to learn more about fathering. Here you can join an email mailing list by following the links on the resources page.

www.athomedad.com is dedicated to at-home dads who are doing the majority of child rearing. The site includes a newsletter and networking system with other dads. The Parents Place hosts the At-Home Dad site and also has special pages for fathers.

The National Center for Fathering presents articles on various aspects of fatherhood to inspire, equip, and prepare dads for nearly every fathering situation. The site at *www.fathers.com* provides research and surveys about fathering and includes chats, bulletin boards, and links. In addition, you can receive a magazine called *Today's Father* through this site.

The National Center for Fathering home page at www.fathers.com has links to practical fathering tips, humor, research articles, and more.

e-Parenting Resources for Special Problems

By now, you e-Parents know how to find information on very specific subjects such as divorce, death, moving, adoption, and more. You know how to do searches, use several search engines, and narrow your search; you know that links, newsgroups, and bulletin boards can also be useful, just as can the special forums or sections in a large parenting site.

Try It Yourself ▼

It would have been nearly impossible and certainly very time consuming to do comprehensive research on the topics of death or divorce before we had the Internet to help us.

1. Suppose that you want some information or help on the subject of divorce. Start at the home page of the TNPC at *www.tnpc.com* and click **Articles**.

2. Use the internal search engine to search for **divorce**. Our search yielded 11 articles written by professionals. Some will be better than others for your purposes, but you'll find that out very quickly.

3. Click one of the age-group categories for lists of links to articles about even more subjects related to divorce.

   A new, recently launched Web site that's a great resource for parents going through a divorce or thinking about a divorce is *www.divorceonline.com*. This site has many resources, and it also enables you to talk with others about the ramifications of divorce on children. Articles on legal, financial, psychological, and other aspects of divorce are also provided.

▲

Here's another "special problems" example: For information on blended families, go to *www.women.com* and choose **Family Channel**. Choose **Family** again from the Family Matters topic box. You'll see a large archive of parenting information, called **Parenting Topics**. The **Blended Families** section of **Parenting Topics** gives six articles on that subject.

As these Web sites expand (more and more experts are writing articles for them every week), the archives of parenting information will grow even larger.

e-Parent Resources for Children's Health

e-Parents know how to find children's health information on the Net. With a simple search, you can find information about concerns such as safety, prevention, and recipes for diabetics. In addition to sites devoted to specific topics like these, general sites like the ones discussed here cover a variety of issues. Sites devoted to children almost always have sections on health. You can also use the Net to search for software on general health or on a specific topic.

The American Academy of Pediatrics Online is at *www.aap.org*. There you will find a section called You and Your Family, which includes all kinds of children's health information. Many books and pamphlets are available for you to order as well. Other areas include research and advocacy, professional education, and a members area.

Another national organization is Healthfinder at *www.healthfinder.com*, a service of the U.S. Department of Health and Human Services. The site includes information and links by age and topic, government health news, and databases for searching.

Dr. Koop's site is a great all-around health site. The *www.Drkoop.com* site has medical news, special features, and health and wellness resources. There's drug information, too, and a medical encyclopedia. The community section has lots of message boards, personal stories, and chats, including scheduled chats on specific health topics.

You can email your health questions, take a "preventionnaire" survey, or find an online pharmacy. You will want to visit the Family Health section for information on children's health issues such as general health, sickness and infections, emotion and behavior, nutrition and fitness, and safety and prevention.

Another site, which we've mentioned before, is Kids Health at *www.kidshealth.org*. Like *www.kidsource.com* it has a health section with articles, forums, and lots of good links. You'll find information on topics such as infections, behavior and emotion, and food and fitness. Kids Health was created by the medical

Help for Families on AOL:
For AOL users, click the Family channel and choose whatever topic you need from the categories in the pull-down topic list.

Video Help:
Also available are videos on health issues. You can find software and videos online; note that you will find more choices online than you would shopping in the real world.

experts at the Nemours Foundation. You can read more about them, too.

We went to *www.excite.com* and chose the topic **Health**. Then we clicked the **Family Health** link and then clicked **For Children**. There were still more topics to choose from! We saw Crisis and Abuse, Dental Health, Emotional Health, Illnesses and Conditions, Prescription Drugs, Nutrition and Fitness, Organizations, Safety, Immunization, Disabilities, Substance Abuse, and Treatment Centers and First Aid.

Clicking any one of these topics brings up more choices of topics until you get exactly what you want. On this health page, the topics to choose from appear on the left. Results (such as sites, clubs, and message boards) appear on the right.

While clicking through topics, we found a site called Dr. Greene's House Calls at *www.drgreene.com*. You can ask a question, or you can read other question and answers from pediatric expert Dr. Greene. You can get on his mailing list and read about his presentation and event schedule. His site offers articles on many health issues, including links and a section on developmental stages. If you want, you can use a scroll-down window to pick a topic from an extensive list. Books and tapes are also available. A similar site that uses about the same approach is The Kids Doctor at *www.kidsdoctor.com*.

Summing Up

We hope you have found this chapter on Web resources for e-Parents useful. With its information as your jumping-off point, you should be ready to find information about anything an e-Parent might face.

This chapter covered child development and general parenting resources, as well as resources for parents of special-needs kids, alternative families, special parenting challenges, and health. The chapter talked about getting information by using searches, newsgroups, forums, classes, and professional advice.

We hope that you will use the evaluation checklist at the beginning of this chapter to recognize and evaluate good sites—and that you will also encourage your kids to use it. Talk with your kids about critical thinking and help them use these eight criteria (or others) to evaluate sites they find on the Net.

Keep hanging in there and be proud of what you are doing as both a parent and an e-Parent. You'll find that e-Parenting challenges seem to grow as children grow, but at the same time your kids are growing, you are growing wiser and more experienced about parenting.

Stay up-to-date with information and practical ideas by using the support of the Net while you stay positive, have fun, show an interest, and provide guidance to your kids.

CHAPTER 9

Internet Safety for Online Kids

We think you will get a lot out of this chapter. In it, we discuss the major issues and approaches to dealing with the challenge of online safety, as well as some of the industry and public-interest efforts to address the problem.

We also give you lots of information on safety resources, safety tips, safe sites, and parental control. Knowledge is power for e-Parenting. More power to you!

Safety Issues

The ongoing debate about potential dangers on the Internet and what do about them is not easy to resolve. The issue is much bigger than protecting kids from possible encounters with strangers or preventing kids from seeing or reading something their parents don't approve of. The issue is also about censorship and how to give kids safe access to all the good things the Net offers without depriving their parents full freedom of choice about the approach they want to use to accomplish this goal.

The issue also concerns individual beliefs about censorship and access to information. Because the Net offers easy access to the world and all its diversity, its users hold widely different beliefs about what is good, bad, decent, indecent, or moral. These concepts probably even mean different things to you than they do to your next-door neighbors; imagine what they mean to a family in another part of the world.

How can any single system of censorship or access be fair to everyone? That is the problem Internet industry and public interest groups are struggling with. It is clear to us that the industry is genuinely concerned and working hard to come up with fair solutions.

What You'll Learn in This Chapter:

▸ How to weigh the positives and negatives of using online parental controls to protect your child's Internet adventures

▸ Where to go for help in making the Internet a safe place for your child

A Look at Some Short-Term and Long-Term Fixes

The sides of this debate on Internet censorship are bounded by those who actually want government censorship of the Internet and filters galore and those who want absolutely no controls whatsoever. And there are many positions on this issue all along the spectrum.

Of course, the "quick fix" is to have nothing to do with the PC and Net or to massively censor its information. Because this solution is not realistic in terms of raising e-Children from birth to 18, e-Parents need to know about other options. Long-term "fixes" for protecting children and teaching them appropriate use of the PC and Net include many approaches, from no controls to gentle filtering to strict filtering. Parents need to understand the impact of each of these options on their parenting and decide for themselves how they want to proceed.

Open All the Doors

Way over on one side of the censorship debate are those who believe that if we show kids enough of the really great stuff on the Net and how to access and use it for fun, for learning, for research, and for working with others of like interests, everything will be fine. The kids won't even bother with the "bad stuff" because they will enjoy using the Net appropriately. These parents believe the emphasis should not be on fear but on freedom of choice.

This long-term approach to Internet safety could work only if many other things happen, also. Although we agree with this approach in principal, we know that it's unrealistic and just a bit naïve as it's stated here. Obviously, some kids will need more help and supervision than others. The big danger in complete freedom of access to the Internet is that parents may give children unlimited access with no supervision or guidance at all.

This casual but positive approach would work only if e-Parents were highly involved at all times *and* if they also realized (and taught their kids) that the freedom of an *informed* choice is more important than simple freedom of choice.

The freedom to choose comes hand in hand with the responsibility of making informed choices—choices that are not harmful to ourselves or others. Modeling, good parenting, and good communication are the best ways to ensure that children make wise, safe, and informed choices.

In addition, this approach could work well if e-Parents made sure that their children were aware of the dangers of the virtual world and how to deal with them, just as parents should always teach kids about how to protect themselves from dangers in the real world.

Close All the Doors

Way over on the other side of this issue are parents who believe that we should protect kids by using software or Internet service provider filters that completely prevent access to sites that have certain words embedded in the text.

Parents who want to go this route won't have to teach children as much as other parents do about evaluating information, doing critical thinking, or making safe and wise choices. Someone else will be making lots of those decisions for them.

We believe that the fine-filter approach is a quick fix because it will work only until children find out how to get around the filters or use other people's computers to access the Net. What happens with this approach when children begin using the Net without filters, as they eventually will (and probably before they are teens)?

Here's our concern: We wonder how kids who have never had much chance to practice evaluating information or making good choices *with* their parents will ever be able to make such decisions on their own?

One other problem with the close-the-doors approach is that information an older child legitimately needs may be inaccessible. For example, a student doing a report on breast cancer would be blocked from doing research on this topic, just as any teenager would be blocked from any site that included the word *breast* in its text.

Who's Deciding for You?

Many filters do not state the criteria being used to make blocking decisions—or exactly who makes these decisions. Some parents may implicitly trust the entity making these decisions. Personally, we would not use a filter if we did not know the criteria and the source of the decision making.

Is this a case of throwing the baby out with the bath water?
A teenager whose family PC is filtered can simply use a friend's
unfiltered computer or a PC at the local library. What good is
your home PC filter if you have not taught your kids how to make
good choices without it?

Unfiltered Libraries:

The American Library Association does not recommend filtering for PCs in public libraries, but allows individual libraries to modify this position to fit the needs of their local communities if they so choose.

Even if parents choose to use filters, if they want their children to
be able to live successfully and safely in an e-World, parents cannot avoid their responsibility. They must still teach kids about
potential dangers and how to cope with them. They must still
teach kids to use critical thinking skills to evaluate information
and make wise choices.

It Won't Go Away If You Close Your Eyes

Of course, there are always a few parents who just won't have a PC in their homes. They choose to ignore the fact that even if *they* never become computer literate, their children *will* be and will live and work in the e-World. And some parents who do have PCs may pull the plug and not let their kids use them. This attitude is totally unrealistic and rather dangerous. Avoiding the e-World and denying its many opportu-nities for positive discovery and learning is not in a child's best interest. We are all e-Parents; let's be the best e-Parents possible.

Open the Back Door (or Maybe a Window)

Some families have adopted another long-term approach to teaching Internet safety to kids: the middle-of-the-road approach. This
system supports filters (along with rules for limiting Net access to
"safe" sites, child-safe browsers, and so on) as useful tools for
young children—children who are just beginning to use the
Internet but who have not yet developed all the critical-thinking
skills they need to make safe choices.

With this some-doors-open system, ongoing parent involvement,
e-Parenting basics, and good parent-child communication are
essential.

As they begin to use the PC and Net with this approach, children's experiences would be something like learning to ride a
two-wheeler bike. Children would use the filters and the safe sites
as training wheels, and their parents would watch carefully to see
when those training wheels can come off.

As children grow into beginning drivers, there is dual control; parents drive with them until they can go solo. Children will undoubtedly make some mistakes, but because good parent-child communication is in place, the kids will come to their parents with these fender-bender mistakes or concerns, learning better and better Internet superhighway driving skills through experience.

As kids mature, more driving freedom (freedom of access) is allowed. In the interim, e-Parents have helped their kids to internalize critical thinking skills and self-discipline. We can see why, in this approach, e-Parenting involvement and parenting basics are essential. For example, who decides when kids are ready for dual driving or free access? Who supervises this transition? We believe that parents, not the government or some third-party filter manufacturer, should make these important decisions.

In this long-term approach to self-disciplined protection, e-Parents will need comprehensive information to make good choices about filters and access to information, as well as a good handle on their own beliefs. And because each child is unique, parents will have to make decisions based on what they know about the maturity of their individual children.

The Bottom Line

We come back to the fact that, with any of these three approaches, if you want to raise successful e-World kids, you have to understand the issues, gather information, and take responsibility. You have to be involved with your kids' developing use of these technologies from the get-go.

No matter which avenue you take to the information superhighway, you still have to teach children how to use the PC and Net in appropriate ways.

Information Is Knowledge, and Knowledge Is Power

We think that to make informed choices about these issues and to take responsibility for them, e-Parents need all the information they can get. Ignorance is dangerous because it makes you vulnerable. Knowledge is empowering. Knowledge lets you make informed choices and act on those choices.

Actually, groups representing differing sides or opinions on Internet safety issues do agree that parents should be informed and that the responsibility for choices about the use of the Net is up to the individual family. This agreement has been the starting point and touchstone for some cooperative efforts to address these issues.

Online Safety Information Resources

We believe that all e-Parents need to have a working knowledge of Internet safety issues, so we start out with some suggestions for general reading. As you will see when you do some browsing, some of these sites lean more toward filtering solutions and some lean more toward emphasizing good Net resources. Some take the middle road.

The Children's Partnership site at *www.childrenspartnership.org* is committed to getting parents involved in children's online activities as well as in protecting the interests of children. The organization recently helped launch the *www.GetNetWise.com* site, and the brochure, *Parent's Guide to the Information Superhighway*, is available at the Web site.

The Family Education Company has more than 16,400 community-based Web sites nationwide that emphasize the "good stuff" and provide valuable information on Internet issues. The organization's main site is at *www.familyeducation.com.*

At *www.larrysworld.com* you'll find the site of Larry Magid, columnist for the *LA Times*, who is known for his work in the areas of Internet safety and his practical, commonsense writing about Internet issues. Some of his online articles include the "Virtual Sandbox," "Kids Need to Learn to Sift out Net Junk," and "Lessons Children Learn in Internet Safety Can Be Lessons for Living."

The Family Education home page at www.familyeducation.com *has links to children's development information, parenting strategies, fun activities, and help for families with special needs.*

You've read about the Net Parents site at *www.netparents.com* in other parts of this book. Net Parents is a nonprofit organization designed to educate parents about Internet safety and technology. In the America Links Up pages, you'll see that this site also focuses on lots of good stuff. It provides tips for guidance as well as many activities for fun and learning for all ages.

The Internet Online Summit: Focus on Children site at *www.kidsonline.org* offers detailed information about the Internet Online Summit and similar events and issues, such as the Communications Decency Act (CDA).

www.americalinksup.org is a site that grew out of the Internet Online Summit. It is an ongoing Internet public awareness and education campaign sponsored by a broad-based coalition of non-profit organizations, education groups, and corporations concerned with providing children safe and rewarding online experiences. The campaign and its Web site are designed to reach families through grassroots efforts in schools, libraries, nonprofit organizations, and community centers.

The Electronic Frontier Foundation has its Web site at *www.eff.org*. This nonprofit organization opposes the CDA and is an excellent resource for information on the CDA hearings. Following the hearings is a good way to get well-documented information about Internet safety issues.

The National Law Center (*www.filteringfacts.org*) and the American Civil Liberties Union (*www.aclu.org*) have sites where you can find facts about Internet legislation and learn about relevant laws and cases.

Enough is Enough is a nonprofit organization dedicated to protecting children. Its Web site at *www.enough.org* offers advice on ways to prevent Internet crimes against children and other resources and links.

www.safesurf.com is a company working hard to develop and implement a SafeSurf Internet Filtering Solution based on a voluntary and comprehensive SafeSurf Rating System installed at the Internet service provider (ISP) level. The company believes that self-regulation by the Internet community is the best way to resolve Internet safety issues. (You'll find more about this topic later in the chapter.)

www.safetyed.com is a nonprofit organization that works to protect children in cyberspace. Along with many other organizations, SafteyEd.com is assisting the SafeSurf Organization in its rating-system efforts.

Web Wise Kids at *www.webwisekids.com* is an online safety resource center for parents, children, and teachers. The goal here is to encourage families to discover and enjoy cyberspace opportunities, but the center also advises Net users of potential dangers and how to equip themselves to deal with those dangers.

The site includes an excellent letter of safety and education advice for online parents, sponsors a Web safety program for classrooms, presents updated lists of Internet-related safety legislation, and lists pages of Internet safety sites as well as other safe, interesting sites for families. Web Wise Kids works closely with Enough.org and SafetyEd.com, and suggests that parents visit those sites and *www.research.att.com* to learn about the technology tools being used as filters.

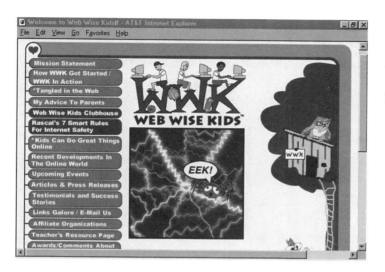

Check out the link to Rascal's 7 Smart Rules for Internet Safety at the Web Wise Kids home page at www. webwisekids.com.

Cooperative Internet Industry Efforts

The internet industry itself is concerned with making the Net safe for children and with making it a great resource for discovery, learning, and enjoyment. Concerned public interest groups working together and also working closely with the Internet industry are trying to accomplish these goals. We want to share a few examples of these efforts.

GetNetWise

We chose the dozen or so sites described in the last section after researching more than 30 sites. But the site we actually like best in this area is *www.getnetwise.com* because it has some unusual qualities. For one, the site and its content are an excellent example of cooperative efforts by the Internet industry and the nonprofit community to address online safety issues.

Launched in the summer of 1999 and operated by the Internet Education Foundation, GetNetWise is a public service site sponsored by a coalition of Internet industry corporations and public interest organizations.

It was organized by AOL, AT&T, BellSouth, Bell Atlantic, MCI WorldCom, and Microsoft Corporation; its steering committee is composed of Commercial Internet Exchange, Disney Online, Excite@Home, Lycos, MindSpring, Network Solutions, Yahoo!,

Big Corporations, Big Ideas:
You may begin to see what we mean by the "unusual qualities" of GetNetWise. The brainstorming power possibilities combined in those groups is pretty amazing.

and Zeeks. Supporting partners are AltaVista, Ameritech, the Association of American Publishers, CyberPatrol, Dell, and IBM.

The 35 advisory board members for GetNetWise represent the entire spectrum of views on online safety issues, from Net Nanny and other filtering software to organizations like the American Library Association, which has taken a stand against filters.

It is really encouraging to see these people working together to ensure that families get *all* the information and resources they need to make informed decisions and to help parents and kids have safe, entertaining, and educational online experiences.

The challenge for e-Parents is to educate themselves and their kids about how to use the Internet safely; we think that GetNetWise has put together excellent resources to help them do just that.

From the mission statement at the top of its home page at www.getnetwise.com *to its inclusion of information supporting positions all along the Internet safety spectrum, GetNetWise is a great place to start forming your opinion on how to make your family's online experience what you want it to be.*

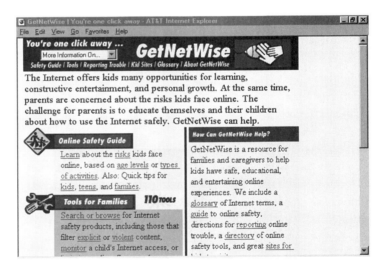

On the GetNetWise home page, you will find categories for What's This All About?, How Can GetNetWise Help?, 102 Tools for Families, Reporting Trouble, and Web Sites for Kids, as well as the best Online Safety Guide we have seen. Each category's contents are clearly described, and you can find hyperlinks to other areas of the site throughout the descriptions. As promised in the header, these links make navigation really easy. Just one click on the underlined topic of your interest, and you are there.

About the Online Safety Guide.... Because we are involved in the fields of education and child development, we were really pleased to see that this guide does much more than list the familiar good rules about online safety that you see in almost all sites. Although it doesn't hurt to repeat and reinforce the basic do's and don'ts, parents find these rules much more helpful when they are placed in perspective for the age, maturity, and development of their children. Online safety tips in this guide are arranged in six well-thought-out age groups that cover ages 2 to 17.

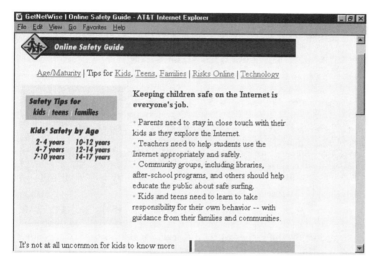

In addition to its online safety tips by age, GetNetWise has links to good discussions about the kinds of risks you may encounter online. Go to http://www.getnetwise.org/safetyguide/ to start.

When rules match up with what parents observe and know about each of their children at different ages, the rules make more sense and it's easier to implement them. In this online safety guide, a tip on guidance specific to a toddler or a four-year-old is, and should be, quite different than tips for eight-year-olds or preteens. Here's an excerpt from the guidance for children age 4 to about age 7:

Click to Find More Information:

As does any good site, the advice in GetNetWise is filled with hyperlinks (shown underlined in these excerpts) to take the user to additional information in one click.

> Children begin to explore on their own, but it's still important for parents to be in very close touch with their children as they explore the Net. When your child's at this age, you should consider restricting her access only to sites that you have visited and feel are appropriate. For help with this matter, you can consider using one of the prescreened Web sites in Get Net Wise, as well as child-safe search *engines.*

© 1999 by Internet Education Foundation

Now look at excerpts from what the guide says in its tips for 7 to 10 year olds:

> During this period, children begin looking outside the home for social validation and information. This is when peer pressure begins to be an issue for many kids.... During these years, children should be encouraged to do a bit more exploring on their own, but that doesn't mean parents should not be close at hand. Just as you wouldn't send children at this age to a movie by themselves, it's important to be with them—or at least nearby—when they explore the Net.

> For this age group, consider putting the computer in a kitchen area, family room, den, or other areas where the child has access to Mom or Dad while using the computer. That way, they can be independent, but not alone. Also consider using a <u>filtering program</u> or restricting them to sites that you locate via a <u>child-safe search engine</u>. Another option for this age group is a <u>child-friendly browser</u>....

> Be sure that his time on the computer and the Internet doesn't take away from all his other activities. Kids need variety, and it's not a good idea for them to be spending all of their time on any single activity.... One way to deal with this might be through the use of a software time-limiting tool.

> © 1999 by Internet Education Foundation

And in the guide's tips for preteens, here is the age-appropriate advice you'll find:

> At about age 12, children begin to hone their abstract reasoning skills...they begin to form more of their own values and take on the values of their peers.... It's important at this age to begin to emphasize the concept of credibility. Kids need to understand that not everything they see on the Internet is true or valuable, just as not all advice they get from their peers is valuable.

> © 1999 by Internet Education Foundation

Wow! Great child development information and great information on wise Internet choices, all stated in a clear, practical, straightforward manner—a rarity, and one that e-Parents will appreciate.

A few more points about the online safety guide of this site. Parents can find safety guidance based on the age and maturity of their children and also learn about various kinds of online personal risks; risks are also listed by technology. In addition, there are pages of tips for kids, teens, and families that are written in a personal, candid, readable style, customized to each of these groups of readers. These tips, for example, are tips teens would *keep on reading* after the first paragraph.

SafeSurf

Another very interesting joint industry effort is the site at *www.safesurf.com.* The goal here is to implement voluntary Internet standards throughout the Internet by promoting the SafeSurf Rating Standard. Perhaps the most helpful pages for e-Parents trying to understand how SafeSurf works are the Frequently Asked Questions (FAQ) pages.

The founders of this site joined the Platform for Internet Content Selection (PICS) along with 22 other top companies such as Microsoft, Netscape, and AT&T. PICS is an industrywide effort to create a new protocol that would be included in new releases of Internet software and browsers. PICS is not exactly what we usually think of when we think of a rating system; it is an Internet protocol to allow ratings to be transferred and understood across the Internet.

Basically, it works like this: Content providers rate their pages, parents set passwords for their children, and PICS-compliant software/browsers read the settings and the ratings. The SafeSurf system is quite extensive compared to other systems, which usually have three or four categories of criteria (such as nudity, profanity, sex, and hate).

The intent of having more categories or criteria is to give parents more opportunity for freedom of choice and more control over the flow of information. (Similar efforts for creating fair rating systems with more categories of criteria are also underway elsewhere among other groups and companies.)

The SafeSurf Rating System will identify adult themes as well as child-safe sites. The goal is to get all sites on the Net to voluntarily participate in coding the kinds of information on their sites. The code inserted in the content of a site will allow parents to make specific decisions about what kinds of materials they want or will allow their children to use, which will, in turn, determine what sites children can visit.

The system is put in place at the ISP level, not at the end user's computer, to avoid tampering. The codes that describe a site's content are interpreted by the computer as they are encoded. By using the computer to do the translating, the system of content coding can be very complex, and information can be classified very precisely, but the system is still easy enough for parents to understand and use.

Founders of the SafeSurf site say this:

> Choice is what it is all about. By grouping everything (categories of information) together, we take the choice away from everyone. We are in no way stating that one group is right or wrong, good or bad, but that they (sites) contain different types of resources and information, and should be classified per those differences.

> We believe that standards should be implemented in cyberspace. Children should be protected on the Internet; however, parents should have the choice to raise children as they see fit and define the word "indecent" for themselves...the only way we will be able to achieve freedom of choice by parents is to implement an Internet-wide rating standard.

> We believe in the power of the Net. Our system will demonstrate that cooperative self-regulation is a million times more effective than government censorship.

© 1996 by SafeSurf

Safety Tips

Let's get away from sites and resources for a while and just talk about some commonsense Internet safety tips and the reasons for them.

We have to be realistic about the potential dangers of the Net. There are predators on the Internet, just as there are predators in the real world. Wise e-Parents will need to think of ways to help kids transfer the concepts of "stranger danger" in the real world to the virtual world.

Nothing Beats Good Parenting

Something that may be reassuring to some parents is what Larry Magid said in his *Los Angeles Times* column on July 12, 1999:

> When it comes to dangers on the Internet, the most serious problem one can imagine is a child who turns up missing or is molested as a result of an online contact. It is tragic, but it doesn't happen very often.

> Of the millions of children who surf the Net, the National Center for Missing and Exploited Children has information on about 130 cases where a child has left home or been targeted by an adult to leave home.... The reported cases are almost all kids who have left home on their own, usually after meeting someone online....

> And they're generally not little kids. About 72% are over 15, and
> 83% are female.
>
> We believe that if those teenage girls had received the e-Parenting guid-
> ance and good parent-child communication we are advocating in this
> book, the numbers might be much smaller.
>
> When those teens were little, parents were not as aware of the need
> for computer literacy and supervision as are the e-Parents of today.
> The awareness and understanding of today's online parents will lead to
> action that will help prevent problems.

One of the biggest problems with trying to help little kids and
school-age kids understand the concept of stranger danger is that
after they talk to someone a few times on the Net, they think of
that person as an online friend, not as a stranger. And they don't
have the life experience or critical-thinking skills to be very cautious about what they say.

In addition, the Net doesn't provide the visual or body language
cues that help kids sense that a person may be a predator: no car
with someone leaning out with candy or something in a facial
expression that makes kids uncomfortable. Kids need to understand that what a person says online could actually be totally
untrue. For example, someone can easily pose as another child;
would your kids know the difference? Would you? Probably not.

Fear of online chats resulting in abducted children leads many
parents to forbid chats. But don't forget that your kids can go
elsewhere to chat. It is imperative to tell kids that predators on the
Net can and do sometimes pretend to be someone else; they can
use seemingly innocent conversations and subtle questions to get
more information about your child in order to identify or find
them.

Prove the Point:

Try this experiment:
Make an arrange-
ment with an adult
family member to go
online to your child's
interest group or
chat room to try to
fool your child into
thinking the adult is
the child's peer. How
savvy is your child?

Teach your kids some "red flags" to watch out for in online conversations:

- Someone who asks what school you go to or what grade you
  are in at the school

- Someone who asks about neighborhood landmarks, such as
  the movie theaters or malls you go to

- Someone who asks what team sport you play or what your uniform number is (predators sometimes go to even adult-monitored interest or chat groups, pretending to be kids)

- Someone who asks what you are wearing because of the kind of weather we are having

- Someone who asks that your conversation be "our secret"

- Someone who asks to meet you someplace without your parents

- Someone who asks for your phone number, address, or any other personal information

- Someone who sends you a photo and asks for yours

- Someone who uses profanity or sexual innuendoes in the conversation

Help your kids understand that even when you are home in what you think is a safe place, it is possible for strangers to come "into your home" through the Internet.

It is easy to see why we have recommended throughout this book that parents supervise and be there or at least nearby when kids use the Net and why we firmly believe that the PC should be treated as a family resource and appliance and be placed in a family room or den, never in a child's room.

Here is an analogy. You know that your young teen is going to take drivers' education and that next year he or she will be driving a car independently. But you don't give him or her the keys to the family car and tell the teen to start practicing now, do you? You won't give your child the keys and let him or her take your car solo until the teen has had driving lessons in a car with dual controls. And even after your child gets a driving permit, you are going to do about 25 hours (minimum) of supervised driving with your child—when your child drives, but you are in the car for support, coaching, and supervision.

After all that, you are still going to make some rules about the use of the car. It is the *family* car, not the teen's car, and it is a lethal weapon in the hands of an irresponsible driver. You don't want your child or others to be in danger because your teen driver is too inexperienced to make wise choices.

We hope you see that you can substitute the word *PC* for *car* in this example. You would not give your kid—a pretty inexperienced user—the "keys" to unlimited use of the PC. This behavior is just as dangerous as giving a kid the keys to your car before he or she is ready and trained to drive.

If you want to raise responsible kids who make safe and wise choices, it won't happen automatically, any more than expert driving can happen without study, supervision, driving experience, and some mistakes along the way. You have to be there. You have to be involved with your children as they learn to drive or learn to use the PC and the Net.

Scary but True

Here are some facts we found in the May issue of *Time Magazine*. In the article, "Raising Kids Online: What Can Parents Do?," by Daniel Okrent, we read that 43% of parents don't have rules about Internet use!

The article went on to state that 83% of kids say they place a great deal of trust in the information they get from their parents. Other kids listed teachers, religious leaders, friends, and TV news and newspapers as sources they trust. Only 13% of kids said they trusted the Internet for information.

Isn't it interesting that a large 83% of kids are willing to trust and listen to their parents, and yet 43% of parents in the study—nearly half—are not putting rules in place for the use of the PC and Net?

Here are a few more safety tips:

- Never let your child post an online profile. These profiles are targeted by predators. No one should have any personal information on you or your child.

- Be cautious about your family Web sites. Do not put up your children's photos on sites that can be publicly accessed. Don't include personal information about where you live or the schools your kids attend.

- Firmly instruct your child to tell you if anyone approaches them for an offline meeting or makes them feel uncomfortable in a conversation. Assure them that you won't be angry

or blame them. Also tell them not to respond at all if they
receive something offensive, and that they should show you
anything they receive that makes them feel ill at ease.

• Don't overreact if your children come to you with this information. Never punish kids for telling you about an uncomfortable online encounter. Be reassuring and praise them for
  telling you; notify the authorities if that seems appropriate.

• Establish clear ground rules for Net use in the family and
  consider making contracts with your kids that state the rules.
  Involve the whole family in the decision making about the
  rules for a contract; kids usually keep the rules they help
  make.

• Learn about the parental control tools, protective software,
  and controlled access options that are available and decide
  whether any of these options interest you or meet your needs.

• Use e-Parenting basics! Show a real interest in your kids'
  online activities. Have fun learning about the technology
  together and enjoying discoveries together. Ask lots of questions and let your children teach you things, but at the same
  time, teach them what you believe and think they should
  know.

Remember that the challenges of the Net can be positive. When
kids learn to use critical thinking to make wise, safe choices
about the Net, they are also learning life skills they will need in
the real world.

e-Kids will learn how to know whether something they see or
hear about is too good to be true or whether the advice of a friend
is dangerous. They will learn to ask questions and find their own
answers about peer groups, fads, and political candidates. They
will know that when others say "everyone does it," this kind of
generalization is simply not true.

Safe Sites

The Internet community is making real efforts to help parents and
kids have safe, exciting, and enjoyable online learning experiences. This concern is evidenced by the speed with which safe

sites for kids are being created and shared across the community. Providers are anxious to offer their own safe sites and refer and link parents and kids to other safe sites. You can find leads to kid-safe sites at all the sites we have listed, and that's a good sign.

You will also quickly discover that certain links to recommended safe sites for kids and teens come up again and again. For example, if you go to the two pages for Web Sites for Kids at GetNetWise (*www.getnetwise.com*), you will find links to NetMom at *www.netmom.com*, the American Library Association with its 700 great sites at *www.ala.org*, Children's Partnership at *www.childrenspartnership.org*, Enough is Enough at *www.enough.org*, and Cyber Angels at *www.cyberangels.com*. You will find recommendations for these five safe sites and others in many places on the Net.

In addition, GetNetWise links users directly to its partners Lycos, Excite, Yahoo!, AT&T, Disney, AOL, Microsoft, and Netscape so that you can get directly to *their* safe site lists.

One more thing: GetNetWise also links to *www.safekids.com* and *www.safeteens.com*. These are excellent resources for parents and kids, not only for safety information but also for even *more* safe sites for kids and teens, categorized by topics.

Another place to find good lists of safe sites is *www.netfamilynews.org*, the home of the Net Family News site and newsletter. We found nine pages of links in 10 categories, plus an interesting newsletter especially designed for online families.

It's like grandma often said: Good company leads to more good company, and You may be known by the friends you keep.

Just as you always find certain parenting sites listed in all recommended lists (for example, The National Parenting Center, Parents Place, Parent Soup, Earlychildhood.com, Women.com), you will also find certain safe site recommendations repeated again and again. That means credibility to *us*, what about you?

Out of curiosity, we went to *www.netmom.com* to see what Jean Armour Polly had to say about safe sites. Sure enough, in her hotlist of parenting sites from *The Internet Kids & Family Yellow Pages*, we found another referral and review for Safe Kids.com.

Tip:
In addition, Safe Kids offers immediate access to two kid-friendly, safe search tools: Ask Jeeves and Yahooligans.

You Are Your Child's Keeper:
You should always make the effort to know your kids' friends and welcome them into your homes. It's well worth the extra soft drinks and potato chips to know the company your kids keep, both online and in the real world.

> ### What Criteria Is Used to Define a "Safe" Site?
>
> One of the very best things about the GetNetWise pages of safe sites is that every listing includes not only a description of what the site offers but also a link to the *criteria* used at each site to determine its safety and usefulness to parents and kids. GetNetWise is the only site where we found instant access to the criteria used in determining safe site quality. For e-Parents who want comprehensive information, this is a real plus.

Netmom also recommended *www.family.go.com*, which is presented by Disney Online and offers lots of interesting articles about family activities (such as camp crafts, kindergarten activities, and stuff to do with grandparents). You can even "get local" to see what's happening for families in your town.

The Family.com home page at www.family.go. com (from Disney Online) is full of interesting activities and information targeted for the family.

Filters

We believe that the use of any filtering tool for blocking, browsing, and searching should be carefully researched by parents and should be carefully chosen, based on the particular needs and values of the family.

Most important, we believe that parents should not choose a filtering tool without knowing its exact criteria, who developed it, the particular biases of the developers (if any), and how the tool can best be used in the family. For example, young children may need filtering help as well as parental supervision with tools for blocking or browsing. Older children may not need these tools if they are self-disciplined, responsible, and working closely with their e-Parents in online activities.

In other words, no filtering device can be a substitute for good e-Parenting. Filters just won't do that job *for* you.

Here are some of our suggestions for evaluating filtering tools:

- Explore and investigate many and varied tools, (easy to do on the Net). Don't just pick one on impulse or on a friend's advice.

- See which tools your ISP can offer; usually ISP filters work best because they prevent tampering.

- See SafeSurf at *www.safesurf.com* to learn about and consider using its voluntary Safe Surf Rating System.

Find Filters on AOL:
In AOL, click the Family channel and then choose Parental Controls from the pull-down topic list. The directions for using these controls and selecting and storing your password are very clear.

- To start exploring your options, go directly to the Safe Kids Home page at *www.safekids.com* and click on the Directory of Parental Control Software.

- If you want to immediately download an ISP filter, you may want to consider Microsoft's Content Advisor. (Remember that Microsoft is using SafeSurf.) Refer to *Teach Yourself the Internet in 24 Hours* (Sams Publishing), in "Important Family Safety Tips," to get step-by-step help for installing Content Advisor.

- Other filtering software programs we have researched and that you may want to consider are CyberPatrol, SurfWatch, and NetNanny (all about $30). These programs are not completely perfect, but they do let parents specify the type of material they feel is not appropriate in categories such as sexually explicit, violent or hateful, and dangerous substances.

- You may also be interested in Edmark software's Kid Desk Internet Safe (about $30). This kid-friendly Web browser keeps out inappropriate content and is also a personal desktop for kids, allowing them to keep their programs separate alongside your existing browser. (This product works seamlessly with AOL.)

Check Your Kid's History:

You can also do a little checking with the history or cache file in your browser. Both Microsoft's Internet Explorer and Netscape Navigator keep a history file of sites visited.

- Rather than block access, you may want to get some help in monitoring your older kids' activities with a program such as CyberSnoop (from Pearl Software at *www.pearlsw.com*). This tool creates a log of where your kids have been or what they have typed in email, chats, sites, and newsgroups. If you learn something that concerns you, you can have a serious, real-world chat with your kids.

Summing Up

We hope you have found the information in this chapter useful and challenging in terms of your own values and decision making. We wanted to give you some things to think about, not just a quick fix regarding online safety.

We have covered some of the major issues and approaches to resolving the challenge of online safety and some of the cooperative efforts to resolve problems fairly. We have given you safety tips, safety resources, safe sites, and parental control information.

You have to gather and digest good information to make your own decisions about your children's safe use of the Net. But we hope you got our message loud and clear. Nothing you do will substitute for your own good e-Parenting and your own ongoing and genuine parent-child communication.

Life is full of risks and rewards. Educate yourself about the wonderful benefits as well as the risks of the Net. Keep using e-Parenting basics every day: Show an interest, provide guidance, and have fun together. Filtering programs may help you with short-term goals, but talking with your kids, good parenting, and doing things together on the Net will have far greater long-term benefits.

CHAPTER 10

Saving Family Traditions in New Ways

In this final chapter, we are going to leave you with something to think about as we begin the new millennium. Every generation has had traditions, special things that always stayed the same and are cherished because of their very sameness. (The phenomenal success of the *Chicken Soup* series of books can be largely attributed to that human need for sameness; chicken soup is certainly a universal and timeless tradition.)

We believe that this generation of e-Parents and children will also cherish the traditions they have grown up with, but that they will take advantage of the PC and Net to reinvent some of those traditions in new ways and will enhance others with a twist of e-World technology.

Along those lines, we want to talk first about family craft traditions and homemade gift and card traditions. Then we talk about using the Net to enhance family traditions such as vacations, family history, and family reunions.

In closing, we suggest that certain traditions must be saved in real-world time. We must always value some things because of their sameness, not because of the changes we make to them.

What Are Family Traditions and Why Are They Important?

Everyone knows what family traditions are, right? Most people would agree that family traditions are the simple, ordinary things that families do together regularly, such as playing cards, playing games, taking fall color drives, going out for Mothers Day brunches, and going on Labor Day picnics. Traditions are things like having Thanksgiving dinner together, going home for the

What You'll Learn in This Chapter:

▶ A definition of what makes a family tradition, and how some old standbys can benefit from technology

▶ Ways you can apply your Internet savvy to tried-and-true family activities

▶ Why some old-fashioned, non-virtual traditions shouldn't be turned into online adventures

holidays, putting up certain holiday decorations, going on an annual family trip, or making homemade gifts and cards.

When someone asks why your family does a certain thing a certain way every year, you might say it is because you have always done it or that your grandparents started the tradition and you are keeping it going. That's what makes it a tradition.

When families keep on doing a certain thing regularly and pass it on, it means that activity is important to them. The dictionary tells us that traditions are beliefs, customs, activities, and tales that are felt to be important enough to be passed on from generation to generation.

Most of us don't notice that something else, something very special, happens when we do that simple, ordinary "family stuff" together. At the same time that we are enjoying whatever we are doing, we are actually passing on those beliefs, tales, and customs the dictionary mentions.

For proof that family traditions have a long-term impact on our lives, ask most adults what they remember about growing up. They will get nostalgic as they recall something their family did together that was fun, where people were talking, laughing, and enjoying each other face to face.

They didn't notice, but at the same time they were having fun playing a board game, playing cards, or baking cookies, they were also valuing family togetherness, valuing sociable conversation, enjoying family humor, relaxing, getting a feel for their roots, and feeling a sense of "belonging" to the group. These are important things that traditions do for us. They are things children need and that e-Parents will want to find ways to preserve.

Can't Find the Time:

The e-World, which was intended to save us time, has brought us so much information and so many choices that we *think* we have less time for family than our parents did. But we can still find the time.

Because we are all so busy these days, we have to look at our choices and our time more critically and make a commitment to saving time for e-Parenting and other things that are important to us.

We know e-Parents can do this because e-Parenting means working much smarter, not necessarily harder. e-Parents are smart, and what they will do is use the best of e-World technology to prioritize ways for families to enjoy each other. They can carve out time to save the traditions that are important to them, or they can create new traditions. They can discover new ways to pass on family traditions, even if it means reinventing some of them.

Family traditions are grounded in a sense of security and comfort that comes with belonging to a group. e-Children need this connection, this anchor to hold on to as they grow into a world full of speed and changes.

It is important for e-Parents to provide that anchor by learning to use the e-World to enhance family traditions and to save or re-create other traditions in both old and new ways.

Starting or Enhancing Craft Traditions

Many parents enjoy making handmade crafts because the work is relaxing and creative, and you can make crafts at home. When crafts are a tradition in a family, parents usually give craft items as gifts and also teach their children how to make simple homemade gifts at an early age.

The core of the craft gift tradition is that you are giving something of yourself when you make something by hand. When children feel the joy of giving something they made to someone they care about, they are learning much more than a creative craft.

Perhaps you are an e-Parent who has a new interest in trying some crafts, or perhaps you feel that your children would like them. You may even think craft gifts could teach your child something new. In that case, your PC and the Net can help you find out everything you want to know.

The resources available on the Net allow people to push the envelope of their creativity, making it easy for them to expand on old interests or explore new ones. A Net search might spark an interest that will become a hobby and a family tradition now, and possibly become a retirement income activity down the road.

Exploring Crafts Ideas

Okay, so what do you do first? You already know that you need to narrow your search if you have something specific in mind, instead of searching the Net using the words **crafts** or **"homemade crafts"** or **"children's crafts"**.

If you have nothing specific in mind, you can just start with those words and continue to browse until you find something intriguing. On the other hand, you can go to a house and garden or home decorating site first, just to look at images and get some ideas.

After you find an idea you like, you can continue your search with words that are more specific. Keep in mind that, as e-Parents, you want to involve your children in the craft activity tradition, so get them involved in helping with these searches, too!

Dogs Need a Home, Too:

If e-Children want the privilege of having a dog, they can take some responsibility by helping to build the dog house.

Searching for Ideas

We used the search terms **home, garden, decorate,** and **projects**. In less than 20 minutes, we found several sites that gave us some good ideas. One was *www.HGTV.com*—a group everyone is familiar with because of the associated television channel.

HGTV.com has a shopping village, a gardening and landscaping section, building and remodeling ideas, a food and lifestyle section, design and decorating tips, chats, and more! We even found an example of how to make a clamshell quilt—with step-by-step pictures.

Lowes.com is another familiar site because of the chain of home improvement stores. *www.lowes.com* is a huge reference site; we immediately found 150 how-to projects in various categories. Under the Family category, you can find out how to build a dog house; instructions are clear, and they come complete with a supply list.

Other sites we found were *www.homefurnish.com* with decorating tips, projects, forums, and a feng shui section, plus lots of links to direct us to more specific sites. At *www.living.com*, we found an archive of home projects and techniques, a forum, and a chat.

Another great find, and a very original site, is Gothic Martha Stewart at *www.toreadors.com/martha*, an adaptation of Martha's decorating and craft projects with a special twist in colors and fabric for "special kinds of tastes." Its creative ideas might appeal to teens. Gothic Martha is not a "dark" site; it even discuses the negative effects of smoking in the home.

Still another way to go about your search is to ask yourself what kinds of things in nature are free or easily obtainable in the area where you live. It's possible that you and your child could have a great time gathering the materials you need to create unique homemade craft items. These items could be used for decorating your own home or for giving as homemade gifts for others.

Here are some examples of ways real-time e-Parenting experiences can be enhanced and made even better by using the Net together.

- If you live near the sea, a river, or a lake, you can go on a shell, beach stone, or driftwood gathering expedition with your child. Then you can use the Net together to see what crafts can be done with stones, shells, and driftwood. This e-Parenting strategy also teaches your children the value of saving money by using natural materials in new ways. Any time kids figure out how to use materials in new ways, they are practicing creative problem solving.

- If you live where there are many wildflowers, you can gather and dry them to use in making potpourri. If you are able to grow herbs in your yard (easy for a child to do in any type of flowerpot as long as there is sun), you can even add certain herbs to the potpourri for a customized aromatherapy gift.

- You may be interested in showing your child how to use wildflowers for decoupage, how to mat and frame them, or how to use them to create original notepaper gifts.

- If you live where you can walk in the woods with your child and gather pine, cedar, and other greenery as well as bark, pine cones, acorns, and unusual fungus or moss, you may want to make holiday wreaths, swags, bird feeders, small terrariums, driftwood centerpieces, or Christmas tree ornaments. If you have access to grape vineyards and grapevine brambles, all the better.

Flower Projects Online:

To avoid retailers while searching the Net, narrow your search by using phrases such as *"growing fragrant herbs"*, *"aromatherapy projects"*, *"making wild flower potpourri"*, and *"wild flower decoupage"*.

Now you can do a search for sites that can tell you what other materials you might need, where to get them, and ways to put these natural things together for your creations.

Your search words should be phrases such as **"making small terrariums"**, **"making Christmas decorations"**, **"making Christmas wreaths"**, **"making creative door decorations"**, **"grapevine craft creations"**, **"grapevine wreath crafts"**, **"making tree decorations"**, **"making bird feeders"**, **"driftwood arrangements"**, and so on.

- You may live in a part of the country where you can easily find discards from furniture manufacturers, or an area where it is not difficult to collect inexpensive architectural pieces such as table legs and parts of staircases. These can be "crafted" into unusual antique-looking candlesticks or candleholders.

Perhaps your older child would love working with the wood, sanding it, staining it, or rubbing in oils. And your younger child might like making homemade candles that would make the creation complete. Your search can tell you how to make your own candles safely, what to use to add color and scent, and what to use for forms. Your Web search for enhancing this craft tradition might include words such as **"how to make candles"**, **"candle making safety"**, and **"candle molds"**.

As you do these searches, you are likely to discover other people who are interested in the same craft. You'll be able to find a newsgroup, chat room, or bulletin board on just about any craft topic, and then you'll be able to exchange ideas that will enhance your craft choices and make new online friends.

Use Newsgroups and Chats to Narrow Your Craft Search

Earlier in this book, we discussed bulletin boards, chats, and newsgroups. Remember to use relevant bulletin boards and chats to narrow your search. You can even search with terms such as *"candle making chat rooms"* or *"candle making bulletin boards"* or *"candle making message boards"* or *"candle making forums"*.

Check newsgroups for *"homemade candles"* or *"candle sticks"*. For better results, look for and sign up with candle-type newsgroups. Review the archived messages or post your own candle-making questions.

Remember that large sites employ internal search engines that search specific words within the site! In addition, the site's index is a very helpful search tool. If an index is listed on the site's home page, you can often use that index to find exactly what you want within a site.

For example, if you want information about making a candelabra for your outdoor garden, you can use a garden site's search engine and search with those words first. If nothing comes up right away, try a big garden reference site for help.

Our point is that using the major search engines (such as AltaVista, Excite, and Yahoo!) is not the be-all and end-all for finding information. And don't forget to check the links at sites, which often lead you to a more specific site.

You'll also find how-to-do-it sites in your search, and you may find that sometimes there are classes or seminars or workshops online that can enhance your craft tradition.

Because the Net is a marketing tool (millions of dollars are spent annually online) as well as an information highway, there are countless virtual storefronts and "pay for it now" sites. To avoid these virtual stores, use the phrases we've mentioned (*how to*, *making a*, *projects on*, *free classes on*, *virtual workshops and seminars on*, and the like).

How-to videos and books are sold on the Net, and can often be much less expensive if ordered online. Even virtual storefronts may offer free tips or options or lead you to free classes online.

The site www. familyplay.com, sponsored by Crayola and part of the Women. com network, may give you some good children's craft ideas.

Quilts: A Special Craft Tradition

Let's consider quilts. Quilt making was a practical craft in the past when quilts made good use of scrap materials and were a necessity for warmth. Long ago, special quilts were made for weddings, births, and other occasions. Making quilts was a family tradition passed on through the generations, and quilt restoration has become a popular hobby.

Quilts Then and Now

You can learn about the history of quilts on the Internet, and you can also find people who will appraise the value of your antique quilt or who specialize in restoring quilts.

The settlers passed on their interest and skills in quilt making to the Plains Indians, who still make elaborate Star Quilts today. More recently, special quilts have been made to remember AIDS victims and to celebrate a particular school, city, state, or event.

The renewed interest in antique patterns and fabrics has started a huge revival of the craft of quilt making. One neat thing about quilt making is that it can be done as a parent-child or family group activity; sometimes members of the extended family get together to quilt one evening a week. A family-made quilt can also be passed on as an heirloom.

If you are an e-Parent who is interested in starting a family tradition of collecting quilts or of quilt making, the following sidebar will help you with your search.

Where to Look for Quilting Sites

When we looked for quilting sites, we first typed in **"how to make a quilt"**. We found *www.palaver.com/mountainmist/welcome.htm*, a site that had such a large list of related links that it would be a good candidate for saving in a Favorites folder about quilting.

We also found The Quilt Shop. This is a good beginner's site, offering "classes" such as Quilting 101, Quilting 102, and so on. Links to getting started, supplies, sewing, patterns, and more are listed. Go to *www.cranstonvillage.com/visitor/visitors.htm*. Under **Places to Visit**, click **The Quilt Shop**.

Another good beginner quilting site with lots of good links is Quilting for Beginners by Beginners at *http://www.sostre.com/beginnersquilts.htm*.

We decided to try a search for **"quilting bee"** and found the Quilters' Newsletter at *www.quiltmaker.com*. This great site has quick technique lessons, contests, a gallery, bulletin board, articles, back issues, and more. In about 15 minutes, the Net gave us lots of information about quilts and quilting.

The Quilts Online site at www. quiltmaker.com, sponsored by Primedia Special Interest Publications, is a good place to start learning about quilts.

Greeting Cards: A New Take on an Old Tradition

Sending greeting cards for various occasions has been a tradition for a hundred years or so, and the greeting cards tradition has grown into an enormous industry. Today's cards are not only unique, they are darned expensive. People were finding so many occasions to send or give cards that many parents and children started making their own cards.

The card industry recognized this situation as a way to fill a need and found a new way to market cards. Now you and the kids don't have to make your own cards (unless you want to), nor do you have to drive to a store and stand in the card section for hours figuring out which card to purchase.

You can design your own greeting card using your PC and the Net. This activity is a good example of the way e-Parents can use e-World technology to carry on a family tradition in a new way.

e-Parent alert! Something you should know is that kids are much more likely to take an interest in the family tradition of sending greeting cards when family members make their own cards. Your kids not only want to do things with you but also because they love the creative option of making their own cards on the PC. For example, kids love to point and click and hear the noises on musical or talking cards they can create.

Quilts on CompuServe:

If your Internet service provider is CompuServe, you can go to the section called **Go Crafts**, where you can log onto a quilting bee at 10 p.m. eastern time on Tuesdays.

Today, you can get or make online cards for any kind of occasion; personalize the cards; and choose music, animation, and so on. You can use *www.urbancow.com* to send cow-type cards; E Online at *www.eonline.com/Fun/Cards* has a card section with cards for celebrity watchers; Warner Brothers (at *www. warnerbrothers.com*) offers Looney Tune cards, and there are retro sites with cards for lovers of vintage things.

Your make-a-gift-card search can start with the biggies: Hallmark and American. Both of these sites can help you create and print cards, personalize paper cards that they will mail for you, and can even send you email reminders about dates you register with the service.

Making your own cards is also useful for gatherings of family or friends. You can send mass e-Card invitations to a birthday party, a wedding, or a family reunion.

Try It Yourself ▼

Cards are also lifesavers for important e-Parenting messages on nonoccasions. Suppose that you're out of town away on business and you miss your child's hockey game or piano recital. You will be able to find or create the perfect card for that situation and send it to your child from your laptop computer.

1. You can use some nontraditional methods to make an original greeting card. (We decided to do a birth announcement for our cat because she is our newest baby. Why not?) After doing a search for **"greeting cards"**, we found a good site in just minutes called Pacific Products Gallery (at *www.pacprod. com/card.htm*).

2. At this site, you can create a card with a computer image, or you can scan in your own photograph to use. We have a picture of our cat, so we scanned it on to our computer. If you don't have a scanner, you can use any image file on your computer; just follow the simple directions to locate the file.

3. Select the type of card you want to create (we choose **New Baby**) and choose the musical accompaniment for the card from a drop-down list. (We scrolled to find "Alley Cat"— appropriate, don't you think?) The site has tons of music choices, from TV show themes to classics to Tarzan yells.

You can click to preview the music; if you want, you can change your choice.

4. Type or select the appropriate information into the following fields:

   - Title (we typed **Our new family member**)

   - Email recipient

   - Graphic for the title from a drop-down list (we picked **It's a Girl** in animated balloons)

   - Greeting (we typed **Introducing Sabrina, our 3rd adoption, 5 lbs, 15 inches, looks like…neither one of us!**)

   - Ending image or animation (we chose nothing)

5. This may sound like lots of steps but the whole process takes less than 5 minutes. Your child can then click Preview to see just how the card will appear when it's sent. There's also a chance to go back and edit any part of the card. When you're ready, confirm the email address of the recipient and click Send. The program automatically confirms where the card is going and will tell you the password that they will give the recipient to view the card.

Your children can create and print out cards with software you can purchase, or they can use the Net to create and email cards. As your children become even more experienced PC users, they can even use special software to create their own animations for cards.

To find software, you might think to search the Web sites of specific software companies, but don't forget about searching for **"children's software reviews"** or **"education software"**. Craft sites, parenting sites, or technology sites such as *www.cnet.com* often advertise related software or have links to sites about software.

In our search for some good card-making software, we decided to visit the Igive Mall at *www.igive.com*. We found software called Printmaster Gold, which contains more than 100,000 images on

CD-ROM; you can use this software to make greeting cards, invitations, stationery, flyers, banners, and Web pages.

We also found the Creataparty package by American Greetings, which has templates for coordinating designs for parties. You can make invitations, hats, thank-you cards, package decorations, centerpieces, napkin rings, and more.

> **Shop Online and Donate to Charity**
>
> We like to shop in the Igive Mall because a percent of every purchase there goes to our favorite charity. (You can sign up your favorite charity if it isn't already listed, and you can view your charity's stats with a password.) The Igive Mall is a great example of ways that nonprofit organizations are taking advantage of Net resources. For you online shoppers who want to make a difference, visit *www.igive.com*.

American Greetings has lots of creative software and paper supplies. You can even make your own T-shirts, costumes, picture frames and puzzles! (See how easy it is to stumble upon more than you hoped to find!)

Enhancing the Tradition of Family Vacations

When we began to write this chapter, we quickly discovered that we could have written an entire *book* about how e-Parents can use the PC and Net to enhance or reinvent family traditions.

Because you already know a lot about searches and software, we decided to limit this section about e-Travel to general e-Parenting tips and strategies with only one walk-through example.

Family vacations continue to be a family tradition, and more families take vacations together than ever before.

Tip:

You'll find some great travel deals on the Net for airline fares, train tickets, and hotel and travel packages.

The first thing e-Parents need to do is involve the whole family in deciding where to go. Start by having a casual family meeting, perhaps around the dinner table, to brainstorm for ideas about a family vacation.

Even though you, the parent, will make the final decision, your children will feel like important members of the family group if they can suggest ideas and share in the discussion. Jot down everyone's ideas. Then get your kids involved in the brainstorming. You know why: Brainstorming is process thinking and critical thinking!

Find out the special interests of family members and ask them where they would like to go and why. Give them some parameters based on your finances and the time available for the trip. For example, perhaps you cannot afford to go to Hawaii, but perhaps you can afford to go to a destination in the United States, Canada, Mexico, or the Caribbean.

When you narrow down the choices, you can ask your older kids for help in doing Net searches and getting printouts of the alternatives so that you can all get together and make a decision. After you know where you want to go, the Internet will continue to save you time and money by giving you helpful information about that specific location.

Make a list of all the things you want to find out about your destination. The preplanning you do on the Net can help you make the most of your e-Parenting time together as a family. You can start to enjoy your vacation as soon as you get there and not waste time by having to gather information after you arrive. Here's a sample list.

- Campsite; campgrounds and fees

- Dock or marina; boating fee

- Beach

- Hiking and nature trails

- Bike trails; resort rental bikes

- Water sports

- Ski rental; golf

- Groceries

- Medical facilities; decompression chamber (for those deep-sea diving adventures)

- Maps; directions

- Area attractions and fees

- Photos of area scenery

- Amenities; prices

- Public transportation

One advantage of using the Internet to enhance the e-Family vacation tradition is that kids can be involved in different parts of your searches. For example, you can delegate different parts of the preceding list to some of the kids, and they can find and print the information for the whole family to review.

Another e-Parenting advantage is that the Net makes choosing and planning so much more fun and so much easier that families may go on more trips together or discover an entirely new interest as a family group.

For example, a whitewater rafting trip may lead the family to go rafting each year on different rivers. A trip that begins as curiosity may turn out to be a special place that the family returns to each year, starting a new family tradition.

The e-Family Plans a Vacation

If you know what kinds of things everybody in the family wants to do on a vacation, you will find it easier to search for just the right location.

Let's take a fictitious e-Family. Suppose that the father wants to go deep-sea fishing, the mother wants to sun and shop, and the teens want to snorkel and maybe try scuba diving and parasailing. (It's hard to know with teens because they change their minds so often.) The school-age child loves to swim and has a tropical fish hobby, and the youngest cannot swim but loves the water and sand.

Now suppose that the family wants a resort in the Caribbean that offers all of these activities.

Use these search words and phrases: **"snorkel and scuba"**, **"deep sea fishing"**, **"parasail"**, **"Caribbean beach resort"**. The sites that come up will allow you to continue the search to find a location that has everything the family wants to do. In this fictional search, Cozumel, Mexico, will come up as one of the options.

If you want to know more about Cozumel, you can search for Cozumel chat rooms, fan clubs, and bulletin boards. You will find out from people who have been there about the best places to snorkel and eat; where to parasail; typical taxi fares, water temperature and clarity, and weather; where to go for live music or medical care; and the best time of year for deep-sea fishing. You may also find out what some folks *don't* like about Cozumel, but that's okay, too.

For more help in planning an e-Family vacation, see *Sams Teach Yourself e-Travel Today* by Mark Orwall.

An e-Travel site you may want to check out is www.FamilyFun Vacations.com, which has lots of its own advertising and some good information as well.

The Family History Tradition

Some of us tend to take our family history for granted—the photos; the great-grandmothers' maiden names; the family jokes, stories, heroes, and rouges; the family struggles and successes. If we could put ourselves in the place of people who have lost their family histories, we might realize what a precious gift our family history really is, and why we should find ways to preserve it for our children and grandchildren. Histories can be saved with photos, scrapbooks, movies, videos, audio tapes, printed books, and more.

Saving Family Photos and Tapes in New Ways

Who doesn't have boxes of family photos waiting to be put in the albums? (Probably Martha.) These photos are very important to children. Photos are not only visual records of children's lives they are another way to help kids feel connected to the family group. Photos tell family stories and save special moments or cherished memories.

Photos nourish self-esteem and preserve family history.

The e-World has brought us new ways to save these photos, and possibly save time as well. Now e-Parents can use software and scanners to organize their photos on the PC and share them with other family members and friends by email (for details of this process, see Chapter 4, "Using the PC and Net to Nurture Self-Esteem").

Digital cameras are eliminating the need to develop film (digital images feed right into your computer) or make costly reprints. Kodak will even send you your photos by email or put them on CD-ROM.

You can visit *www.Kodak.com* for loads of information about digital cameras and creative things to do with your photos through new technology. Visit the how-to section of Kodak's digital learning center for lots of ideas. This site also presents an imaging technique of the month—for example, how to make a background image on your monitor with your own photo. Very cool.

And then, of course, there is the "scrapbooking" craze! Every family has some sort of scrapbook, and children are often encouraged to make scrapbooks about their hobbies, sport activities, and trips or vacations. Scrapbooks have endured as a great way to save family history and personal memories.

Scrapbooking was a real-world interest that grew from a hobby into a multimillion dollar business. If you search the Net for the term **scrapbooking**, you will find lots of sites or pages in sites. Many will be suppliers of scrapbook materials, but you will also find opportunities to use chats, bulletin boards, and newsgroups for sharing ideas.

Tip:
Visit the Scraphappy site at *www.telepath.com/ bcarson/scrap_happy/ indexo.html* for lots of great creative advice on scrapbooking.

Technology has also given us a new way to save video tape. Many parents have put slides, photos, and movies on video, but video tape may soon be outdated by the Digital Video Disc (DVD).

You can rent DVD players and movies, and some families are setting up DVD home entertainment centers. Compared to traditional video media, movies in DVD are cleaner and crisper. DVD discs also hold more information and last longer than traditional video media. Search the Net for the term **DVD** to learn more. Or visit *www.cnet.com/gadgets/special/DVD* and search for **DVD** with the site's internal search engine.

No matter which way you choose to do it, it is good e-Parenting to save your family photos and family history. It is an important family tradition. Sorting, enjoying, and saving those images in new ways is a very good thing. Get the kids involved!

Family Newsletters, Stories, Sayings, and Jokes

Here is a tradition that has always been predominantly an oral tradition. When the elders pass on, later generations may not continue the tales they've been told. Not many families have a volunteer scribe, so it's all too easy for families to lose much of their most interesting family history.

But now, with the PC and the Net, it is easier, faster, and cheaper for families to reinvent this oral tradition. e-Parents can save money on phone calls, keep in frequent touch with family members, and share the latest stories and events with email.

In addition to news, many e-Parents are remembering family tales, writing them down, and passing them on. Some e-Parents collect stories, jokes, and sayings in a "family history" folder over time. Then they create family newsletters with simple software (such as Microsoft Publisher) and post the newsletters on their family Web sites.

e-Parents can combine their efforts in collecting the family's stories and jokes. (Delegate one person to get grandma's stories, one to get Uncle Joe's, and so on.) Each family can also have its own page in the newsletter, which can be distributed as an attachment to email. When all the pages are received by the leader of the project, they can be assembled to share on the Net or made into a physical booklet.

This project is a great way to remember all the little sayings, wisdom, risqué tales (we all love those), and family stories that might otherwise be lost.

e-Children will want to know the family history if it's interesting, accessible, and fun to read. The more interesting history there is to look back on, the more e-Children gain a sense of family, belonging, and traditions.

Family Genealogy

Many people these days are interested in finding their roots, and
the PC and Net are helping families to both trace their genealogy
and to contact distant relatives. Some children are very interested
in genealogy, and in finding out about the countries of the world
that their family members came from. Encourage this interest and
lead your child to sites that help him or her to discover and learn.
The bigger the picture of the family group, the more the child
sees that he or she "belongs" to it.

Sams Teach Yourself e-Genealogy Today, by Terri Stephens Lamb,
will be particularly helpful to e-Parents interested in discovering
their roots.

Family Ties and Family Tree Maker Deluxe are two genealogy
software programs that can help you keep track of the ancestors
you dig up. We found other genealogy software at The Learning
Company at *www.shoptlc.com*; click the Genealogy link to continue your search.

The *www.escore.com* site has a genealogy section. Another site,
www.familytreemaker.com, looks like it has everything you need
to pursue this family tradition. Broderbund at
www.broderbund.com has a genealogy section of special pages on
creating a family tree; My Family at *www.myfamily.com* also has
an excellent genealogy section.

FamilyTreeMaker.com has links to just about everything you can imagine to facilitate your genealogy search and record keeping.

Adopted Kids Can Search for Genealogies, Too

Adopted children can legally search for their biological parents, even though their biological parents cannot legally search for them. Increasing numbers of adopted children are using the Internet to search for and find their biological parents.

In some of these cases, it is important for an adopted child to learn his or her family medical history. Knowing one's "medical genealogy" can help prevent or predict possible medical problems and give a person important information about certain hereditary diseases.

Family Reunions

Family gatherings help everyone feel a strong sense of belonging. Children at such gatherings have fun, find cousins who become new friends, and are amazed at how big their family really is.

e-Parents will want to use the PC and Net to enhance this tradition, whether the gathering is for a funeral, a christening, a wedding, birthday, bar mitzvah, anniversary, or an annual family reunion.

e-Parents will find that email can make planning easier and can save money on phone calls. Searches for information can be an effort shared by family members. Families will have to decide where to go, how to get there, where to hold the celebration, where to stay, and whether they want a caterer, flowers, a theme, or live music. All aspects of planning can be done online.

If some family members are vegetarians and some are not, for example, the Net can help you find an appropriate caterer who can solve that dilemma. If the family wants a photographer with a digital camera or a digital video camera, the Net can help find those resources, too. Planning a wedding at the reunion? There are lots of wedding planner sites.

The more people involved in gathering information and planning, the better—because it will help you save time, and lead to more informed choices. Families may find that the PC and Net make planning and communicating so much easier that they will have family gatherings more often, which is all the better for e-Children.

Tip:
The FamilyTree Maker.com site may be helpful in locating "lost" family relatives.

e-Parents can enhance this tradition in other ways, too. e-Parents and children already know how to use PC and Net resources to make invitations to the event and how to make family history books that can be distributed at the reunion.

Part of such a booklet can include an updated directory of everyone's name, address, job, children, grandchildren, and email addresses or Web sites. Delegate an older child to collect the information by email.

Another special project that children can handle in preparing for a reunion is to collect family recipes by email, save them in a "cookbook" folder on the PC, and then print them out to distribute as a family cookbook to be enjoyed by all.

When children make comments and do line drawing illustrations to accompany the recipes, family cookbooks become truly unique. (We have seen some, and the kids' additions to the recipes are creative, delightful, and often hilarious.)

A Family History Site

The computer savvy e-Parent can arrange a larger family site where every family member, no matter where he or she lives, can post pictures, stories, and so on. Everyone can share a password that allows access to the site's server. Files are transferred by File Transfer Protocol (FTP).

Cherishing Traditions in Real Time

Some real-world traditions are so important that real time must be saved for them. Remember that the core of any family tradition is face-to-face interaction, conversation, and a sense of belonging to the group. However, most of these real-world traditions can also be enhanced with a little e-World technology.

Family Meals

One tradition we may lose unless e-Parents see its value and save it is the family meal. When children eat with their parents they learn what their parents believe is important, they practice table manners, and they learn to carry on a conversation with an adult (a simple skill that is becoming rare these days) .

Family mealtime is one of the first and most important ways children learn about social interaction. Family members talk about their days, their work, their friends, their interests and activities, and what is going on in their lives.

The hour of conversation and interaction in this simple tradition has been proven to give kids a sense of connectedness with the family, which can help prevent problems in the teen years.

Whose Fault Is It?
Don't be angry when you discover that your children can't converse with adults at age 13 if you never gave them any practice.

The Family That Eats Together Is Safer
The American Psychological Association published a study in 1997 that stressed the importance of the family meal in the lives of teens. Teens who ate with their families an average of five days a week had better relationships with peers, better grades, and few, if any, problems with drugs or depression.

We think e-Parents will see the importance of saving real time for this tradition and try to stop or prevent the "grazing" habit that all-too-often replaces dinnertime.

Technology can help put family meals back into the daily routine. The e-World brings us a zillion easy ways to "cook" dinner—witness microwave entrees and fresh produce from the entire world.

We should also trash the idea that every single thing must be ready to eat at exactly the same time. That expectation is unrealistic and is not practiced in most other countries.

The first family members to get home can start dinner or just eat their salad or snack while they wait for the others. Even if the last person home eats the main course while the others eat dessert, you will all be eating and talking together around the table, which is what really counts!

Family picnics and barbecues are another form of family meals. Treasure them. If kids are young, creative e-Parents can have a picnic on a rainy or snowy day right on the living room floor. Put down a blanket and make some "summer food" you can serve right from the picnic basket. We guarantee that this event will be a cherished family memory.

Family Games

Family games are another real-world, real-time tradition that is often enhanced by technology as games are played online or with video and electronic games. (Chapter 5, "Using the PC and Net to Enhance People Skills," discusses family games in more detail.) But if games are violent or played alone, the entire benefit of the tradition is lost. e-Parents should take a stand on this issue.

The deal with family games is that the family plays them *together*, face to face, and does lots of laughing, joking, talking (and snacking) at the same time.

That's where e-Children will gain the sense of belonging to the group that they need. That's where they will learn who you are as a person as well as what you think is important.

In addition, while kids are having fun with you, they are practicing both educational skills and life skills. What life skills, you say? Just think about it.

> All games teach taking turns, cooperation, patience, perseverance, following the rules, honesty, fairness, and making choices and accepting the consequences of those choices.

Family games help children actually practice the life skills that e-Parents think are important. So get those games off the shelf! Play them! Having fun together is an e-Parenting basic. For more helpful tips about family games, see the Hasbro Family Game Night site at *www.familygamenight.com*.

Baking Cookies and Other Delights

We think everyone will agree that baking and cooking together as a family is an important tradition and one that is very special in most families. Here is a way to celebrate your own heritage and also enjoy the diversity of other cultures!

The PC and Net can give us the world when it comes to recipes. Recipes appear on virtually every family site. And you know how to do searches.

But e-Parents need to carve out a little real time to let their kids help them with the searches, to let kids help cut up the veggies and make dips in the kitchen, and to help make the pizza.

Whenever possible, e-Parents, save some time to bake cookies with your kids, taste the warm ones, and talk while the smells swirl into those memories that will last a lifetime.

Family Walks

We are talking here about slow, leisurely walks along a beach or down a path in the woods, where e-Parents can talk and listen to their kids and where they can enjoy the natural "high" of nature and its beauty.

At times you might take along a snack with that water bottle, or a book to read with your child under a tree. You can also take along a flashlight, a handheld magnifying glass (binoculars if you have them), and a little bag to carry home any treasures you find.

The flashlight and magnifying glass will help children really see their treasures as they find them. They'll focus, observe, and tell—all skills that you learned are important in Chapter 3, "Using the PC and Net to Nurture Creative Problem Solving."

The e-World can enhance the family walk in many ways. What if you find some red, funny-shaped fungus on a tree, or a really weird beach shell? You can help your child learn about those treasures when you get home.

Perhaps you'll see an unfamiliar bird. The Net can help you get to know that bird. A fox may run past you, looking back over its shoulder, or maybe you'll see a fawn. You might see a beaver while you are fishing. Suppose that you see animal tracks with your child and your child wants to know what animal made them?

You're an e-Parent! You know exactly how to learn lots of things with your child about foxes, deer, beavers, and animal tracks. Go do some searching on the Net about animal tracks.

Family walks in the real world can remain a cherished tradition and still take you to new e-World discoveries. At the same time, an e-World discovery can take you to a new real-world activity to share with your child.

The Night Sky

It takes only a few minutes to go out and look at the starry sky on a clear night and begin to feel the wonder of the awesome galaxy in which we live. As adults, many of us still remember the first time our parents showed us the Big Dipper or Orion's belt. Over the centuries, children have always been fascinated by the stars and moon.

And what fabulous opportunities are here for e-Parenting enhancement! After looking at the night sky together, you can use the computer with your kids to learn so many more interesting things about the night sky, the Milky Way, the galaxy, the stars....

Studying the stars on a computer can spill over the other direction into a real-world experience. After learning about the life of a star or about some of the constellations on the computer, looking for them at night and pointing them out in the real-world sky is really exciting to kids.

Check out Izzy's Skylog at http://darkstar.swsc.k12.ar.us/~izzy/ *to see constellations and learn about the stars. You can find a link to astronomy software on this site, too.*

An e-Parent always looks for and recognizes opportunities to enhance parenting activities by combining e-World and real-world experiences.

Summing Up

We hope you have enjoyed the final chapter of *Sams Teach Yourself e-Parenting Today,* and that you have recognized that family traditions can actually help us accomplish all three basics of e-Parenting! Traditions help us do the following:

- Show an interest in our children

- Provide guidance that tells them what we believe and what we think they should know

- Have fun together

In this chapter, we have blended the old and new, shown ways to reinvent and enhance family traditions with the PC and Net, and asked you to cherish traditions with your children. Kids need new ideas, but they also need some things that stay the same.

Please remember, too, that kids need support systems and traditions that involve members of *all* of their extended families, including those from other marriages.

We hope you have enjoyed our book and that you will find the appendixes useful. We'll see you on the Internet at *www.askevelyn.com* and at other good e-Parenting sites.

APPENDIX A

A Brief Guide to Child Development

Authors' Note

All children grow and develop at their own pace. The indicators listed for each age group are based on national averages for most children. It is more important to note the sequence of events or milestones of growth in each area (physical, intellectual, social, and emotional) than the exact age at which the milestone occurs.

All skills are learned bit by bit, in sequence. For example, a child learns to play with blocks in a natural sequence of small events. First, as infants or toddlers, they handle (and probably taste) the blocks. Then they put them in a container and take them out. Next, they carry blocks around or lay them flat on the floor, or stack a few. Later they will "bridge" three blocks and set them in a pattern to enclose a space. Still later, by the time they are 4 or 5, they will build taller structures, repeat patterns, and eventually plan and name their buildings.

Growth sequences like this can be seen in each area of the charts (for example, the progression of sit, crawl, stand, walk, run, jump, and hop). If a child is continuing to follow the sequences in each area of the chart, he or she is developing normally. Relax and enjoy each small miracle!

Warning Signals of Possible Problems

There are some simple warning signs that can indicate a possible problem. Problems are easier to solve if they are found early. If you see more than one of these warning signs in your young child, make an appointment with your pediatrician for direction and assistance.

3 months

- No weight gain—Does not smile; cries most of time
- Does not look at things or respond to sounds

9 months

- Not sitting up with support
- Not holding head up
- Not making sounds

1 year

- Not pulling self up to stand
- Not trying to help self
- Not tripled birth weight

18 months

- Not walking
- Not saying words

2 years

- Not running
- Not putting words together

3 years

- Not able to stand on one foot
- Not able to alternate feet while climbing steps

Thumbnail Sketch of the Preschool Years

Before we look at the checklist profiles for each age within the 2- to 6-year-old category, let's just walk through what these years are like. Here is a thumbnail sketch of the years from infancy through age 5.

Development researchers agree that, at each stage of growth, the child has particular goals to accomplish. Sometimes the child's goals—whether conscious or subconscious—mesh well with the parents' goals. Sometimes they do not. This is why occasional conflicts between parents and children are a normal and natural part of the child's growth and of parenting.

Infancy is one of the most amazing periods of human growth! In just two short years, the child changes from a helpless, dependent, demanding and noisy, damp bundle into a walking, talking individual who persistently expresses a personality and will of his or her own.

During infancy and toddlerhood, one of the child's goals is the security of having his or her physical needs met. More than that, the infant or toddler is trying to establish a sense of trust—in spite of the fact that he or she is totally dependent and helpless. This trust in the surroundings and trust in the caregivers or significant others around the child will be the foundation of his or her self-esteem.

What Are Infants Like?

In addition to the obvious goal of the parents to adjust to a new person in their lives, get enough rest, and incorporate new changes in their daily schedules, parents are concerned about the physical and emotional needs of the infant. Parents of infants and toddlers usually ask questions about the child's health and growth, safety, and the needs for immunizations, food, rest, stimulation, and security.

As soon as the child begins to respond and interact, parents begin to be able to interpret what the child tells them with facial expression, body languages, crying, and cooing. It's quite normal for parents to ask about the baby's alertness and how they can stimulate the baby's intelligence. The best stimulation is the parents' own attention, including voice, face, and body language.

What Is a Toddler Like?

As the infant becomes a curious and mobile toddler, parents discover that there is an even greater need for safety-proofing the home. Parents ask questions about physical skills and coordination, as well as questions about finding toys or activities to keep the child safely occupied and interested in appropriate things to look at and handle.

Parents often wonder why toddlers between age 1 and 2 develop fears of strangers or particular adults, or why their children imitate adults and repeat actions that get attention. The reason is that this age group is increasingly conscious of adults and adult reactions. During this time of first steps and first words, the toddler also expresses a wide range of emotions, sometimes has tantrums, and begins to want to do things for himself or herself.

The two-year-old poses new kinds of problems. In addition to being extremely curious, mobile, and sensory in experimenting with everything around them, two-year-olds are beginning to understand being "persons" in their own right—separate from their parents. Their emerging sense of individual identity makes two-year-olds highly aware of "me" and "mine." They test their parents to see what reaction they will get and how much control they really have. This new assertiveness is normal, healthy, and basically temporary, even though temper tantrums and conflicts at mealtime, during dressing, and at bedtime are common.

As parents try to be patient, keep their tempers, and stay in control, they ask many questions about these daily power struggles. They wonder about bottle breaking, security objects, tantrums, and toilet training. They begin to have more questions about the child's reactions to themselves and others—children, relatives, and sitters. They have more questions about childcare; parents should observe potential child care centers carefully and ask many questions. Being firm, "very positive," and very diplomatic is the best way to cope with two-year-olds who are trying hard to establish their identities.

What Are Three-Year-Olds Like?

Three-year-olds are more relaxed, more cooperative, and very eager to please adults. They're more verbal and social and more interested in other children. However, their world still revolves around their home and their own family where they feel more secure. Three-year-olds begin to express their ideas and identities; they practice their language and use their imaginations. They still explore the world with their senses; they pretend, and they often have imaginary friends. They like to do things for themselves; if parents can be patient while three-year-olds dawdle, parents will find that the children really are capable of many things…they can help themselves and help out in small ways at home.

Parents wonder why their loving three-year-olds may still have tantrums at the store, or why they are so extremely jealous of new babies, other people, and telephones. These behaviors are normal.

Three-year-olds do not like changes in routines! They don't like changes at all, unless they are reassured and prepared for them. The security of daily routines and rituals is important to them. Meanwhile, parents sometimes worry about fairly normal things for this age, such as thumb-sucking, bed-wetting, developing language, and discipline. Parents become concerned about safety, social behavior, and intellectual development. The most important thing parents of threes need to know is that three-year-olds are concerned about feeling loved by their parents or caregivers and being proud of their growing accomplishments.

If parents want to begin to set patterns about using the PC with threes, they should occasionally hold children on their laps at the PC and do simple point-and-click games that are fun ways to show cause and effect.

What Are Four-Year-Olds Like?

Although the three-year-old may have been fairly relaxing for parents to live with, four-year-olds probably are not! Four-year-olds seem to be in a constant state of motion, eager for new experiences of any kind! They are very active and very verbal; this is the age of constant questions! It's an age of hands-on experimenting and learning about the give-and-take of friendship and cooperative play. Fours are workaholics about play. They also make messes as they play, and get grouchy when they are overtired. Parents often worry about hyperactivity at this age.

Fours insist on doing everything themselves, are often boastful about what they can do, and often bite off more than they can chew. They love to pretend and role play, but are still unsure of the difference between reality and fantasy. They're extremely friendly and outgoing with adults and are interested in everything adults do—which often causes parents to worry about their safety and about strangers.

If parents are trying to start setting patterns of PC and Net use, they should always be with the child whenever he or she uses the computer and software or safe web sites where the parents have taken the child. Remember that their attention span is short and that there is a great need for active play; keep it simple and short.

Parents ask questions about four-year-olds' very normal interest in their bodies and their sex; they worry (quite unnecessarily) about boys who play dress up. They ask questions about kindergarten readiness, about discipline, about helping out at home, and about the new fears that fours develop as they learn more about the real world. Pediatricians, extended family, Net resources, and books can all help ease these fears and provide information.

Fours also love name-calling, "naughty" words, silly jokes, and tattling. They frequently test their parents in a battle of wills in public places. Parents find that fours can be embarrassing and exasperating, but they are always exciting and interesting!

What Are Five-Year-Olds Like?

Five-year-olds are more likely to tell you they are 5 before they tell you their names! They are excited about new experiences such as school, but are also very vulnerable, needing reassurance and support to face these new experiences. Calmer, more confident, and more cooperative than at age 4, fives want to be liked by others and thrive on adult praise. Although they are very practical and industrious little people, fives also love fun and jokes. They love to learn, and they love to laugh, but they hate to be embarrassed or wrong. They are beginning to like rules, especially if the rules are for other people. They still tattle. Generally, however, fives have good self-control and can understand and follow through on adult expectations.

Parents will find that fives are cooperative about PC and Net rules for use. Fives will enjoy simple games and safe children's sites in the company of parents. They will be able to work on their own for short periods if parents are close by.

It's normal for parents of fives to ask questions about their child's learning, or how they can get along better with friends, or their school progress. Good communication with teachers and caregivers, as well as common sense (don't overreact and don't overschedule the child) will resolve these concerns. Parents will want to continue to teach personal safety and good health habits. Parents may notice that some fives whine or interrupt, which is attention-getting behavior; give attention for the behaviors you want children to repeat. Fives can clean up their rooms, but they still need adult help to organize this process.

By the time he or she reaches age five, the child has developed a sense of trust (or sometimes, mistrust) about the world, as well as a sense of his or her own identity. By the early school years, the child also has developed a drive to express his or her own initiative and a sense of industry and accomplishment. Self-concept is growing, based on feeling both capable and lovable.

What are Six- and Seven-Year-Olds Like? A Look Ahead...

During the early school years, parents sometimes believe that they don't need to do much listening or praising because the child appears to be so confident and independent. The truth is that this age group is actually very vulnerable and still needs reinforcement, reassurance, hugging, and attention.

The fact that six- to eight-year-olds still need attention is obvious when you look at many of their behaviors. It's quite normal to hear parents asking questions about why their children act out by interrupting, whining, having school problems, fighting with friends or siblings, telling "tall tales," maintaining continually messy rooms, and being naughty on family trips. Sometimes parents focus on these very normal problems and forget that the need for "quality time" and attention is still very important during these formative years. Children this age not only need clear, firm guidelines for their behavior, they need adult attention, praise, and support.

They also need to be involved as team members of the family. They are capable of helping at home and are capable at expressing ideas, feelings, and input that can be very valuable during family discussions. They love family games, and although they develop many life skills through playing them, the greatest benefit is the sense of belonging and "connectedness" that children get when they play games with their parents.

This age group is increasingly interested in the PC and Net; parents should consider restricting access to only those sites they have visited and feel are appropriate. Parents can also make use of prescreened "safe" sites and child-safe search engines. Some parents may want to investigate a "kids desktop." The most important thing to do is continue to work with your child whenever he or she uses the PC and Net.

Talk with your child about the sites you visit and why these are good sites. Be sure that children have positive experiences with sites that are easy to navigate, and be sure that they don't sit too long. Active play is still important to physical development.

Children at any age are miraculous and fascinating to observe; they are lovable, interesting, and challenging. What we need to keep in mind is what research has already proven. The things we do—the ways we interact with children from infancy to about age 8—have the greatest impact on the kinds of persons they will become!

Profiles

Now let's look at the profile checklists for each of the preschool age groups.

Profile: Infant to 6 Months

Physical

- Grasps objects, rattles, or hair

- Wiggles and kicks

- Turns toward bright lights or sounds

- Rolls over

- Reaches for objects

- Sits with support

Intellectual

- Knows that crying will bring attention

- Carries hand to mouth

- Watches and listens to surroundings and people

- Enjoys splashing in bath with supervision

Social

- Coos and smiles; recognizes familiar faces

- Responds to familiar voices and sounds

- Babbles at adults; enjoys people talking to him or her

- Babbles to self, laughs

Emotional

- Expresses emotions: anger, fear, hunger, joy, sadness

- Holds out arms or legs to assist in being dressed

- Wants to feed self with finger foods

Profile: 6 Months to 1 Year
Physical

- Follows moving object with eyes; sits alone; crawls

- Pulls self to standing

- Transfers objects one hand to another, and rolls ball to imitate adult

- Drops and picks up objects

- Walks around furniture, using it for balance

Intellectual

- Amuses self for short periods

- Drops things to observe what happens

- Observes people and surroundings carefully

- Attempts to imitate sounds

- Responds to body language, gestures, and simple words (such as *stop*, *hi*, and *bye*)

- Puts things in container and takes them out

Social

- Smiles and laughs; babbles and squeals

- Cries when interrupted from play

- Plays pat-a-cake and peek-a-boo; imitates adults

- Responds differently to familiar people and to strangers

- Responds to *No*

Emotional

- Drinks from a cup

- Begins to use spoon

- Pays attention to own name

- Feeds self finger foods

- Knows own name and responds to it

Profile: Ages 1 and 2

Physical

- Can stand alone for brief period

- Climbs as much as possible

- Learns to walk alone—forward and backward

- Pulls and pushes toys; moves to music

- Lacks depth perception; runs clumsily, often falls

- Begins to turn book pages

- Scribbles; likes painting

- Throws ball and turns knobs

Intellectual

- Very curious; explores, pokes, tastes, probes, opens things

- Does not understand danger; explores with all senses; loves water play

- Learns by trial and error and by experimenting

- Points to objects named by adult

- Builds tower with 2 or 3 blocks; puts rings on stick

- Says first words; vocabulary grows; begins naming body parts and objects

- Initiates own play; very short attention span

Social

- Recognizes "no-no"

- Imitates adults and repeats actions that get a response

- Imitates adults in his or her play; plays alone

- Helps put things away

- Responds to simple directions and questions

- Can find self in picture of small group; names familiar people

- Learns *please* and *thank you*

- Understands rituals such as *hello* and *good-bye*

Emotional

- Continues to show wide range of emotions

- Reacts to emotions of adults; may have tantrums

- Impulsive; moves quickly; rapid shifts of attention

- Thinks world revolves around self; loves mirrors

- Awareness of ownership; refers to self by name; uses "mine"

- Learns to feed self and remove clothing; may indicate toilet needs

Profile: Ages 2 and 3
Physical

- Scribbles

- Much body activity and climbing

- Walks, runs, falls easily, jumps, rolls

- Needs help in dressing; dawdles

- Begins to toilet self (frequent accidents)

- Drinks from a cup; uses spoon (many spills)

Intellectual

- Uses 2-to-3-word sentences; usually hard to understand

- Very curious; likes to examine and explore with all senses

- Good observer, listener; understands more than is communicated

- Interested in books; turns several pages at once

- Names familiar objects, people, and pictures; can associate functions of familiar objects

Social

- Often watches other children but plays alone

- Little interest in peers; hits, pushes, grabs

- Is very possessive

- Begins to "play house" or pretend

- Watches and copies family and caregivers' modeling

Emotional

- Suspicious of new situations

- Power struggles and tantrums are common

- Needs security of consistency in routines and guidance

- Shows independence of spirit

- Loves praise

Profile: Ages 3 and 4
Physical

- Helps dress and undress self fairly well

- Toilets self; accidents still common

- Climbs steps alternating feet

- Runs well; pulls, pushes, or steers wheel toys; jumps

- Throws, catches; begins to be able to balance on one foot; can hop and walk balance beam or line

- Can do simple puzzles and stack blocks or rings

- Enjoys using dough, clay, paint, and so on; moves with music

Intellectual

- Listens to and repeats stories, rhymes, songs

- Talks in simple sentences; can be understood

- Knows age and name; talks a lot

- Begins to recognize (match) colors and tells about own "art work" after it's done

- Begins to ask questions and make associations

- Understands "today" and often "tomorrow," but lives in the *now*

- Learns through hands-on activity and the senses

- Can sit on adult's lap at PC and begin to use mouse to see cause and effect

Social

- Plays well with 1 or 2 peers sometimes, and participates in group activity for short times

- Learning to tell own wants or needs with words to others

- Plays with same toys as others in a small group: sometimes will take turns or share

- Watches and copies adult modeling; begins to show sympathy

- Pretends; plays house or imitates family; notices sex differences

- Enjoys own birthday and simple celebrations, especially at own home

Emotional

- Still fears new things; likes rituals and consistent routines

- Wants to please; generally cooperative with adults

- Can become jealous and revert to babyhood for attention

- Wants to try to do things independently (self-care)

- Thrives on praise, hugs, and positive reinforcement

- Sense of pride in accomplishments

Profile: Ages 4 and 5
Physical

- Handles blunt scissors and simple tools safely with adult guidance

- Very active; uses slides, climbers, tunnels, and balance beams in many ways

- Hops, gallops, begins learning to skip; pumps swing

- Toilets self; washes self; helps clean up toys; helps with "jobs"

- Enjoys using variety of open-ended art media, and creative movement to music (all kinds)

- "Workaholic" about learning through play; often becomes over tired

Intellectual

- Talks a lot; compound sentences and increased vocabulary; the "age of questions"

- Loves to experiment; wants to know how and why; learns by doing and can tell others his or her observations; can play simple computer software games with parents

- Likes books, stories, and acting them out; can make up own stories, songs, and "jokes"

- Designs and constructs; uses original ideas with art and blocks

- Still confused about "real" or "pretend"; understands yesterday, today, and tomorrow

- Can match and sort; makes many associations; enjoys nature and cooking activities

Social

- Enjoys peers, makes "friends," and plays cooperatively; often plays or builds with a purpose and delegates roles; interested in the world outside the family

- Can share and take turns, but sometimes teases or calls names

- Enjoys participating as member of group; enjoys "jobs" and holidays

- Enjoys imitating adults and using positive social language and manners (copies "bad" words, too)

- Empathy, sensitivity, and conscience start to develop

Emotional

- Fours show many emotions, most of them loudly

- Fours can separate from parents fairly easily for child care

- Fours are impatient, change moods often, and test limits; fives are more even tempered and cooperative

- Fours want to be more independent then they are able and still resist unpredictable changes; fives can accept change more easily and are comfortably independent

- Fours still need lots of praise and reassurance; fives do less "showing off" and begin to have a comfortable sense of who they are and what they are able to do

The School-Age Child (Ages 6 through 12)

The school-age years are a period of unusual growth and change for children. Children continue to soak up an enormous amount of information and now begin to use it to develop very individual and unique personalities.

Developmental Information

Great physical changes begin to occur. The child moves from being an egocentric being to a person able to observe and accept the view of others. Children begin these years by learning through concrete, hands-on experiences and end this period beginning to be able to do abstract thinking and conceptualizing.

Parents are often unaware of the complex growing that children are doing during the school-age years. These are usually years in which both parents become part of the work force, increase their socializing, and develop hobbies and interests they had put aside while the children were younger. Unfortunately, many of the problems that occur in the teen years begin in the school-age years. It is vital that parents remain highly aware of their children's need for input, attention, praise, and guidance during these years.

Think of school-age children as your perennials. They may continue to grow every year in the garden of your family, but even perennials need care and nourishment. Especially during these growing years, when you may take them for granted and believe they're just fine, they can become sickly or grow wildly out of control. You still need to keep out the weeds, trim them up as necessary, and give them the basic nutrients and fertilizers of good e-Parenting.

Prevention of problems in the later years will be more probable if parents understand the ways children of age 6 to 12 are developing mentally, physically, emotionally, and socially. Listening and talking with your kids, noticing when they may have problems, and getting kids to talk about them (even when they don't always voluntarily share them) is very important.

In addition, remember that there are things you, as a parent, should be sure to tell them during these years. Talk and listen more, not less. Tell them how you feel about drugs or smoking or sexuality. Tell them what you believe and value. Sometimes what you do *not* say to kids can hurt them.

Playing family games is highly important at these ages, not only because kids love them and practice many life skills through games, but also because of the sense of belonging and connectedness that playing games gives to children. Family games also help cement your child's relationship with you; making sure that your parent-child relationship is strong in these years before adolescence is very important.

Kids between the ages of 7 and 10 begin looking outside the family for friendships and information, so be sure that your kids' friends are welcome in your home any time. You want your child to continue to see you as both a parent and a friend they can trust. Having their trust can prevent peer-pressure problems.

These are also important years in terms of the child's use of the PC and Net. Patterns you have put in place must remain consistent. Continue to use these tools with your children, or be nearby whenever they use them. Be sure that the computer is placed in the den, family room, or a place where it is completely accessible to everyone. Play games with your child, visit sites, and talk about your child's online activities.

As you will see in the profiles, children in this age group are quite capable of comparing Web sites and doing critical thinking about them. They like gathering information and will understand why it is important to gather it from several sources. Demonstrate the advantages of this.

Many parents of this age group restrict children to Web sites they have visited and approved or may use a filtering program, a child-safe search engine, a child-friendly browser, or even a "kids desktop." Kids this age fully understand the need for rules, and they can both follow rules and help develop consequences for forgetting or breaking a rule.

Encourage this age group to have many other interests in addition to the PC and Net. They need active play, fresh air, hobbies, sports, and groups such as scouts and 4H. The Net may lead them to new interests or find them some resources for interests they already have. Be sure that they have a good balance of varied activities daily, but do this without over scheduling them. Continue that practice into the next several years.

From ages 10 to 12, many kids will want more independence. You will need to help them manage that independence. Set limits or parameters within which they can have freedoms, and be sure that all freedoms come with responsibilities. For example, if they are able to join a club or chat online, they may need to do the interacting when you are nearby. If they have an online pen pal, they will share the correspondence with you. Set limits for how long kids can be online and make rules about having other jobs done before using the computer. Let them find ways the Net can help them do homework and research, but have them continue to share information with you. Show a genuine interest and praise them for gathering information from more than one source.

Children from 10 to 12 are beginning to use their abstract reasoning skills. They can understand the need to check information, and they understand the concept of credibility. Discussions with parents will help them find ways to check out things and discover what is true and what is exaggeration.

If children this age experiment and make mistakes, be sure that you do not overreact, and that you praise them for telling you about the mistake. Decide together what the consequences should be, and plan ways the child can avoid making the same mistake again. Working with preteens as you guide them is the best way to keep their trust and respect.

Profiles

Now let's look at the profile checklists for school-age children. Each child will grow in all these areas at his or her own pace. However, the following "milestones" are generally accepted in the fields of health, human development, and education as "normal" expectations for growth in school-age children.

Profile: The Six-Year-Old
Physical

- Bursts with energy, always on the go, overtires easily
- Loses baby teeth, molars erupt

- Can skip, hop, ride a bike easily, tie shoes, jump rope

- Growth slackens at 6; needs 11 to 12 hours sleep a night

- Boisterous, likes to wrestle but doesn't know when to stop

- Demonstrates more activity than actual accomplishment

- Is awkward at some fine-motor tasks but very interested in manipulating

- Is self-conscious about work being done, often tries too hard

Mental

- Likes to work, especially likes to begin something new, but often gets confused and needs help and praise to finish

- Not ready for purely formal abstract instruction in reading, writing, and mathematics

- Works best through creative activity, life experiences, and hands-on learning

- Interested in reading; likes to recognize words and enjoys printing letters

- Span of concentration is still short

- May create stories or drawings at the PC

Emotional

- Not moderate; does nothing by halves; demonstrates much emotional intensity

- Wants to cooperate but at times wants own way and is often bossy

- Success and a sense of achievement are of utmost importance

- Always wants to win and be first; begins to like rules, especially for others

- Needs to feel loved; wants much attention

- Feels guilt about own negative feelings

- Jealous of anyone becoming between him or her and mother

- Unable to easily consider compromises

- Takes criticism badly; thrives on praise; is possessive

- Lives intensely in the present and may worry about problems in the family

- Begins to understand and accept reality

- Dramatic play and block play helps organize thoughts and feelings

- Has an inner self, which he or she keeps secret and in which grievances are hidden

- Has nightmares about wild animals, darkness, fire, thunder, monsters, lightning, and so on

Social

- Can play with one playmate best; inconsistent with relationships

- May find it hard to fit into the group; daydreaming is common

- Likes social routines that provide a senses of security; plays with both sexes, though beginning to prefer same gender

- Needs guidance in deciding what to do in school but often responds slowly and negatively to direct demands; very sensitive to criticism

- Cannot distinguish between good and bad clearly; still needs much practice in critical-thinking skills

Profile: The Seven-Year-Old
Physical

- Activities come in spurts; generally calmer than at age 6

- Must constantly be manipulating things

- Physical skills are imperfect and inconsistent

- If pushed into physical activity before he or she is ready, may become stubborn and may never try again; organized sports may cause undue stress

- Needs balance of rest and activity

Mental

- Good understanding of time; "easy" to teach

- Makes generalizations (sometimes incorrect) based on own observations

- Has an almost scientific interest in causes of things

- Becomes absorbed in classroom work; likes to debate

- Able to concentrate harder

- Logic and reasoning still based on personal and real hands-on experiences

Emotional

- Often calm and self-absorbed; resents intrusions on thoughts

- More inhibited, more controlled, and more aware of others

- Gets angry with self if cannot do something

- Often lacks confidence; withdraws from new or unsure situations

- Very sensitive to being laughed at; ashamed of fears

- Has difficulty starting something but once started, becomes over persistent

- Assumes responsibility and takes it seriously

- If under too much pressure, may exhibit regressive behaviors

Social

- Begins to be more detached from mother; forms peer friendships

- Enjoys "clubs" and buddies; may try to "buy" friendships

- Learning laws of group living; very loyal to group

- Sensitive to attitudes of others

- Begins to discriminate between good and bad in others and self

- Tries to settle question of authority; "who is boss"

- More companionable; likes to do things for adults; is a very good helper if tasks are not solitary or too hard

- Becomes very fond of teachers

Profile: The Eight-Year-Old
Physical

- Looks more mature; seeing and hearing should be very well developed; eye exams are very important

- Nervous habits are common in children under pressure or trauma

- Athletic games and skills are of high interest, but child is often a poor loser

- Wants to excel in skills and works at it

- Loves computer and video games

Mental

- Books have meaning; reads for pleasure and for information

- Can obtain information both directly and indirectly

- Continues many avenues of active curiosity; loves hands-on learning activities

- Beginning to have historic perspective of self and behavior

- Interests are often short lived; shifts from one thing to the next, but is very creative

- Enjoys school; has good attendance; enters with enthusiasm

- Is interested in babies, origins of life, marriage and reproduction (especially own birth)

- Begins to see fundamental differences between the impersonal forces of nature and the psychological forces of man

- Growing conscious of own cultural or ethnic status and heritage

- Impatient; wants to get things done fast; does not enjoy long demonstrations

Emotional

- Susceptible to jealousy and still can be easily hurt

- Begins to doubt the infallibility of parents and adults in general

- Sensitive to criticism, whether actual or implied

- Does not like to be criticized about shortcomings, even humorously

- Self-conscious; may feel impelled to assert scorn of demonstrative affection when around peers

- Begins to desire to stand alone and judge for own self, to "be somebody"

- Does everything in "high gear"; courage and dare are characteristics

Social

- Has accepted parents' prejudices and attitudes towards others

- Feels more at home with adults and talks with them freely; likes to ask riddles they cannot answer

- Shows strong admiration for parents in words and actions; hero worship begins

- Discovers teacher can be a friend; likes teacher involvement and feedback

- Conscious of belonging to his or her school group; understands responsibility to this group

- Likes to work with and to be with other people

- Sees self more clearly as a person participating among other persons

- Wants to be "good"; is aware of good and bad forces; is willing to take consequences but often apt to pass the blame

- Admits wrong doings, but rationalizes the reasons; has aversion to falsehoods; tall tales usually have some truth in them

- Much dickering, bickering in games

- Interest in barter, exchange, and collecting; value is less important than numbers and quantity

- Likes to argue; is aware of other's mistakes; is self-critical

- Exaggerates and uses slapstick humor; gets excited and often interrupts adults

Profile: The Nine-Year-Old
Physical

- Apt to "overdo" and get overtired; still has difficulty calming down; less restless than at age 8

- Sports or athletic games are of high interest, as is television; eye exams are important

- Wants to excel in a skill and works at it; eye-hand coordination is good

- Nervous habits are common, especially in tense or pressured children

- Skillful in computer and video games

Mental

- Self-motivation is a common characteristic; often plans own time

- Persistent and wants to complete what is started

- Wants teacher and peer "feedback"

- Familiar with surprising array of facts, figures, and words

- Still enjoys hands-on learning activities

- Curious about happenings in other parts of the world, in discoveries, inventions, prehistoric animals, science, movies, books, and personalities in the news; loves to gather facts and information

- Wants things that can be quickly demonstrated to peers and adults

- Creative activities like music, painting, or writing may appear, unless child becomes too self-conscious about efforts

- Skills in abstract thinking and reasoning are beginning to grow

Emotional

- Desire to stand alone, to judge for one's self, to be somebody and not merely to take part in someone else's plan

- Growing hero worship; has definite likes and dislikes

- Afraid of failing; worries, but is more able to accept criticism

- May be self-conscious about showing affection but wants it

Social

- Demands little of mother's time; extremely busy in chosen activities

- Wants to be independent of teacher; peers are main social interest

- Great desire to be useful, needed, and to be like an adult

- Much time spent in solitary activities or in sports for "fun"

- Great talker; is factual and open to instruction; is fairly dependable

- Can accept blame but wants it apportioned fairly

Profile: The Ten- to Eleven-Year-Old
Physical

- Beginning of preadolescence; growing interest in sexuality
- Girls more physically mature than boys
- Good coordination and attention span
- Plays and works hard; needs balance of rest and activity and healthy foods
- Physical and eye exams important

Mental

- Often reads independently on variety of topics
- Uses language well as a tool to express feelings and wants
- Mastering many intellectual concepts
- Great interest in how and why things happen or work
- Often enjoys detailed drawings

Emotional

- Self-assured at home; questions parent's ideals and values
- Strong sense of humor; modesty about body increases; sex conscious
- Responds best to suggestion and reasoning rather than to a "dictator" approach
- Begins qualitative "collections" and creative hobbies

Social

- "Gang" or "club" stage is at a peak, as is hero worship
- Likes rituals, codes, and passwords
- Able to be very courteous and cooperative with adults
- Enjoys group projects, sports, outings, camps
- Strong preference for same-sex peers
- Enjoys cards and table games, family games, cooking, and crafts

Profile: The Eleven- to Twelve-Year-Old
Physical

- Very energetic; more "adult" physically; good coordination

- Growth spurt for girls; boys have more physical strength

- Individual differences between sexes is more apparent

- Eruption of permanent teeth is complete except for third molars/wisdom teeth

- Menstruation in girls may begin

- Growing interest in sexuality

Mental

- Able to think about social problems and morals

- Likes reading stories and mysteries

- Able to see other's point of view

- Impressed with own knowledge

- Interested in the whys of health practices

- Understands reproduction and life cycle

- Can conceptualize and do abstract thinking

- Self-critical and reflective; very observant

Emotional

- Intense emotions; has or wants a "best friend"

- Often wants unreasonable freedom and independence; often argues

- May be rebellious about routines

- May appear tense and often has wide mood swings

- Boys begin teasing girls; girls begin flirting with boys

- Needs daily privacy; may need help in relaxation techniques

Social

- Continued hero worship

- Intense group or team loyalty

- Loves to talk with friends on the telephone

- Likes to do errands and earn money

- Likes projects, sports, acting, dancing, and music

What's "Normal"?

As we stated at the beginning of this appendix, these developmental milestones are set into growth *sequences*. If your child is "behind" in some areas and "ahead" in others, that may just be just a normal part of his or her growth and development rate. The *sequence* and the patterns of development are more important than is a particular milestone. The pace of the child's development in each growth area is influenced by many factors such as experiences and personal learning styles. Some growth spurts can and do occur along the way; so do developmental lags. These derivations should be considered a possible problem to be investigated when there are *patterns* of *several* lags in *several* areas over time.

Safety

Safety is a primary concern in the school-age years. Although children 6 to 12 years old have a great deal of unsupervised freedom, they are immature. They are often impulsive and reckless. This is why parents of 6 to 12 year olds must strictly enforce safety concepts and rules.

- Teach safety related to hobbies, crafts, and tools.

- Teach and reinforce bicycle, moped, and traffic safety through age 12.

- Teach safety about "strangers" in the real and online worlds.

- Teach and set good examples regarding harmful drugs, use of alcohol, and smoking.

- Teach and reinforce health habits to prevent illness.

- Stress safety with firearms: remove or keep them under lock and key.

- Teach water safety and supervise swimming activities.

- Know who your children's friends are and monitor friend selection as much as possible.

Tips for Temporary Latch-Key Situations

We hope all e-Parents understand that they are fully and legally responsible for the safety of their minor children. It is always best to find appropriate after-school care for children, whether it be with a trusted relative or friend or with an after-school program. However, if temporary latch-key situations are unavoidable, here are some safety tips to consider when making your plans.

- List all emergency numbers and parent work numbers near the telephone.

- Keep flashlights in working order.

- Develop and practice a fire exit plan.

- Practice telephone safety. Role-play what to do or say if someone calls or knocks at the door.

- Designate several neighbors to call in an emergency.

- Make home as hazard free as possible.

- Lock up or remove firearms from the home.

- Consider a pet for the child if possible.

- Prepare a first-aid kit that can be used by the child.

- Practice for weather-related emergencies.

- Maintain strict rules on cooking.

- Be home on time or call if you will be late.

- Leave tape-recorded messages and notes for child. In any specialty catalog, you can find all kinds of recording devices. Some motion-activated figures will play a recorded message; you can place the device at the back door so that kids get your message as soon as they walk in the door—no more excuses!

- Leave ideas for things to do; include alternatives to television.

- Help child feel successful and appreciated.

- Try to find an after-school program; your child should not be left alone.

Parental Guidance for Television

Television has a powerful impact on children. It is estimated that American children watch 30 to 40 hours of television per week. Increased children's television viewing has precipitated grave concerns about increased aggression, indifference to violence, increased materialism, unrealistic expectations, stereotyped attitudes, and increased escapism. Television decreases the physical activity your children need for health and fitness, can cause eye problems, and does not motivate creativity. When parents and children do not view and discuss television together, communication in the family decreases. Children often form misconceptions about what they see and may form attitudes that differ from parents' values. Parents can obtain information about the ways they can minimize the harmful aspects of television from Action for Children's Television, The National Council for Children and Television, and local PTA or PTO groups.

- Do your own survey. Total the hours of actual TV viewing and then establish limits on viewing per day or week.

- Try not to increase the importance of TV by using it as a reward or punishment.

- Supervise what is watched and set limits on times for viewing.

- Spend time watching TV with your children and discuss your feelings, the characters, and possible alternative story lines.

- Teach children critical thinking about programs and commercials; help them sort out fact and fantasy.

- Encourage alternatives to television such as reading, hobbies, creative activities, games, and active play.

Teenagers (Ages 13 to 17)

The most important thing we can say to parents of teenagers is to "hang in there" during the turbulence that often occurs in the early and middle teen years. Keep showing that you love and support your teen, even when it may appear that the teen is rejecting you or is responding with what looks like indifference. This is a time to "let go" of the child your teenager used to be, and to accept and guide a new young person on the path toward adulthood.

The teenager's drive for freedom and independence is both important and necessary for development into adulthood. To accomplish this sense of individual, independent, young-adult identity, the teenager has to "let go" of the child he or she once was, just as the parent has to let go. This "giving up" of childhood is so hard for teenagers that they feel they must actively reject their childhood and, often, the people they connect with their childhood: their parents.

Teens act out this rejection and assertiveness in a variety of ways. They "hang out" with peers and avoid family activities; they "try on" different roles as they search for their own real identity; they say shocking things to get a response; they wear clothes and hairdos to get a reaction or to present their current "persona"; they argue and debate; they withdraw and evade. All in all, parents can be as confused as teens are about the new person who is evolving in the household.

This is why the best approach for parents of 13- to 17-year-olds is to try to accept these changes as normal, to try hard not to overreact, and to try even harder to stay calm and consistent about the rules and belief systems of the family.

Parents need to take the time, not only to say *no* when it's necessary, but to explain *why* the *no* is in the best long-term interest of the teenager. It helps to look at every debate, every power struggle, as a learning opportunity. Try to look at these times as a challenge to your maturity and patience, not as a challenge to your power as a parent. At the same time, remember that you are still "in charge" when your teen needs firm guidance.

During these years, it's very important for parents to make no assumptions that they "know" their teenager thoroughly. As objectively as possible, parents must observe, accept, and understand the new person the teen is becoming. Take time to listen and talk with teens as they "work out" and make conclusions about their ideas, fears, and feelings. Realize that what teens "conclude" will continually change. Know that no matter what they say, their values are still generally the same as yours.

Obviously, parents know lots more about life than teens do. Don't "rub it in." Instead, provide as much information as possible to teens so that they can make informed, responsible choices. Gradually, teens need to learn to make their own decisions. Give them chances to do so, but also be sure that they always experience the consequences of every one of their choices. This is the only way they will learn that freedom goes hand-in-hand with responsibility, and that every choice has a consequence.

This is particularly true with the teen's use of the PC and Net. The patterns and understandings you put in place in earlier years should still be there. Now the teen can be independent in the use of the Net, but will still need your supervision. (Think of it as drivers' education in a dual-control car.) You still expect your teen to talk with you about online activities, and you still show a genuine interest. You continue to compare and evaluate sites. You continue to ask the teen to get more than one source for information.

Teens are complex. They want guidance and independence at the same time. You need to remember when you were a teen, and try to understand, even though it is frustrating at times.

Teens think they are invincible. Remind them that people online (and offline too) may not be who they seem to be. If they engage in risky behavior and make a mistake, don't overreact; make it a learning experience, and make sure that the teen faces the consequences he or she helped to develop. If the teen confides in you about a mistake or something uncomfortable encountered online, be proud that he or she trusts you; work together to make sure that this does not happen again.

Keep reminding your teens that you believe they can make wise and healthy choices in their best interests. Expect their best.

At times, in order to get the somewhat detached and objective approach you'll need during these few short years, you may find it helpful to pretend that your teenager is an exchange student who is living with you! But remember this: Your teenager needs you, your maturity, your modeling, your patience, your discipline and your love now, as never before! Hang in there. It will be well worth the effort. Your teen will become more than your child; your teen will become a lifelong friend you'll be proud to have.

Most parent-child conflicts occur in the early and middle years (from 13 to 16). Most of these tensions and disagreements are caused by the social and emotional development of children during these years. It is helpful for parents to know what's "normal" and what to expect, socially and emotionally, between the ages of 12 and 17. This is why detailed lists are presented in this appendix for the social and emotional "milestones" of 13-, 14-, 15-, and 16-year-olds.

The physical and intellectual "milestones" of teenagers are so individual and varied that detailed lists will not be presented for these areas. We can summarize the major physical characteristics by saying that puberty and its accompanying physical changes occur generally between the ages of 11 and 15. The age of puberty varies, but is usually two years earlier for girls than for boys. Both sexes experience growth and height spurts. Both sexes mature earlier and grow taller than in past generations. Youngsters need to be reassured that their body changes are normal. Parents should encourage diets and exercise that keeps teens physically fit.

Why Are Kids Developing Faster?

Many development authorities and researchers are studying the phenomena of faster physical maturation in today's children. Most believe this is because of healthier diets and an interest in fitness over the span of the last two generations.

Children's exposure to more information and their highly developed language and communication skills often fool us into believing that children are more mature in all other ways. However, in most cases, the veneer of "maturity" is only physical and verbal or intellectual; it does not extend to the growth areas of social and emotional maturity.

Today's e-Parents should take steps to ensure that they are raising kids who not only look and sound "grown up" but who actually *are* mature and responsible in the social and emotional areas of development.

It is important that teens have a daily balance of restful pastimes and activity, as well as at least 8 hours of sleep. Teach your teens ways to prevent or relieve stress; share techniques and help your teens learn to manage and prioritize their time.

Intellectually, youngsters begin their early teen years (10 to 13) in the stage of concrete, not abstract, thinking. They tend to make broad generalizations based on their limited concrete information and experiences. They make vague and unrealistic plans. During the middle stages of the teen years (14 to 16), they develop and become very interested in their growing abilities to do abstract thinking.

During these years, they often "test" the morals or belief systems of adults and exhibit rigid concepts of their own about right and wrong. In the late teen years (16 to 18), they begin to be able to set specific goals and develop steps to achieve their goals. They are able to do abstract thinking and become more "other" oriented, rather than self-oriented.

They are also just beginning to see that there are many "gray areas" between the black and white of right and wrong.

Social and Emotional Profiles

Remember that these milestones or guidelines are based on research on overall norms for most children. Every child goes through these stages at his or her own pace.

Profile: The 13-Year-Old
Social

- Changes in friendships and peer groups

- Increased use of telephone and gossip

- Teasing and critiquing members of opposite sex

- Increased movie going and use of arcade electronic games

- Often has adult "crushes" (idols, teachers, and so on)

- Interested in chats and clubs

Emotional

- Moody, touchy, sometimes "silly," grouchy

- Anxious about appearance

- Self-critical, introspective

- Self-conscious

- Secretive, reclusive

- Preoccupation with self

- Begins emotional break with parents

Profile: The 14-Year-Old
Social

- Socialization increases on all fronts

- Interest in dances, parties, dates (interaction between sexes)

- Increased use of telephone, particularly by girls

- Interested in social issues, current events

- Enjoys expression of self (oral reports, drama)

- Interest in study of people (psychology, the human body)

- Closely knit cliques among girls

- Loosely knit "gangs" among boys

- Increased interest in sports

Emotional

- Outgoing, enthusiastic

- Improved relations with parents

- Increased sense of humor

- Less anxiety

- Better acceptance of self and own strengths and weaknesses

- Dislike of bragging by others

- More open in sharing feelings

- Can tolerate own failures but hates criticism

- Often makes complex plans about school, clothes, and activities to gain a sense of security

Profile: The 15-Year-Old
Social

- Often appears in a "slump"; apathetic

- More withdrawn, less outgoing

- Boys and girls move in groups

- Dating and double-dating common

- Boys intensely interested in cars

- "Spectator" activities increase

- Critical of teachers, school, parents

- Wants peer acceptance and approval

Emotional

- Begins separation from parents and adults

- Concerned about own future

- Feels sense of loss about childhood

- Hard to "read"; keeps feelings inside

- Resents intrusion of privacy

- Often "guarded," evasive, and uncommunicative

- Interest in self-improvement

- Detachment from family activities

- Wants and needs love and acceptance in spite of apparent indifference

Profile: The 16-Year-Old
Social

- Aware of interpersonal dependencies and reciprocity in relationships; friendships are less superficial

- More sociable and outgoing; socially busy

- More comfortable with using manners and "social graces"

- More relaxed; improved relations with parents, siblings, and adults

- Interest, hobbies, and activities are integrated into life style

- Girls begin to enjoy some boys as "just friends"

- Most boys still see girls as sex objects

- Girls often host "parties"

- Boys more interested in cars and in jobs

- Avid interest in magazines

Emotional

- Begins to be less fearful of future and to set career goals

- New sense of confidence and independence; more relaxed

- Less likely to need to "prove" independence with defiance

- More open about feelings, even with parents or relatives

- Enjoys "big brother/big sister" role

- More receptive to constructive criticism

- Can handle feelings more calmly

- Shares feelings with friends and sometimes with parents

- More accepting of self

APPENDIX B

e-Parenting Web Site Directory

Authors' Note

We want readers to understand that there are thousands of great Web sites on the Net for fun, for information, and for discovery learning. We cannot begin to list them all—nor was that the purpose of this book. Our intent in this appendix is to make it easier for you to find sites you have read about in the chapters, and also to provide a few examples to get you started with your own exploring. Please remember, too, that Web site addresses (also called URLs) frequently change.

Chapter 1: Being an e-Parent

www.aquarium.org	Oregon Coast Aquarium

Chapter 2: Why a PC Can Be More Useful to Families Than a TV

www.tnpc.com	The National Parenting Center
www.netmom.com	Net Mom
www.netfamilynews.com	Net Family News

Chapter 3: Using the PC and Net to Nurture Creative Problem Solving

www.weather.com	The Weather Channel online
www.sln.org	Science Learning Network
www.infosee.com	Infoseek
www.yahoo.com	Yahoo!
www.excite.com	Excite

www.altavista.com	AltaVista
www.powerup.com.au/ *~glen/spider.htm*	Spider Pages
www.mindspring.com/ *~nlgray/ttour/index.htm*	Tarantula Tour
www.cochran.com/theodore/ *beritsbest/*	Berits Best Sites
www.cochran.com/theodore/ *beritsbest/seriousstuff/science/* *index.html*	Berits Best Sites Science Category
www.chem4kids.com and *www.kapili.com*	Chem4kids (part of Kapili Islands)
http://sciencemadesimple.com/ *~science/ck.html*	Science Made Simple
www.zoomdinosaurs.com/ *subjects/dinosaurs/toc.shtml*	Zoom Dinosaurs
http://spaceplace.ipl.nasa.gov/ *spacepl.htm*	The Space Place
www.madsci.org/experiments	The Mad Scientist Network; Edible/Inedible Experiments Archive
www.nj.com/yucky/worm	Worm World; the Yuckiest Site on the Internet
www.smarterkids.com	Smarterkids.com
www.thereviewzone.com	The Review Zone
www.naturalchild.com	Find the Global Children's Art Gallery
www.arts.ufl.edu/art/rt_room/ *@rtroom_doorway.html*	The Art Room
www.askevelyn.com	Ask Evelyn
www.earlychildhood.com	Earlychildhood.com
www.classroomdirect.com	Discount School Supply
www.theideabox.com	Idea Box

www.hasbro.com	Hasbro
www.fgn.com	Family Game Night
www.littlejason.com/lemonade	Lemonade Stand by Jason Mayans
www.thefunplace.com	The F.U.N. Place (Families United on the Net)

Other Recommendations

- *http://www.cochran.com/theodore/beritsbest/seriousstuff/science/index.html*
  Berit's Best Sites—Science. All 10 site entries are great for creative problem solving.

- *www.kids-space.org/hpt*
  Hop Pop Town. Interactive musical games and other fun preschool activities.

- *www.nickjr.com*
  Nick Jr. Lots of thinking games for preschoolers.

- *www.onramp.ca/cankids/*
  Canadian Kids Home Page. Links to hundreds of pages by age or topic; designed to encourage parents and young school-age kids to explore together.

- *http://www2.arkansas.net/~mom/bonnie.html*
  Bonnie's Fun Things to Do on the Computer (and Off). Many creative games and arts/crafts activities. Internal links; quick navigation.

- *www.odyssey.org*
  Odyssey of the Mind. Ideas for creative problem solving and guidance for competing school teams.

- *www.zuzu.org*
  Zuzu. A kids' magazine that exhibits kids' art work, stories, and poems. Encourages original writing about yourself and your activities.

Chapter 4: Using the PC and Net to Nurture Self-Esteem

www.my-kids.com	My-Kids.com
www.custombooksandmore.com	Custom Books and More
www.horsenet.com	Horsenet.com
www.countrybarn.com/pace/ equestrian-search1.dbm	Equestrian World Directory
www.equivision.net	Equivision
www.yahoo.com	Yahoo!

www.getnetwise.com	Get Net Wise
www.cyberangels.com	Cyber Angels
www.purple-moon.com	Purple Moon
www.freezone.com	Free Zone
www.enough.org	Enough is Enough
www.kidscom.com	Kidscom
www.netmom.com	Net-mom
www.safekids.com	Safe Kids
www.liszt.com/news	Liszt Usenet Newsgroup Directory
http://clubs.yahoo.com/ clubs/youngaspiringartists	Young Aspiring Artists Club
http://clubs.yahoo.com/clubs/ aalllyricsclub	Lyrics R Us Club
www.musictherapy.org	American Music Therapy Association
www.courttv.com/choices/ yourturn/stereotype	Your Turn
www.newmoon.org	New Moon
www.chaqueen.com	Jennifer Esperante Gunter
www.widesmiles.org/ useful/serious.html	"Mom We Need To Talk: Serious Issues Facing Children and Teens" at Wide Smiles
www.gogirlmag.com	Go Girl! Magazine
www.parentsoup.com	Parent Soup
www.parentsplace.com	Parents Place
www.tnpc.com	The National Parenting Center
www.drkoop.com	Dr. Koop
www.kidshealth.com	Kids Health
www.amazing-kids.org	Amazing Kids!
www.kidssource.com	Kids Source

Other Recommendations

- *www.girlpower.com*
  Girl Power. A site to encourage and motivate young women toward creative self-expression, specifically through writing.

- *www.webehave.com*
  Site includes advice and products to help parents and teachers with issues such as self-esteem, discipline, and responsibility.

- *www.campfire.org*
  Camp Fire Boys and Girls. Resources for building self-reliance, self-confidence, and self-esteem.

- *www.kids-space.org*
  Kids Space. Creative activities to build self-esteem. Example: Choose some art and make up a story, or choose a story and illustrate it. Provides a wide range of interactive activities for 4- to 12-year-olds.

- *www.sanford-artedventures.com*
  Sanford Art Edventures. Art experiences online for every age.

- *http://library.advanced.org/tq-admin/month.cgi*
  ThinkQuest Library of Entries. Here you can create your own Web site. You can also visit all the wonderful sites created by high school students and younger kids.

- *http://www.kids-space.org*
  International Kids' Space. Be inspired to participate. See the art galleries and music by kids, and the original stories. Also find pen-pals or chats.

Chapter 5: Using the PC and Net to Enhance People Skills

www.iamyourchild.org	I Am Your Child
www.babyhood.com	Babyhood
www.parenttime.com	Parent Time
www.hasbro.com	Hasbro
www.fgn.com	Family Game Night
www.kidscom.com	KidsCom
www.familyplay.com	Crayola Family Play
www.nickjr.com	Nick Jr. (Nickelodeon Online)
www.theideabox.com	The Idea Box
www.randomhouse.com/ seussville/games	Random House; Seussville games page
www.funbrain.com	Funbrain

www.kidsdomain.com	Kids Domain
www.ysn.com/gameroom	Youth Sports Network; Gameroom (note that YSN has merged with MyTeam.Com; the page you actually reach when you type this URL is located at *www.myteam.com/ysnim/ templates/main.jsp?i=new_ ysn.txt*)
www.thefunplace.com	The Fun Place
www.ffn.org	Family Fun Network
www.tnpc.com	The National Parenting Center
www.netmom.com	Net-mom
www.brushstrokes.com/ games/intro038.htm	Enter the Game Zone from this site (*www.mega-soft. com/games/*)
www.links2go.com/ topic/chess_clubs	Links 2 Go; chess clubs
www.Yahooligans.com	Yahooligans
www.ajkids.com	Ask Jeeves for Kids
www.zeeks.com	Zeeks
www.alfy.com	Alfy
www.webwisekids.com	Web Wise Kids
www.getnetwise.com	Get Net Wise
www.safekids.com	Safe Kids
www.kidscom.com	Kidscom
www.kidscom.com/orakc/ Friends/newfriends.html	Kidscom; Graffiti Wall Chat
www.afs.org	American Field Service
www.yfu.org	Youth for Understanding
www.yforum.com	National Forum on People's Differences

www.yahoo.com   Yahoo!

www.altavista.com   AltaVista

Other Recommendations

- *http://kids.library.wisc.edu/*
  The KIDS Report. A resource magazine published by kids K–12 and for kids K–12. Archives. Classrooms across the U.S. contribute.

- *www.inkspot.com/young*
  Young Writers. Activities and advice about writing, and the opportunity to submit and post original work.

- *www.freezone.com*
  Free Zone. Homework help, activities, creative writing opportunities, e-Pals, and supervised chats.

- *www.headbone.com*
  Headbone Zone. Brain teasers, opportunities to solve Web mysteries, riddles, games, and monitored chat rooms.

- *www.kidscom.com/orakc/pwdkeypal.html*
  Kids Com. A good place to find a pen pal; requires parents' permission.

- *www.agirlsworld.com/geri/penpal/index.html*
  A Girl's World Pen Pal Spectacular. A safe way for girls to have pen pals without giving out email addresses.

Chapter 6:Using the PC and Net to Teach Self-Discipline and Responsibility

www.pfmagic.com   Pfmagic's Petz Central

www.altavista.com   AltaVista

www.waltham.com/   The Waltham World of
pets/select/f1.htm   Petcare; select a dog
                                 questionnaire page

www.canismajor.com/   Dog Owner's Guide;
dog/topic1.html#choosing   choosing a breed page

www.howtoloveyourdog.com   How to Love Your Dog

www.storknet.org/articles/sibs.htm   Storknet; articles page

www.hcpl.lib.tx.us   Freeman Memorial Branch of
                                 the Harris County Library in
                                 Houston Texas

www.kids.maine.org   Kids Can Make a Difference

www.areyouintoit.com   4-H site about volunteering

www.mightymedia.com/youth.asp	Mighty Media Network and also Youth in Action Network
www.nwf.org	The National Wildlife Federation
www.savethemanatee.org	Save the Manatee Club
www.arborday.org	The Arbor Day Foundation

Other Recommendations

- *http://gpn.unl.edu/rainbow*
  Reading Rainbow. Kids can submit original writing for contests for all age groups.
- *www.webehave.com*
  Site includes advice and products to help parents and teachers with issues such as self-esteem, discipline, and responsibility.
- *http://kidswriting.miningco.com/*
  Creative Writing for Kids. Lots of links and articles to help kids develop writing skills. Exercises for different grade levels; kids submit and critique each others' work.

Chapter 7: Online Resources for Schooling

www.tnpc.com	The National Parenting Center
www.parentsoup.com	Parent Soup
www.worldvillage.com/wv/ school/html/schoolrev.htm	School House Software Review
www.smartkidssoftware.com	Smart Kids Software
www.edmark.com	Edmark
www.dearparents.com	Dear Parents; sound advice on learning and technology (part of Edmark)
www.childrenssoftware.com	Children's Software Review
www.mindplay.com	Mind Play
www.sunburst.com	Sunburst Communications
www.learningco.com	The Learning Company
www.broderbund.com	Broderbund
www.elibrary.com	The Electric Library

www.ala.org/iconn/kidsconn.html	Kids Connect
www.netmom.com	Net-mom
www.bjpinchbeck.com	B.J. Pinchbeck's Homework Helper
www.mtsu.edu/studskllhsindex.html	Study Skills for Teens
www.npac.syr.edu/textbook/ kidsweb	Kids Web; when you type this URL, you may be "forwarded" to another site (*www.kidsvista.com/index. html*)
www.metalab.unc.edu/ cisco/schoolhouse	The Virtual Schoolhouse
www.funbrain.com	Fun Brain
www.schooltime.com	School Time
www.familyeducation.com	Family Education
www.eb.com	Encyclopedia Britannica
www.comptons.com	Compton's
www.m-w.com	Merriam Webster
www.worldbook.com	World Book
www.nypl.org	New York Public Library
http://ipl.org	Internet Public Library
www.comlab.ox.ac.uk/ archive/other/museums.html	Virtual Library Museum Page
www.whitehouse.gov/WH/ kids/html/home.html	White House for Kids
www.askJeevesforkids.com	Ask Jeeves
www.studyweb.com	Study Web
www.icq.com	ICQ (I Seek You)
www.ed.gov	Department of Education
www.collegenet.com	College NET
www.jayi.com	Fishnet College Guide
www.embark.com	Embark College Guide

www.universities.com	Universities.com
www.testprep.com	SAT Preparation
www.kaplan.com	Kaplan
www.jobprofiles.com	Job Profiles
www.monster.com	Monster.com
www.hslda.com	National Center for Home Education at the Home School Legal Defense Association
http://members.tripod.com/maaja	Home School Resources and Supplies
www.n-h-a.org	Home School Advocacy
www.sound.net/~ejcol/ confer.html	Home School Conferences
http://www.computerage.net/ homeschool/findit/	Curriculum Planning and Resources for Home Schooling
www.homeschooldad.com	Home School Dad
www.athomedad.com	At-Home Dad
www.midnightbeach.com	Midnight Beach
www.hsc.com	Home School
http://learningfreedom.org	Learning Freedom
http://homeschooling. miningcp.com	Home Schooling
www.homeschoolarts.com	Home School Arts
www.dimensional.com/~janf/ homeschoolinfo/html	Home School Information
www.waymarks.com/homeschool	Homeschooling—Who Me?
www.childu.com	K–6 interactive virtual school
www.academyonline.org	Another virtual school
www.netfamilynews.com	Net Family News
www.kaleidoscapes.com/	Kaleidoscapes Home School Networking

www.iser.com/nps.html	Internet Special Education Resources; Special EducationLinks
www.mindplay.com	Mindplay
http://www2.edc.org/ncip/	National Center to Improve Practice in Special Education
www.funtasticlearning.com	Fun and Games for Special Needs Kids
www.dreams.org/index/html	Dreams for Kids Inc.

Other Recommendations

- *www.funschool.com*
  Fun School. Free interactive learning software for kids covering many topics.
- *www.giftedpsychologypress.com*
  Gifted. Articles, resources, and links for parents of gifted children.
- *http://homeschooling.miningco.com*
  Home Schooling. Articles, links, chats, forms, and resources.
- *www.sunsite.berkeley.edu.kidsclick*
  Kids Click. Offers comprehensive homework help by topic with thousands of matching sites selected by librarians.
- *http://whitney.artmuseum.com*
  Whitney Museum of Art. Museum tours.
- *www.ala.com*
  American Library Association. 700 great sites.

Chapter 8: Online Resources for Parenting

www.askevelyn.com	Ask Evelyn.com
www.parentsplace.com	Parents' Place
www.tnpc.com	The National Parenting Center
www.earlychildhood.com	Early Childhood.com
www.women.com	Women.com
www.quick.org.uk	Health Education Authority; London
www.nmchc.org	The National Maternal and Child Health Clearinghouse

www.babycenter.com	Baby Center.com
www.babyhood.com	Babyhood.com
www.totalbabycare.com	Pampers Parenting Institute
www.parenttime.com	Parent Time
www.escore.com	eScore, (formerly Parent Partners at *www.parentpartners.com)*
www.naeyc.org	The National Association for the Education of Young Children
http://ericeece.org	The ERIC Clearinghouse on Elementary and Early Education
www.iamyourchild.org	I Am Your Child
www.kidsource.com	Kidsource Online
www.parenthoodweb.com	Parenthood Web
www.parentsoup.com	Parent Soup
www.kidshealth.org	Kids Health
www.virtuescalendar.com	Virtues Calendar
www.lycos.com	Lycos
www.gcccd.cc.ca.us/ grossmont/internet_guides/ newsgroups.html	Usenet Newsgroups through Netscape
www.primocomputers.com/ public/learn/23nwsgrp.htm	All About Newsgroups
www.jameswindell.com	Effective Parenting with James Windell
www.ablelink.org	Ability Online Support Network
www.chadd.org	Children and Adults with Attention Deficit/ Hyperactivity Disorder

www.nichy.org	The National Information Center for Children and Youth with Disabilities
www.dssc.org	Disabilities Studies and Service Center
www.eparent.com	*Exceptional Parent* magazine
www.ldonline.org	Learning Disabilities Online
www.interdys.org	The International Dyslexia Association
www.DrKoop.com	Dr. Koop
www.families.com	Families.com
www.go.com	Go network
www.blendedfamily.com/ blendedfamily/blendring.html	Blended Families
www.grandsplace.com	Grands Place
www.daddyshome.com	Daddy's Home
www.athomedad.com	At-Home Dad
www.fathers.com	The National Center for Fathering
www.divorceonline.com	Divorce Online
www.aap.org	American Academy of Pediatrics Online
www.healthfinder.com	Healthfinder (U.S. Dept. Health and Human Services)
www.excite.com	Excite
www.drgreene.com	Dr. Greene's House Calls
www.kidsdoctor.com	Kids Doctor

Other Recommendations

- *www.thecybermom.com/chat.html*
  Cyber Mom. Parent chat forums on a wide variety of topics.
- *www.parenting-qa.com/*
  Parenting Q & A. Very credible resources and parent advice.

continues

continued

- *www.parentingteens.com*
  Parenting Today's Teen. Resources and support on a wide range of topics.
- *www.talkingwithkids.org*
  Talking With Kids. Great resources and forums to help parents talk to kids about tough issues such as drugs, sex, and so on.
- *www.webehave.com*
  Site includes advice and products to help parents and teachers with issues such as self-esteem, discipline, and responsibility.

Chapter 9: Internet Safety for Online Kids

www.childrenspartnership.org	The Children's Partnership
www.getnetwise.com	GetNetWise
www.familyeducation.com	Family Education
www.larrysworld.com	Larry's World (Larry Magid)
www.netparents.com	Net Parents
www.kidsonline.org	Kids Online
www.americalinksup.org	America Links Up
www.eff.org	Electronic Frontier Foundation
www.filteringfacts.org	The National Law Center
www.aclu.org	American Civil Liberties Union
www.enough.org	Enough Is Enough
www.safesurf.com	SafeSurf
www.safetyed.com	Safety Education
www.webwisekids.com	Web Wise Kids
www.research.att.com	AT&T Research
www.netfamilynews.org	Net Family News
www.netmom.com	Net-mom; Jean Armour Polly
www.ala.com	American Library Association
www.childrenspartnership.org	The Children's Partnership Online

www.cyberangels.com	Cyber Angels
www.safekids.com	Safe Kids
www.pearlsw.com	Pearl Software
www.safeteens.com	Safe Teens
www.family.go.com	Family.Com Home Page (Disney)

Other Recommendations

- *www.freezone.com*
  Free Zone. Homework help, original writing, e-Pals, and supervised chats.
- *http://greenroomonline.com*
  Green Room Online. For older kids and teens; chat and meet celebrities.
- *http://sunsite.berkeley.edu/kidsclick/*
  Kids Click. A Web search engine for kids by librarians; links to many resources.
- *www.headbone.com*
  Headbone Zone. Great brainteasers, riddles, and mystery activities; monitored chat rooms.
- *www.kidscom.com*
  Kids Com. A safe electronic playground.

Chapter 10: Saving Family Traditions in New Ways

www.hgtv.com	House and Garden TV
www.Lowes.com	Lowe's Home Improvement
www.homefurnish.com	Home Furnishing Netquarters
www.living.com	Living.com
www.toreadors.com/martha/index.html	Gothic Martha Stewart
www.familyplay.com	Crayola's Family Play
www.palaver.com/mountainmist/welcome.htm	Mountain Mist quilts
www.cranstonvillage.com/visitor/visitors.htm	Cranston Village; the Quilt Corner
http://www.sostre.com/beginnersquilts.htm	Quilting for Beginners

www.quiltmaker.com	Quiltmaker
www.urbancow.com	The Urban Cow
www.hallmark.com	Hallmark Cards
www.americangreetings.com	American Greetings
www.eonline.com/Fun/Cards	E! online; card section
www.warnerbrothers.com	Warner Brothers
www.pacprod.com/card/htm	Pacific Products; cards
www.igive.com	The I Give Mall
www.cnet.com	Cnet
www.familyfunvacations.com	Family Fun Vacations
www.kodak.com	Kodak
www.telepath.com/bcarson/ *scrap_happy/index1.html*	Scraphappy
www.shoptlc.com	The Learning Company
www.escore.com	Escore.com
www.familytreemaker.com	Family Tree Maker
www.broderbund.com	Broderbund
www.myfamily.com	My Family
www.familygamenight.com	Family Game Night
http://darkstar.swsc.k12.ar.us/ *~izzy/*	Izzy's Skylog

Other Recommendations

- *http://family.go.com/categories/activites*
  Disney site for families. Traditional crafts, recipes, and projects.
- *http://family.go.com/categories/travel*
  Travel advice and destinations for families.
- *www.xe.net/currency*
  Here you'll find rates of exchange for your money in any country.
- *www.ctw.org*
  The Children's Television Workshop—Family Workshop. Articles, activities, and traditions enhanced by Sesame Street characters.

INDEX

Symbols

4-H Web site, 128
8 Weeks to a Well-Behaved Child
class, 174

A

abandoned animals, 123
abducted children, statistics, 198
Ability Online Support Network Web
site, 176
abstract skills
  reasoning , 250
  thinking, 11
Academy Online Web site, 154
accepting
  responsibility, 12, 112, 118, 120
  teenagers, 263, 266
access
  global, 185
  Internet, 188-189
accessing, information, 11
  libraries, 143
achievement, personal, 77
acquiring skills, children, 10
active learning, 39
activities
  balancing, 250
  hands-on, process thinking, 43
  newsgroups, 173
  physical, 144, 262
addressing behavior problems, 116
ADHD (Attention Deficit Hyperactivity
  Disorder), 171
adopted
  animals, 129-130
  children, Me books, 71
  trees, 130-131
adult roles, pretending, 52
adults
  children, imitating, 235
  irresponsible, 118
  rules, following, 115
advertising, 28-30

advice
  free, 172
  professional, 162, 172, 174
advocacy, 119
  encouraging, 127
  environment, 128
after-school care, 261
aggression, increased, 262
aims of Web sites, evaluating, 166
albums, photos, 68
Alfy Web site, 104
allowance, choices, 12
alt.parenting newsgroup, 173
alt.support.attn-deficit newsgroup, 173
AltaVista Web site, 44, 121, 193
alternative-families, 178
Amazing Kids Web site, 84
Amazon.com Web site, 59
America Links Up Web site, 191
America Online, homework resources,
  147-148
American Academy of Pediatrics Online
  Web site, The, 181
American Civil Liberties Union Web
  site, 192
American Field Service Web site, 108
American Greetings Web site, 139
American Library Association Web
  site, 203
American Music Therapy Association
  (AMTA) Web site, 76
Ameritech, 193
anemometers, 42
animals
  abandoned, 123
  adopting, 129-130
  unwanted, 123
anonymity, protecting, 174
AOL, 193
AOL Kids Only, 107
appearance, self-esteem, 67, 76-77
applying for computer equipment, 170
appreciation, expressing, 64, 81
approach of Web sites, evaluating, 161
approaches, to e-Parenting, 175
approved software, 27

changes
    coping with, 64, 72
    parenting, 9
    physical, 248
Chaqueen Web site, 77
chats, 74
    advantages, 103
    cautions, 199
    event calendars, 104
    finding craft information, 212
    online support, 172
    safe, 74, 103-104
    searching, 104
    setting up, 147
    warning signs, 199, 201
Chem4kids Web site, 46
chess clubs, 99
child development resources, 167-168
children, 171
    adopted, e-Genealogy, 225
    adults, imitating, 235
    appreciating, 64
    behavior, 174
    beliefs, teaching, 8
    crimes against, preventing, 192
    development, 191
    Down's syndrome, 157
    expectations, 116
    fact versus fantasy, 23
    gifted, 157
    goals, 235
    guidance, 9, 171, 186
    health, 76
    influences, 7
    information, evaluating, 10-11
    interacting with, 91
    interest in, showing, 14, 114
    limits, 116
    maturity, 189
    monitoring, 26
    praising, 80, 82, 117
    preferences, 59
    protecting, 186-187
    roles, 17
    school age, needs, 248
    shy, 104, 110
    skills, acquiring, 10
    special-needs, 155-156, 175
    spoiling, 118
    statistics, 198
    supervising, 186
    trusting, 11
    visually impaired, 155
Children's Partnership Web site, The,
    190, 203

Children's Software Review Web site, 138
ChildU Web site, 154
choices
    allowance, 12
    bad, dangers, 13
    clothing, 12
    considering, 113
    encouraging, 12
    food, 12
    freedom, 186
    friends, 12
    informed, 30, 121, 187
    making, 12
    money, 57
    pets, 12
    preceptions, 12
    smoking, 13
    teams, 12
    unchaperoned parties, 13
chores, 120
citizens, global, 126
classes
    8 Weeks to a Well-Behaved Child,
        174
    Training the Trainers, 174
clay, experiments, 41
clubs
    chess, 99
    online, 75, 106-107
cnet.com Web site, 217
Cochran Web site, 45
collecting quilts, 214
college, preparing for, 148-149
CollegeNET Web site, 148
colleges, 148-149
combating weight problems, 77
Commercial Internet Exchange, 193
commercials, televisions, 28-29
common conflicts, toddlers, 236
communication. See also people skills,
    87, 90
    building, 90, 92
    decreased, 262
    developing, 109
    email, 25
    families, 25
    foundations, 91
    learning, 91
    modeling, 100
    nurturing, 88, 90
    online, regulating, 89
    parent-child, 188
    positive, 93-94
    practicing, 94
    skills, 87, 109

G

X-Z

Tell Us What You Think!

As the reader of this book, *you* are our most important critic and commentator. We value your opinion and want to know what we're doing right, what we could do better, what areas you'd like to see us publish in, and any other words of wisdom you're willing to pass our way.

I welcome your comments. You can email or write me directly to let me know what you did or didn't like about this book—as well as what we can do to make our books stronger.

Please note that I cannot help you with technical problems related to the topic of this book, and that due to the high volume of mail I receive, I might not be able to reply to every message.

When you write, please be sure to include this book's title and author as well as your name and phone or fax number. I will carefully review your comments and share them with the author and editors who worked on the book.

Email: *internet_sams@mcp.com*

Mail: Mark Taber
            Associate Publisher
            Sams Publishing
            201 West 103rd Street
            Indianapolis, IN 46290 USA